MORE

Than

WORDS

Can Ever

TELL

MORE
Than
WORDS
Can Ever
TELL

Jennifer Lansbury

EIGHTY-SIX
SIXTY-ONE
PUBLISHING

Springfield VA

PUBLISHER'S CATALOGING-IN-PUBLICATION DATA

NAMES: Lansbury, Jennifer H., author.
TITLE: More than words can ever tell / Jennifer Lansbury.
DESCRIPTION: Includes bibliographical references. | Springfield, VA:
Eighty-six Sixty-one Publishing, 2020.
IDENTIFIERS: LCCN: 2020918014 | ISBN: 978-1-7356960-0-3 (Hardcover)
| 978-1-7356960-1-0 (pbk.) | 978-1-7356960-2-7 (ebook)
SUBJECTS: LCSH Hobaugh, George Francis--Marriage. | Hobaugh,
Rebecca Gardner--Marriage. | Lansbury, Jennifer H.--Family. | United
States. Marine Corps--Biography. | Marines--United States--Biography. |
Marine Corps spouses--United States--Biography. | Families of military
personnel--United States. | United States. Marine Corps--Military
life. | United States. Marine Corps--History--Korean War, 1950-1953.
| BISAC FAMILY & RELATIONSHIPS / General | FAMILY &
RELATIONSHIPS / Military Families | HISTORY / Military / Wars &
Conflicts (Other) | HISTORY / United States / General | HUMOR /
Topic / Marriage & Family
CLASSIFICATION: LCC VE25 .L36 2020| DDC 301.5/93/092--dc23

Cover & Interior design by Joseph Dente

For Jeff, who all my life has been my big "bubba"
And in memory of our parents, and those in our family who have gone before

GARDNER-HOBAUGH
FAMILY TREE

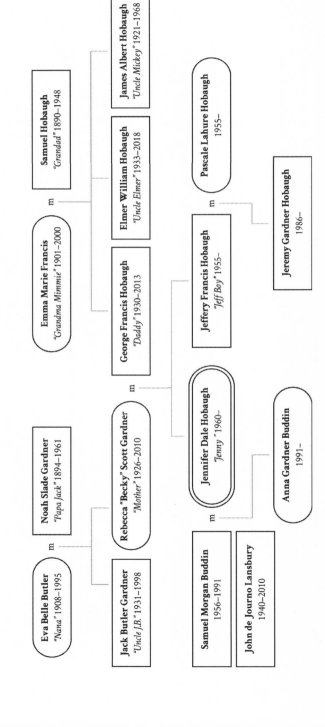

Eva Belle Butler
"Nana" 1908–1995

Noah Slade Gardner
"Papa Jack" 1894–1961

m

Samuel Hobaugh
"Grandad" 1890–1948

Emma Marie Francis
"Grandma Mimmie" 1901–2000

m

James Albert Hobaugh
"Uncle Mickey" 1921–1968

Elmer William Hobaugh
"Uncle Elmer" 1933–2018

Jack Butler Gardner
"Uncle J.B." 1931–1998

Rebecca "Becky" Scott Gardner
"Mother" 1926–2010

m

George Francis Hobaugh
"Daddy" 1930–2013

Pascale Lahure Hobaugh
1955–

m

Jeffery Francis Hobaugh
"Jeff Boy" 1955–

Jennifer Dale Hobaugh
"Jenny" 1960–

Jeremy Gardner Hobaugh
1986–

Samuel Morgan Buddin
1956–1991

John de Journo Lansbury
1940–2010

m

Anna Gardner Buddin
1991–

Contents

Preface

THIS BOOK WAS BORN OF DISCOVERY, A DISCOVERY of letters I did not know existed until a few years ago.

In the early months of 2014, after our father died unexpectedly in late December of the previous year, my brother and I endured the hardship of cleaning out our parents' last residence in preparation for its sale. Our father was the last of our parents to go, and we were working with a woman who would manage an estate sale for us. We did not have to dispense with anything on our own, but we at least had to know what was there—what we would take, and what would be left for the sale.

The larger pieces were fairly easy to figure out—my brother and his wife could use that new king-size mattress, I would like this bedroom suit, and so on, with each of our children asking for a piece here and there until we knew what needed to be sold.

It was the smaller, personal items that bedeviled us—decades of family pictures; piles of birthday, anniversary, and holiday cards; our grandmother's travel diaries and her books and notebooks from 39 years of collegiate teaching; keepsakes from distant lands from our father's time in military service—and we asked ourselves the question that generations of children have pondered...what in the world do we do with *these*?

As we continued rummaging through drawers and closets, I also began assembling a number of letters in my parents' handwriting. I didn't discover them all at once. There were a few in the nightstand drawer on our mother's side of the bed, a stash tucked away in one of the guest bedroom closets, several stacks in boxes out in the garage, all of it typical of our mother, the unorganized saver. I did not stop to read them at the time, worried I would get lost in them and not finish the task at hand, but I could see from the postmarks that they covered different periods in our parents' lives. By the time we were finished going through everything, we had amassed a box full of letters that appeared to number somewhere in the two to three hundreds.

My brother Jeff and I divided up the personal items so we could go through them on our own, trusting each other to pare down the piles as he or she saw fit before exchanging what was left. I offered to take the letters, read them, and then pass them along to him. Six years later, the letters still reside with me.

As I began to read them, I realized what a treasure I had. I was educated as a historian, and so I pushed aside the personal and let my training take over. They spanned some sixteen years, from 1951, when as a young Marine, our father was fighting in the Korean War while our parents were dating, to the final time the Corps separated us from him in 1967, the year before he retired. The letters gave insight into postwar culture and military life, but they also spoke of love, loss, family, childrearing, and what it took to sustain a marriage through the long months of separation that often comes with signing on to serve one's country.

As much as I saw the historical value to the letters, I didn't want the personal story they told to get lost. There seemed to be, in the somewhat flimsy, crinkly pages that I held, a discovery of the underpinnings of a beautiful marriage that had lasted for close to 58 years, a relationship that served as the rock for the family that my brother and I had been privileged to call our own. In truth, more than anything, I wanted to unearth *that* story.

But how to do that, I wondered? The letters are an incomplete narrative, since, on the whole, our parents were together more often than apart, and, even when they were apart, not all of the letters survived. There are periods of separation when many more of Daddy's letters survived and I can only infer Mother's side of the conversation; at other times, the opposite. Their correspondence is also often repetitive in our parents' declarations of love or mundane in their back and forth on the minutia of life. But while reading them, my mind would get lost in what it meant to be a part of our family, in the stories and memories that comprised our family lore, and what it meant to be living through and growing up in the 1950s and 1960s. It seemed that there was a broader story, and so I decided to rely on both the historian and the daughter to tell it.

This is, then, predominately the story of our parents with a bit of my brother and me mixed in, all told against the backdrop of the times and culture we were living through. The overall arc of the narrative is chronological, but my memories enter the story randomly—as they tend to do in our minds—as something in our parents' letters brought them to the forefront of my own. Sometimes excerpts from their letters do the actual storytelling; at other times, they are merely a jumping off point, used more to introduce a section or theme rather than situate the narrative in time or place. It is a story told often in my voice but sometimes in theirs, through their letters. In some respects, if our parents' correspondence were love letters to each other, this book has become my love letter to them and the family they created.

There was nothing particularly remarkable about our parents or our little family of four, no celebrity status, family trauma, alcoholism, or drug use. We had difficulties, to be sure. At the age of 20, our father was sent off to fight in a war that he probably didn't fully understand and witnessed his best friend shot and killed next to him. I'm sure our mother didn't truly grasp the hardship of lengthy periods of single parenting she would face when she married our father. Within our extended family, there *was* alcoholism and instability and those relationships could be strained at times. There were sorrows mixed in with the joy throughout our parents' lives, and financial struggles dogged their early years of marriage.

But the only thing exceptional about the family my brother and I grew up in was the love that sustained our parents through repeated periods apart and through almost 58 years of marriage, and that Jeff and I were fortunate enough to have passed along to us. A friend recently pointed out that perhaps, in that love, lay the extraordinariness of what most would see as an ordinary life. Perhaps. What I do know is that I consider being part of our family the luck of the draw, and I have been thinking about that a lot lately through the lens of these days—what it means to be part of a loving family, to hold that family together despite extended separations. I think about how the social distancing we are living through to suppress covid-19 has made separation real for us in stark and seemingly unending ways. I think about the myraid ways systemic racism and the White privilege it is built upon has separated families of color throughout the long centuries of our country's racialized history. I think about the love *and* resiliency it must take to hold a family of color together in this country, the ways those families are able to acknowledge and lift up such resiliency. While I know I can never truly understand that reality, my hope is that the story in these pages will speak to the memory of love and family for all persons fortunate enough to have lived it, encourage those who have survived far different pasts with the hope of brighter futures, and bring to mind for all who read it, stories of their own to celebrate, and encourage them through separation.

Prologue

OUR MOTHER DIED ON A TUESDAY AFTERNOON IN summer.

I remember the deathwatch as a day of bright sunshine and damp, Southwest Georgia heat, although I cannot say for certain that it wasn't raining. I do not remember the songs of the birds that took up residence in the woods across the pond just out back of our parents' home, but they most assuredly were there.

My son David was saying his goodbye over the phone as she slipped away. The church of my youth would say that the Lord had called her home. As deaths go, it was a good one—calm, full of serenity and grace.

Years before, when our dad's mother had died in a nursing home without a family member by her side, our mother had extracted a promise from me—do not let me die alone, she pleaded. I assured her that I would not, but we really can't script these things, as covid-19 has taught us anew in frightening and horrifying ways. In the end, though, I was able to keep that promise, holding the phone to her ear so that the last words she heard were those of love—love from a grandson that had come into her life when he was 14, and that she had loved as her own. And so it was, Mother and me in her bedroom, and David, 750 miles away.

My brother Jeff had said his goodbye the previous Saturday, probably sensing that the next time he could make the two-hour trip to our parents' house our mother would no longer be there.

Our father—our father, as it turned out, said his goodbye minutes before Mother died.

He had to check on things at the country club he managed and make provisions for someone else to lock up that night. In a scene I had witnessed play out more times than I can recall, he kissed her, told her he was going to check on the club but would be right back, said I love you, and walked out the door. The distance from their golf villa to the club could be measured in yards. He could not have been away for more than five or ten minutes, and she died while he was gone. I knew our father beat himself up for having left, but I came to see the scene as an entirely fitting end to their story, just one more goodbye as he went to check on the club, her way of sparing him a parting that would have seemed foreign. I hope, in time, he came to feel the same way.

Regardless of whether he ever reconciled himself to not being there, something happened to our father that day. A light went out of his eyes that could never quite be rekindled in the three and a half years before his own death. His "dearest, darling wife," had, unwillingly, left him to finish his own journey without her. Some friends encouraged him, after a while, to find someone else. They even laid bets that he would go on a date during his second year alone. But I knew better. On the first anniversary of Mother's death, we talked about how hard that first year without her was. I'll never forget what he said. "One year wasn't enough, 100 won't be." It turned out that three and a half were not.

They were, in some ways, an unlikely couple, she with a degree in music education, he with little more than a high school education; she with a rich contralto voice, he described affectionately as tone deaf; he reveling in the organized and regimented legacy of the United States Marine Corps, she with the secret of unorganized closets and drawers. He loved country music; she adored Mozart. She drank in the beauty of language; he often made grammatical mistakes. He was an accomplished golfer; her few lessons never amounted to much. She would get her extrovert fix at the conclusion of Sunday morning worship, having to almost be pulled out the door; as an introvert, he would often wait for her, by that door. But when they finally started dating—having known one another virtually all their lives—her grandmother told her to hang onto that one, he was "good husband material." And so he was, and so she did, for almost 58 years.

This is their story, told against the backdrop of the world in which they lived, through the fluidity of family stories and memory, and the constancy of their letters. It is their story, but it is also, at least in some ways, Jeff's and mine.

There were numerous separations that prompted them to write to one another, separation being part of their early years together, the stuff that military life is made of.

There was the time before they were married when Daddy landed at Inchon during the Korean War and survived the bone-chilling cold of the Chosin Reservoir. If we needed to look for evidence of why he liked the heat of Southwest Georgia, we could look to Korea.

There was the period as they anticipated the birth of their first child as Mother waited with her parents in Pomona, North Carolina, while Daddy remained at Camp LeJeune. Their letters spoke of their love, the difficulty of their separation, and the anticipation of a new baby.

There were the separations when orders came down for transfer to a new duty station. Daddy would leave, and Mother, Jeff, and I would come later, when transportation and housing were ready. And there were courses on food service management that took Daddy away for the spring and summer while Mother stayed behind with us, knowing that the course was important for her husband's career advancement but longing for the end of the months apart.

The bulk of their time apart, however, was a fourteen-month period during 1957 and 1958, when our father, a twenty-seven-year-old Marine staff sergeant with a wife and toddler son, was sent TDY— temporary duty— to Japan and Okinawa. Mother and Jeff remained in the States, moving back to Greensboro, North Carolina, to live with her parents. Daddy left a 20-month-old son; he came home to an almost three-year-old.

During all these separations, in the age before email, FaceTime, smart phones, and social media, when long distance and overseas phone calls were expensive and connections unreliable, letters brought people together. And so, our mother and father wrote to each other, virtually every day. She wrote to "my darling husband." He wrote to "my dearest, darling wife." She wrote from her parents' home in Greensboro, North Carolina, and from duty stations in Beaufort, South Carolina, and Albany, Georgia. He wrote from wherever he was—a foxhole in Korea, a bunk in Mt. Fuji, Japan, a mess tent in Okinawa and a ship in between, upon arrival at a new duty station in Newfoundland, Canada, and at the Quartermaster School at Fort Lee, Virginia. She wrote of the minutia of daily life, finances, and the excitement of watching their son, and eventually, daughter, grow. He wrote of the disciplined life of a Marine living in a different culture, of the letters he longed for at mail call, of the deals he could find in postwar Japan, and of the things he hoped to send back to the States for his family. They asked each other questions, and waited over the long weeks for the reply. They encouraged each other, and laid bare the difficulty of such a long separation.

No matter where they wrote from, though, they wrote unendingly of their love—of loving one another more than words could ever tell—and of the day they could be together again.

Their letters during each of these separations provide a glimpse into their lives together, lived apart, and speak to a world that was both simpler and more complicated than the one we live in today. They anchor a story that is fleshed out with the tricky substance of my own memories; family stories, passed down, told and retold; and recent conversations with family.

I was reminded of how shifting these things can be recently as I re-watched a favorite movie. At the end of the movie, I was sure the orphan boy left India to live with his surrogate father in Denmark. It was the third, maybe fourth, time I had seen the film, and I would have sworn to such an ending. But unless I was watching a different, remade version, which I was not, the little boy chose to remain at the school in India, saying goodbye to the teacher who wanted to adopt him.

I was able to set that movie ending straight. But life has no rewind button or opportunities for second viewings; we remember events, people, life as we remember them, and our remembering can change over time or differ from others who witnessed the same thing.

I do not, then, imply the following to be our lives as we actually lived them, but rather the way I remember these years and the story that our parents' letters tell about their time apart. It was, in many respects, pretty ordinary. Then again, maybe it was extraordinary after all.

PART I

Beginnings

1

Growing up in Greensboro

November 23, 1957, Okinawa

My Dearest Darling Wife,

I just live for the day when I will get off that plane at Greensboro and into your arms. I lay and think about it at night a long time before I go to sleep. You are the only one for me, darling.

WHEN DADDY WROTE THESE LINES TO MOTHER, he was dreaming of Greensboro, not because it was "home," but because it was where his wife and son were, and he hadn't seen them for five months of what would be a fourteen-month separation. For me, though, who grew up in places often far away, Greensboro had meaning as the place where our grandmothers lived, where we went to spend time with them, and aunts, uncles, and cousins during the summer, where we arrived only after a trip in the car that seemed like it would never end.

My brother and I would start out in the back seat together. He would try to explain to me how he, being five years older and considerably bigger, needed more space. He would draw an invisible line down the back seat, granting me about a quarter of the available area, and tell me to stay on my feebly small side. Right, I thought. I may have been five years younger, but I was not stupid. I knew I had tools in my small but well-used toolkit to combat this extreme injustice.

"Daddy, Jeff's being rouge!" I knew the word was supposed to be *rude* but the four of us still said it this way as a nod to my cuteness factor as a toddler. A girl has to hold on to what she can when her brother has five years on her.

"Boy, you'd better behave," Daddy would direct at Jeff. "You do *not* want me to stop this car." More like it, neither Jeff nor I wanted Mother to stop the car. Our mother was the epitome of Southern graciousness and ladylike hospitality, but boy howdy, you did not want to get that woman's dander up. One stop of the car on a particularly long drive to Greensboro had taught Jeff and me where the line was. We had fussed and argued and gotten on her very last nerve until she saw an open field, told Daddy to stop the car, and instructed us to get out and run in circles around the field until she said we could stop. Jeff and I looked at each other in disbelief and then looked back at Mother. "RUN!" she yelled. We did not have to be told three times. I didn't even consider appealing to Daddy. He kept his mouth shut, thinking he might get the raised eyebrow and be asked if he wanted to join us. So we ran in circles. I lost a flip flop at one point, hopped along feebly but still ended up stepping on a briar. (I've always been a bit of a klutz.) I looked up hopefully at Mother, but she was unrelenting. "RUN!" she yelled again in that same, insistent tone. At some point, Daddy pulled out the 8mm camera and started filming, preserving the moment for a good family story and just in case we ever forgot the consequences of annoying behavior on long road trips. We got back in the car, exhausted, and were miraculously pleasant to one another for the remainder of the trip.

Once in Greensboro, we headed straight to our Nana's. We always stayed with our mother's mother, whose house was not large but a bit bigger than Grandma Mimmie's. Both of our grandmothers lived alone after our grandfathers died, and they only lived about a block and a half apart. Within thirty minutes or so of our arrival, Daddy would announce, "I'm going over to Mama's for a bit." Being a daddy's girl, I would always ask to tag along. Being my daddy, he would always say yes. There was not a lot to do at Grandma Mimmie's, but with any luck, my Uncle Mickey, Daddy's older brother, would be there watching TV. We always seemed to arrive right around the time *The Lone Ranger* was about to come on. I loved that show. Mostly, I think I just loved my uncle, and if that's what he was watching, then I was all in.

So after hugging my grandmother, I would crawl up into my Uncle Mickey's lap, settle into his chest, lay my head onto his smoke-infused blue work shirt, and bask in another exciting episode of the exploits of the Lone Ranger and his Native American side-kick, Tonto. That was before I knew things, like the thrilling theme song was from Rossini's *William Tell Overture*, or that Tonto's broken English had racist overtones, or that the reason my uncle was usually home in the afternoon instead of at work was that he was an alcoholic. But in that moment, I wouldn't choose to be anywhere else.

That our grandmothers lived so closely to one another was something I took for granted. It made sense. I had always understood that our parents had grown up together. Surely, these must be the houses that they had grown up in. Sure, I had heard our parents mention any number of times "the house on Boren Street," which turned out to be a house where Mother had lived with her parents and younger brother, but that was some abstract place that held little meaning for me. Plus, I could be a little dense sometimes.

So I think I was an adult before I discovered that our parents were not even born in Greensboro, but rather in small towns in North Carolina, Daddy in Central Falls, about 30 miles south of Greensboro, and Mother in Four Oaks, a little over an hour to the southeast of the city. Blips on a map, really. My friend Peter, who I came to know in my mid-20s, had grown up not far from our mother's hometown. He delighted in telling her they always referred to the nearby town as "Three Oaks and a Stump." Mother would smile and chuckle at the jab. I discovered years later that if you take I-95 through North Carolina there is an exit for Four Oaks off the interstate. Well now, take that, Peter!

August 15, 1958, Greensboro, North Carolina
My dearest George,

    Tonight we ate out in the yard with Bill and Wade and family. It sure is nice out and we got to talking about how nice it would be if you were here to eat out with us!

At least once while we were visiting each summer, we would eat supper outside in Nana's back yard under the shade of old oak trees. It was hot outside, but at least there was a breeze and it was better than the still, hot air of Nana's house that had no air-conditioning. And the yard provided space for extended family—sometimes Nana's sister and her family who lived next door; sometimes my dad's side of the family; sometimes everyone. A long table got set up out back and the women of the family would bring out copious amounts of food. As children, we were excused from the table to go play as soon as we finished eating, a luxury afforded us thanks to the informality of eating outdoors that was certainly *not* bestowed indoors. Once dusk settled in, my brother, cousins, and I would run around the back yard catching fireflies in washed out mayonnaise jars, breath holes poked in the tops by an adult to keep us from killing these little natural lights before we released them to fly away to freedom.

Sometimes I would wonder to myself what Mother and Daddy's childhoods had been like in what I thought then were those same yards. Did they have backyard suppers in the summer? Were our grandparents' rules to outside eating more relaxed for their own children? Did they race around the back yards of their houses catching fireflies?

Our parents were a little over three years apart, with Mother the older. They both grew up with younger brothers, and while Daddy also had his older brother Mickey, nine years separated the two of them. As children, I imagine our parents spending their summers playing and running barefoot outside in the hot, humid North Carolina piedmont sun, our dad with his brother Elmer and Mother with hers, J.B., short for Jack Butler. Younger brothers to play with, torment, or be annoyed by, depending on the day, the moods, and the severity of the North Carolina heat.

They both grew up with youthful mothers, each having married while still in their teens—one at seventeen, the other at fifteen—to men over a decade older than them. Eva Butler, our "Nana," created a scandal in the family when she married widower Jack Gardner, our "Papa Jack," who was almost fourteen years her senior; she had her firstborn, our mother, two years later at the age of nineteen. Our paternal grandfather Samuel Hobaugh, a granddaddy we never knew, rescued his bride Emma Francis, our Grandma Mimmie, from an abusive household. When Sam returned Emma home late one night after a date, her father stood there waiting for her, strap in hand, telling her he was going to tear her behind up. But Sam stepped in and said, "No, you've whupped her for the last time you're ever going to. Emma is coming with me." And that is when they went out and got married.

Our parents were also both children of the Great Depression. But, surprisingly, my brother and I did not grow up hearing about need, want, or hardship. The one link to that time was the orange, tangerine, and walnuts that would be at the bottom of our stockings on Christmas morning. I really couldn't understand why Santa thought those were good things to put in a child's stocking; it always seemed a bit lame to me, the least interesting of the wonders of the morning. To Mother and Daddy, though, that fresh orange or tangerine had been a treat when they were little, something that was far too expensive to buy on a regular basis. The stories that did get passed down from that time were of our mother's grandmother—Lesta Teague Butler. Her frugality with food was legendary in our family. "Grandmother," as she was always known through the generations, insisted on small portions of meat. When she and Granddaddy visited our parents when they were a young married couple living in Florida and Daddy returned from the market with four steaks, one per adult, she was aghast. "We don't need all that meat. Here, wrap these two up and put them in the freezer for another meal. We can split these between us, and fill up on vegetables and biscuits." Of course Daddy complied, because that is what you did with Grandmother. And he wasn't arguing about the biscuits for they had become a matter of legend in his wife's family lore; by then he knew the drill. Grandmother served them, from scratch of course, at every meal. But she made an accounting of them at meal's end. If she had made eight for breakfast and only seven were eaten, you could be sure it would take several meals of vanished biscuits and people asking for more before eight ever appeared back on the table. She had learned during the Depression years that waste could not be tolerated.

If our parents, as children, did not really grasp the effects of the Depression, it certainly surrounded them. It can be hard now, being close to a century removed from it, to imagine the want, the worry, the sheer deprivation that went on for years. The Great Recession that began in 2008 with its ten percent unemployment rate touched some of us. And as we wait to see the full effects of the coronavirus pandemic on our economy, the word "depression" is again being thrown about as unemployment continues to rise. Sadly, perhaps these economic crises serve as a barometer of sorts for a Great Depression now resigned to the history books. During the height of the Depression, the unemployment rate sat at twenty-five percent. Add in those whose jobs had been cut to half or quarter time, and close to seventy-five percent of the U.S. population probably felt the effects of lost work. An overvalued stock market, over production by U.S. corporations amid lost confidence, and declining demand—I'm not sure the various systemic problems mattered much to those families whose loss of work meant they struggled to feed their families. "At present, I have $.22 in my pocket. I have been out [of work] since 1929 and have used up all my savings," wrote a father living in Chicago in 1933. "Our bank has been closed since March 4th which has tied up my wife's and son's small savings. We are living on what my son gets working three days a week for $9.00." His letter was addressed to "my dear President," and was one of the more than 15 million like it that FDR received while in office. An attorney with the Federal Land Bank in Trinity, North Carolina, about twenty miles southwest of Greensboro, wrote Roosevelt in 1933 about a farmer who came to see him for a loan. "He is representative of thousands of farmers in North Carolina, owning maybe 50 acres of land and doing all of his own work, and about to lose his farm under a mortgage. But to get the loan he is obliged to pay $20 in advance for appraisals, and another $10 for a survey, and he no more has that much cash than he has the moon."

Illinois, North Carolina, the Northeast, West Coast, Deep South, Midwest, the Dust Bowl—it did not seem to matter. There was want and scarcity throughout. But even with such widespread deprivation, Americans moved in search of a better situation. Many rural North Carolinians hoped that leaving a life of farming for the city could mean more opportunity, a better living; so families often uprooted and moved to a "mill town," as places like Greensboro were called.

And so our parents' families followed suit, moving from their rural beginnings to the city of Greensboro at some point when Mother and Daddy were children. Opportunity, or the hope of it, likely brought them work, a job, during a time when it was precious and exceedingly hard to come by.

Greensboro suffered like the rest of the country during the Depression—banks closed, families from across the social spectrum lost their homes, city and county governments laid off workers, schools eliminated "non-essential" programs like music and art. Yet Greensboro, with its textile mills and construction projects, became, if not a Mecca, then a place of some hope. The city's textile mills kept running, even expanded, during the 1930s and insulated the city a bit from the harsh realities of depression. Both of our father's parents—Emma and Sam— worked first for Pomona cotton mill, then moved over to the Cone textile mill. Established by the Cone brothers in the late nineteenth century, by 1940, their enterprise was the world's largest producer of cotton denim.

To us, however, it was always just "the mill." Grandma Mimmie worked as a spinner, running the spinning frames, while Granddaddy was a fixer, working to keep the machinery running. The Cone family compensated their employees with cash and script to be used in the company stores, both precious commodities during the Depression.

Construction projects probably brought our mother's family to Greensboro. Mother's dad was a carpenter and also oversaw the construction of bridges, and there was work to be had in the city. The Public Works Administration (PWA), one of the alphabet agencies created during FDR's administration to help get people back to work, built the city's Country Park and the small bridges in Fisher Park during the Depression years. These, and a number of other city-wide beautification projects, likely provided the employment for Noah Slade Gardner, our mother's dad, that shielded his family somewhat during those bleak years.

Noah Slade Gardner—I always loved that name. It was only as an older child that I learned that his real name *was* Noah. He was known to everyone in the family and community as Jack, a nickname that characterized him as a "jack of all trades." Once our own daddy married into the family, though, "Mr. Gardner" was, thereafter, "dad" to him.

July 10, 1957, Camp Pendleton, California

Honey, tell Mother that I will write her again when I know my new address. Tell Elmer and all I said hello, and be sure to tell dad, his son said hello. He sure has been a good dad to me. I could have never done any better. And that goes for Mrs. Eva too.

By the time Daddy wrote these lines to Mother as he waited to be sent over to Okinawa, he had been without his own father for almost nine years. Cancer, heart problems, emphysema—I heard different stories over the years. When Grandma Mimmie found out he had fallen at work, she put her foot down and told him that was it, he was *not* going back to that mill anymore. And he didn't. She stood barely five feet but that woman was a force to be reckoned with when she made up her mind about something.

Whatever the cause, the disease was physically debilitating. While Granddaddy would spend his days reclined in the glider on the porch, our Uncle Elmer sat with him as a young teenager, having given up playing baseball to look after his daddy while their mother continued to work at the mill, listening to each precious, struggling breath and wondering to himself if his father had just taken his last.

At the time, our own daddy was on a ship in the Mediterranean. He had joined the U.S. Marines in January of that year, and his first post was aboard a Navy ship, realizing the "at sea" part of the Marine Corps hymn. When it became clear that the end was nearing, the family contacted the Red Cross about getting him home. As soon as they arrive at port, we'll get him home as quickly as we can, was the response. It could not have been quick or easy in 1948 to get a young PFC (private first class) from a ship in the aquiline waters of the Mediterranean to a home he would never live in again. But once the ship docked, they were true to their word and got him home in a hurry.

While they waited, the family worried that "Georgie" wouldn't make it in time. But Daddy had always been "doll baby" to his own father. Doll baby. As a little girl, I'd sometimes giggle at the nickname and wonder how it had come about. Did it reflect Daddy's fairly easy-going temperament, one that may have meshed well with his own father's and his role as a traditional middle-child peacemaker? Or was it the way he looked as a baby? Or perhaps it was the joy of welcoming another baby after nine years of waiting? I found it a dear, but funny, nickname for someone I knew as kind and loving, a big teddy bear of sorts, but also a committed, ramrod-straight Marine. But something about it also struck me as right. While our father could sometimes exhibit a gruff exterior, it mostly seemed forced, almost playful. So our grandfather, outlasting the predictions of the doctors, held on until his doll baby arrived so they could have their goodbyes. He died shortly after. Daddy was eighteen.

What he found in his wife's family some years later was love, nurture, and another father. To Daddy, Nana was always "Mrs. Eva, though the "Mrs." got dropped in later years. But Papa Jack was "Dad," a role our grandfather had already cemented with his own children at a time when fathers weren't always expected to be so present.

It would have been easy for Papa Jack to be a sort of standard-issue father of the 1930s. He worked hard, with his hands, and I'm sure came home tired. With a wife fourteen years his junior, a clear delineation of duties would seem to be in order. It would not be surprising for him to come home, eat a dinner that Nana had prepared, and put his feet up so he could read the paper. Spend a few short minutes with the children before they went to bed, perhaps, but most of the childcare for the evening would continue to fall to his wife.

But Papa Jack was far from a standard-issue dad, and Nana was no ordinary mother. Neither of our parents' families had a legacy of being well educated, but that did not stop our Nana. To put it simply, she loved learning. By the time I came along in the 1960s, she was a speech therapist. With her Masters in Religious Education, she also taught at John Wesley College, a Bible college there in Greensboro. But this was a woman who was married at seventeen and a mother of two by her early twenties. Attending college was not in the cards until sometime in the 1930s. How she and Papa Jack, in the midst of the Depression, scraped together the money for her to do it, I'll never know.

Maybe the bigger question was how Nana ever managed to pass the math she was required to take to get her degree. Ask her to recite a poem or a story, write a thesis, study scripture, and she was all over it. She was a woman of words, not of numbers. Her younger sister Bill—short for Villard Novella, so we never questioned why she did not go by either one of those names and simply thought it was cool to have an *Aunt* Bill—had a way with numbers and wondered the same thing. Knowing Nana, it came down to a lot of hard work and perhaps repeated visits to the professor using those words of hers to get help and perhaps some sympathy. She was definitely a "by any means necessary" kind of woman. But she had another resource; Papa Jack would hear her struggling and pull out his slide rule to help her try and figure out the math that stumped her so badly.

"So, how did Nana go to college if you and Uncle J.B. were little and she had to look after you during the day," I'd asked Mother one day when I was old enough to understand the sequence of how this all came about.

"Oh, she would attend classes at night, and Daddy—your Papa Jack—would take care of J.B. and me."

I guess my eyes got big because she quickly continued.

"Yes, I know. A lot of dads back then wouldn't have done that for their wives.

But he always said it was his privilege to take care of his children." She smiled at the memory.

Wow, I thought. That was pretty special. A daddy taking care of his children, putting them to bed on a regular basis! Even in the 1960s there wasn't a lot of that going on. And this was thirty-odd years before! I wondered what kind of things they did. Apparently, it didn't dawn on me to ask Mother; as I said, I can be a bit dense sometimes. So I created my own images—twilight games in the yard, laughter and giggling, Mother and Uncle J.B. crawling up in Papa Jack's lap to listen to his rich, baritone voice sing a song, read a book, or tell a story. I really liked this story, I decided, probably because it put some flesh on a grandfather who died shortly after I was born, who cut a big figure in our family that everyone had memories of but me. As an adult, I understood that it modeled for our mother what it meant for a wife and husband to support one another. It also meant that by the time our father became part of the family, his new "dad" had been practicing fatherhood, *real* fatherhood, for close to twenty years. Taking on another son was as natural as breathing for Papa Jack.

February 23, 1958, On board ship, Okinawa bound for the Philippines

I went to church on ship this morning. There was only about 8 of us there, but we sung a few songs and one of the ship officers spoke. They do not have a Reverend on J.S.T., but the man that did bring the message sure did do a good job. I just sat there and thought of how much I wish I was home to go to church with you and Jeff boy.

MOTHER AND DADDY WERE people of deep faith. Maybe this was easy at a time when church was the only gig in town on Sunday mornings in the South. No soccer games, no stores open, no alcohol served. But they were not just churchgoers, rather holders of an abiding faith that dwelt deep inside and affected the way they lived their lives. Not in a showy, pushy, "religious" way, but with the "Inner Light" that they came to as families of practicing Quakers. It never really dawned on me to question this way of being; it's just how things were in our family.

Quaker meeting is where our parents' paths crossed most often during their growing-up years. The three years between Mother and Daddy must have made a difference, though, and since Mother was older, I'm sure she didn't have much use for a little boy closer in age to her brother. Daddy and Uncle J.B. were in the same Sunday school class at the Pomona Monthly Meeting of Friends, which was unfortunate for their teacher, Mr. Melvin, since they both had a devilish sense of mischief about them, even as adults, and could make Sunday mornings interesting.

I don't really have a good visual on what the Pomona Friends was like when begun in 1909, since it had changed considerably by the time Jeff and I would attend services there during our summer visits. It was part of the Ohio Yearly Meeting of Friends, a "conservative," rather than "orthodox," branch of the Quakers. Conservative Friends adhered to plain speech and dress, and waiting worship. I think by the time our parents came along, the adherence to plain dress, in particular, had fallen off. But Mother said that when she was a little girl, some of the elders continued to use "plain" speech, with their "thee" and "thou" replacing the familiar "you," as in "I hope thee are well this morning." What this meant, practically speaking, is that our parents grew up with worship far different from my brother and me. No pastor, no choir, no beautifully appointed sanctuary. Waiting worship, or sitting, as we would sometimes hear it called. Sitting in silence—what other traditions might refer to as meditation— Friends would wait for the Spirit to speak to someone. And wait they would, for as long as it took. This was not speaking in tongues, not any kind of Pentecostal fervor. It was plain speech. Once someone spoke, those in attendance listened, believing that there was an Inner Light, a spark of the divine, in all people.

I used to think it was a good thing Jeff or I, but especially Jeff, didn't have to do waiting worship. I didn't usually have too much trouble keeping my mouth shut in public, but my brother routinely exercised his gift for speech among family, friends, and strangers. I imagined that he would have tried pulling the stunt Daddy told us had happened a generation before he was born when

Grandma Mimmie's best friend was a child and felt the Spirit's stirrings one Sunday morning. Having waited for forty-five minutes in silence, the six-year-old Mary rose and announced that the Spirit had moved her to adjourn the meeting. And so they did, for Quakers believe that the Spirit speaks through children as well. Brilliant, I thought, when I head the story the first time. I never would have been able to pull it off, being of a shy and reserved nature in public, but I could definitely imagine Jeff doing it. It was a one-time fix, though, for her parents clarified things with little Mary when they got home—not everything one hears is from "the Spirit." The Spirit never moved her again in quite the same way.

But in 1959, the year before I was born, the Pomona Friends built a sanctuary in the Hunter Hills area of Greensboro and became the Hunter Hills Evangelical Friends Church. Evangelical Friends were an outgrowth of what had been the Orthodox branch. Pastor-led and with a sanctuary, there were other, theological differences as well, though evangelical in this case did not have the same meaning as today. But it was the outward manifestations that could seem most significant to those who had not grown up that way. By the time I have any memory of going to Quaker meeting when we visited our grandmothers, a Sunday morning didn't seem much different from the churches we attended growing up. Our congregations were not Quaker, for sure; when you transfer around the country with the Marine Corps, Quaker meetinghouses aren't just everywhere, so we usually attended the protestant service at the base chapel. When we would visit Hunter Hills in the summer, then, it didn't really seem different. There was even music, solos for heaven's sake! Daddy would grouse about it to Mother almost every time we attended. "This isn't a Quaker congregation any more," he would complain. "They have a pastor, music; why, they even have carpet down the center aisle! I can't see how they can still call themselves Quakers."

Despite the changes that rankled our father so, both grandmothers remained in the congregation until they died. Nana was very involved and would often attend what we heard as children referred to as the "Yearly Meeting" in Ohio, when representatives from Quaker meetings affiliated with the Ohio Yearly

Meeting would gather. Grandma Mimmie was a stalwart at Hunter Hills Friends too, faithfully attending services and Sunday school. But Daddy always suspected that his Mother still prayed the rosary, a holdover from her youth. Sure enough, when she died, the rosary beads that she brought with her from Philadelphia as a young bride surfaced. Just in case, I suppose. Some traditions, particularly religious ones, die hard. Those rosary beads now reside, fittingly, with my French sister-in-law, Pascale, who, despite leaving Roman Catholicism as a teen, could appreciate their significance in a way none of her protestant in-laws could.

Our parents' Quaker roots were part of who they were to the extent that when our mother attended college, she ended up at a Quaker school, and when our father chose the Marines, I'm sure it crossed more than one mind to wonder what this Quaker was doing. Their stories, linked for most of their lives through place and faith, would diverge for a time as they both looked to what came after high school.

2

Music and the Marines

March 28, 1951, Korea

Did I tell you that I was a song writer? Well, I am, ha ha. Me and two of my boys wrote a song over here. I will tell you all about it when I get home.

IN THE SUMMER BEFORE I TURNED FIVE, WE WERE transferred, complements of the Marine Corps, from the Naval Air Station in Argentia, Newfoundland, Canada, to the Marine Corps Supply Center (MCSC) in Albany, Georgia. While I have glimpses of memories from Newfoundland, the MCSC in Albany is really the first, and only, duty station I remember. We lived in base housing, in a house with a yard that I can close my eyes and still see.

Every Sunday morning we were in town, which was most of them, we attended the protestant service at the base chapel. Chaplain Howard led the service and preached the sermon, and Jeff and I sat on either side of Daddy while Mother sang in the choir. During what seemed like the interminably long sermon—Really, I thought, isn't there a different way to do church?—Daddy would put his arm around me and I would settle in, nestled in the crook of his arm. Generally a rule follower, though, regardless of what my brain was saying, I would never think of doing anything but sitting still and being quiet. Plus, Jeff and I had both had the fear of the Lord placed in us enough times to know that nothing good came out of acting out in church.

My favorite part of the service was the singing. Here was something I could do, a chance to participate rather than just sit, and, let's be honest, we generally got to stand while singing, which offered a chance to move around a little, even if it just meant we had to sit again when we finished. We might not be allowed to talk in church, but we could certainly sing, at least at the appropriate times.

I caught on to the tunes of the hymns pretty quickly. The Navy hymn, *Eternal Father, Strong to Save*, ended each service, and it didn't take me long to learn the last verse:

> *Eternal Father, grant, we pray,*
> *To all Marines, both night and day,*
> *The courage, honor, strength, and skill*
> *Their land to serve, thy law fulfill;*
> *Be thou the shield forevermore*
> *From every peril to the Corps.*

Each Sunday I looked forward to singing this verse that asked God to protect my Daddy. Well, okay, it also signaled the end of the service, which was an added bonus.

Fast forward to years later when I sang the hymn as a young adult at a church somewhere other than a base chapel for the first time. Some of the words of the first few verses seemed a little different, but they had never been as important to me as the last verse anyway, so I looked forward in anticipation to those final, familiar words. When we arrived there, though, those words that had been a stalwart of my youth were gone. What?, I thought and looked around sure I would see other shocked faces. But the rest of the congregation was singing as if nothing was amiss. Where was the verse asking God to protect our Marines, I questioned silently. It had been there, in print, in the Base Hymnal. What trickery was this? Who had messed with my favorite verse of one of my favorite hymns?! I researched this travesty and discovered that the verse I knew, the one I thought should be inviolate, was actually an alternate one written in 1966, just as there was one written for airmen in 1943. That knowledge didn't really change things for me, though. The Marines' verse would always be, in my personal history, the actual ending of that hymn.

As a little girl at the base chapel, Daddy, Jeff, and I stood proudly singing while Mother sang from the choir, locking eyes with us and smiling. I was smiling too, mostly because I knew I could count the seconds until the service would be over. As we stood there, singing and smiling, I noticed, once again, that there was something different about Daddy's singing. While he sang with gusto, particularly this hymn, his notes didn't match ours. It wasn't that he sang off key, or in another key—he was all over the place. Where the notes went higher, he might sing lower, or higher, or stay on the same note. And however he sang it this Sunday probably wouldn't be the same as it had been before or would be next week. Oh well. Truth was, I loved my daddy, adored him, really, so this was a perceived flaw that I had decided years before to overlook.

WHEN IT CAME TO music, our mother was a completely different story. If golf was our father's mistress, which it *was*, then music was Mother's other lover. Any musical ability Jeff and I acquired naturally came through her. Blessed with a lovely contralto voice (she would disagree, thinking it altogether plain), her love of, and ability with, music passed from her daddy's family, for Nana couldn't sing a lick either. Papa Jack and his brothers had enough voices among them to break into parts on any given song, and they grew up singing at a time when doing so could mean hours of family evening entertainment.

When I ran across these lines from our 21-year-old father claiming to be a songwriter, then, I couldn't help but wonder what Mother's reaction had been when she read them all those years ago. Surely they produced a smile, probably even a chuckle. Did she recognize in them some young men, not far removed from boyhood, searching for a bit of fun in the midst of the brutality of war? She had known for a long time that Daddy was, to put it politely, quite tone deaf. Not to be cruel about it, but he honestly couldn't carry a tune in a bucket. She had told me once that she had tried to teach him early in their relationship, convinced that anyone could learn if they were instructed properly, but that it didn't take her long to give up the notion. Not that any of this stopped Daddy from singing hymns in church. Or singing along to his country music favorites. Or whistling a tuneless melody that consisted of only a couple of notes when he drove us on long trips, a sign that he was relaxed and happy, having left the worries of work far behind.

All of that—the letter, the attempt to cure Daddy's tone deafness, the acceptance that this was part of the man we both loved—all of that would come later. For now, as Mother graduated from high school and thought about what came next, Daddy had just entered his teens and was still simply the annoying friend of her little brother. Options for women at that time didn't really abound, but it seemed clear that, for our mother, what came next would definitely involve music.

IN 1944, SHORTLY AFTER Mother graduated high school and with the war still raging, Nana and Papa Jack moved the family to Cleveland, Ohio, where they had accepted jobs at the Quaker-founded Cleveland Bible College. Mother enrolled at the college in the fall to begin her freshman year. It is likely that Nana was also still taking classes; the long slog to finish her undergraduate degree did not end until the following year.

Mother enrolled as a voice student, becoming part of the college choir and the all female group, the Songsters. Despite the gloom of a war entering its fifth year, the scrapbook she kept shows those to be gloriously wonderful days, full of youth and promise. Days of smiles and laughter, of friendship and silliness. Days of tailored suits and evenings of long, flowing dresses. Days with good friends and nights of dates with young men and outings with her group of fellow classmates.

These were lovely days, yes, but they turned out to be short-lived. After a year in Cleveland, it became clear that the Ohio climate and Mother did not get along. She had survived a bout of rheumatic fever as a child that left her with rheumatic heart disease, a condition that did not respond well, at least at that age, to the colder winter temperatures in Cleveland. Losing class days to illness, she began struggling academically. The college administration allowed her to make up work, at the discretion of her individual teachers. But following her freshman year, the family packed up and returned to Greensboro.

There must have been mixed feelings with the move "home." Leaving Cleveland meant leaving friends, a poignant period of our mother's youth. She was clearly happy there. But her health had suffered and there were days of sickness and sadness. Plus, Greensboro was comfortable, home, and she had left good friends behind there when the family had moved to Cleveland.

As Mother thought about resuming her studies and earning her degree, there was no shortage of options in Greensboro. But two colleges in particular, both with degrees in music and education, looked especially promising. The Women's College of the University of North Carolina, or WC—long since the co-ed University of North Carolina at Greensboro, or UNCG to the locals— was established in the last decade of the nineteenth century as the arm of UNC dedicated to higher education for women. And then there was Guilford College. Another college begun by Quakers like CBC in Cleveland, it predated WC by more than half a century. It was also co-educational from its beginning, the oldest one of its kind in the South. Its first graduating class included both men and women, which had been taught by male and female faculty. Mother applied, and was accepted, to both.

She was offered a full scholarship to attend WC but she chose Guilford, largely because, in the end, she decided she had no desire to attend a college with just women. "It just doesn't seem natural," she used to say. Such thinking must have stemmed at least partly from growing up Quaker. From their origins, the Society of Friends had valued equally the contributions of men and women. But I think there was another reason. Our mother liked men and she felt comfortable around them. I could totally relate, and there should have been little surprise that when I attended Georgia Tech in the early 1980s, women comprised only fourteen percent of the student body, a ratio I felt entirely comfortable with.

Mother did not begin her time at Guilford until the fall of 1947, two years after her freshman term at Cleveland Bible College. The gap could have been due to recovering from poor health while in Cleveland. Or, it could well have been that the family couldn't afford two college tuitions. Nana was still working on her undergraduate degree; she finally reached her senior year in 1946 at the age of thirty-eight. The blurb below her senior picture certainly captured our Nana: "A religion major with a deep twinkle in each eye, Eva is a warm and loyal friend. Serious and studious, at times, she constantly amazes senior Philosophy students with her astute remarks and intelligent manner, even at eight-thirty in the morning."

The year after her own mother graduated from Guilford, then, Mother resumed her collegiate studies. At that time, Guilford provided a five-part educational program: I. Tool Courses, what we now refer to as the general education classes of English, math, science, and a foreign language; II. Essential Cultural Resources, which covered courses in philosophy, psychology, the arts and religion, to enable a graduate to be "intelligently conversant with the culture of his civilization in order to enter more fully into and to contribute more significantly to his social responsibility"; III. Major Concentration in a Selected Field of Personal Interest; IV. Physical Education and Recreational Program; and V. The Creation and Maintenance of a Social Environment, basically, working on living well together, "reflections of the religious spirit in which the institution is nurtured." For Mother, area III, her major field, translated into a heavy dose of music courses, including voice, piano, organ, and music theory, and active participation in the *a cappella* choir.

In its twenty-third season when our mother was a senior, the Guilford College *A Cappella* Choir enjoyed a prominent place among the college's organizations. Known as one of the leading choral groups of the South, its spring tours took it beyond the South's environs to more than seventeen states, including concerts in cities such as New York, Philadelphia, and Washington, D.C. The choir also participated in nationwide radio programs, and, in 1931, President Hoover had invited the group to perform at the White House. It was, without question, our mother's primary social group on campus.

While at Guilford, Mother was an above average student, struggling a bit with math—no surprise, there—and many of the sciences. But she flourished in her music courses to the extent that the college awarded her the David Troll Rees scholarship in advance of her senior year, one of two $100 scholarships awarded to music majors who were "worthy students...young men and women with high standards of mind and character."

Courses, grades, organizations, and scholarships show a part of Mother's Guilford experience, but only a part. What of her social life while there? She lived at home to save money, but our extrovert mother drew energy from being with people; there was no doubt that the choir is where she made most of her close friends. I looked through the college yearbooks of the years she was there, and young versions of our mother stared back at me, smiling and content. When I arrived at her senior picture, the caption next to it told me what I had been searching for—

"Virtue is the true and only nobility."

Four-year choir member...sometimes pitch-giver...kind and helpful...loves a good time...the "life" of the choir trips...day hop...knows any song...pleasing personality...David Troll Rees Musical Scholarship...recital on May 4.

I smiled in recognition, and chuckled in wonder. "Virtue is the true and only nobility," as her quote? Made sense. Kind and helpful? Of course. Pleasing personality? Absolutely. Knows any song? Not a surprise. Loves a good time? Okay, sure. But, the "life" of the choir trips?! Our Mother? She was 24 when she graduated from Guilford. I thought about that as I reread the caption and looked at her gazing back at me. She had always been "Mother" to Jeff and me. But here she was as a young woman with a life and identity separate from who she was to us. It's a little hard to swallow, even as an adult child. But there it was, and there was no denying it. So, what the heck; raise a glass to our mother being the "life" of the choir trips, and whatever craziness that may have entailed.

———

May 18, 1951, Korea

Dear Becky:

I bet you think that I have forgotten about you but I have not. I have been moving around so much I have not had time to do much writing.

Well, I will try to tell you a little of what I have been doing since I last wrote to you. As I said, we have been on the move. Well, the first thing the Marines did was go up and help the army out of a trap they were in. When we got there and were fighting, the army just run off and left us, but you know the "Reds" can't beat the Marines.

IF THERE WAS ANYTHING our father was sure of in his life besides his love for our mother, it was the vast superiority of the Marine Corps over all other branches of the military, *especially* the Army. There was never any doubt in my mind as to the truth of his conviction. My daddy was a Marine, so they must be the best. My brother and I were "Marine brats," through and through. In the 60s, the Corps was even more male dominated than it is today, so Jeff had a natural leg up on me just by virtue of his gender. At our dad's insistence, he also wore a crew cut—although confesses now to having hated it—and stood at attention when we attended military ceremony, particularly Daddy's officer commissioning ceremony. He also went on to become a Marine, graduating first in his class at Parris Island, earning a meritorious promotion to private first class that put him a step ahead of most of his fellow graduates. Always proud of my big bubba, too.

But I was every bit as proud to be part of a Marine Corps family. I was simply not going to be outdone by an older brother just because I happened to born a girl, which, by the way, I was altogether pleased with. So I capitalized on a series of three "natural" events to emphasize my special affiliation with the Corps.

First, I always thought it my good fortune to be born at the U.S. Naval Hospital, Beaufort, South Carolina, located on the mainland across from Parris Island, one of the most "Marine" of duty stations since, as one of their two recruiting depots, literally millions of Marines have started their journey there.

Second, I missed being born on the Marine Corps birthday, November 10, by one day, coming a few hours late and ending up having a Veterans' Day birthday instead. But Mother's due date had been November 10, and Daddy joked with her throughout her pregnancy that they needed to come up with a boy and girl's name with the initials U.S.M.C. I'm pretty sure he was only half kidding. My third and, without a doubt, proudest association with the Corps was genetic. I inherited the same green eyes of my father, a color we proclaimed as "Marine Corps green," since the shade mimics the color of their fatigues. My brother was blessed with a beautiful shade of light blue. Unfortunately for him, though, Daddy and I dubbed them "baby-blue eyes," and I let few opportunities pass to torment him with the fact—"Daddy and I have Marine Corps green eyes, but Jeff's are baby-blue"—being sure to draw out the word "baby" as long as possible. Proud of my big brother, yes; being willing to let him have one up on me, especially when it came to something as important in our father's eyes as the Marine Corps, *absolutely* not.

As an adult, though, I often wondered how Daddy, having been raised Quaker, with their aversion to war, went on to become such a committed Marine. A few years ago, I asked him what made him want to join the Marine Corps. He told me he had always, even as a boy, known that's what he wanted to do. In hindsight, I should have pressed him as to how he reconciled the peaceful ways of the Society of Friends with that elite fighting force. But I didn't, and so that is the only answer I ever received.

And yet I suspect that the three years' difference in our parents' ages and the way that difference altered their relationship to World War II played a part in Daddy's passion. Born in 1926, Mother turned 15 just six days before the Japanese attack on Pearl Harbor brought the United States into the war. She entered womanhood, then, with the world at war. Some young men she called friends in high school never returned. The loss that Mother suffered due to the war was often personal. Our father, born in 1930, was still a boy when America entered the war. While he most assuredly experienced loss, it happened more on a family level. What Daddy also experienced during the war was seeing Marines ship off to the front to fight for a cause they believed in and protect their family and country. It may have been these very images, so powerful to a young boy, that created or at least solidified his dream of one day wearing that uniform.

One thing was certain—intent on becoming a Marine from boyhood, Daddy never wavered on that dream. And in postwar America, with the Cold War threatening to spin out of control, the Marines were eager for willing recruits. Which is how in January 1948, with Becky Gardner still simply his friend's older sister and focused on her first year at Guilford, George F. Hobaugh enlisted in the Marine Corps when he was just a few weeks shy of his eighteenth birthday. Since he was not yet an adult in the eyes of the government, the Corps required him to get his parents' permission. The morning he left to take the bus to Parris Island for boot camp, he was not far from home when he realized he had left behind the form he needed with his parents' signatures granting their permission. He and his parents had already said their goodbyes, but there was nothing to do but hurry back, retrieve the form, and make a beeline for the bus stop. Daddy entered the house and found his mother sitting in the living room crying. I can visualize what that scene must have looked like in my mind and the impact it surely had on our father, for our grandmother simply did not cry. Though pressed for time, he took a minute to comfort his mother, grabbed the form, and headed off again on his journey to become a Marine.

Daddy's destination was Parris Island, South Carolina, a place where the Marine Corps has been making Marines out of men since the early part of the twentieth century and women since 1949. Located near the southeastern most tip of South Carolina about five miles south of Beaufort, the island was a perfect place to train Marine recruits—isolated, difficult to leave, and geographically appropriate for training in amphibious fighting, their specialty. The island acquired its official "Marine Corps Recruit Depot, Parris Island," designation in 1919, shortly after the end of World War I, and the number of recruits swelled during War World II, and the Korean and Vietnam Wars, when over 500,000

Marines were trained during the three conflicts.

Basic training, or boot camp as it is more commonly known, is a grueling, twelve-week effort to strip down men and women and rebuild them into Marines. The week before training starts, the recruits arrive on Parris Island at night, and immediately begin processing—hair cuts, gear and uniform issue, and medical check-ups. After meeting their drill instructor, or DI, at the end of the week, their lives are, as we say in the South, fixin' to undergo a drastic alteration over the next twelve weeks.

Marines are different from the other military branches—smaller, designed to be the readiness corps to be sent in as the first wave, on land, air, or sea. They want an elite corps, and, as the smallest branch of the big four, they can afford to be selective. The Army is made up of soldiers, the Navy of sailors, the Air Force of airmen, but Marines *become* Marines—for life. When we visited the National Museum of the Marine Corps a few years ago, Daddy told the Marine at the front desk that he had been a Marine. A slip up on our father's part, for sure. "You still are, sir," the young Marine reminded him, even though Daddy was, by this time, in his late seventies.

Instilling this level of commitment begins in basic training. During the Vietnam era, the Corps reviewed the skills that must be taught in boot camp versus those that could be deferred to the first unit of assignment. The results of the study were that three things could *not* be deferred: Drill and Ceremony, Rifle Marksmanship, and Marine Corps History. The first teaches immediate obedience to orders; the second is the fundamental skill that all Marines must have; and the last makes Marines part of something bigger than themselves or their current unit. How the specifics are spread throughout the twelve weeks may have shifted some over the years, but the essence of training in obedience, marksmanship, and being part of something bigger has formed the foundation of basic instruction for the last 100 years. Not to be undervalued in the training is the instruction in Marine Corps history. It covers iconic Corps battles that date back to the Revolutionary War and continue through the present, battle names passed down through the centuries, such as Derna, Chapultepec, Belleau Woods, Iwo Jima, Chosin Reservoir, and Hue, and is an essential part of making Marines. Recruits learn about the service and sacrifice of the Marines who came before them and come to understand their own place in a long history of valor and pride.

As a 1948 recruit, Daddy's Marine Corps history lesson stopped at Iwo Jima. The later battles were yet to be fought. He learned about the Chosin Reservoir differently, firsthand, as part of the 1ˢᵗ Marine Division. If I ever question how deeply the making of a Marine goes, I am reminded anew anytime I mention to a Marine I meet that our father fought at the Chosin Reservoir in Korea and watch her eyes widen with respect, or catch an *Oh, shit*, whispered under his breath.

May 18, 1951, Korea

How have you been doing? Do you miss the man you love? And is that me? It had better be. I sure miss the girl that I love and that is you.

WHEN I WAS A CHILD, Mother and I did a lot of snuggling. Okay, maybe not just when I was a child. Once I became a mother with a daughter who is also a snuggler, I began to appreciate the specialness of those times from the other side. A sharing of closeness, warmth, love, mixed in at times with some family stories, and once in a great while maybe a little wisdom.

One of those times that I was curled up with her, I remember asking when and how she and Daddy had started dating. What age I was at the time, where we were stationed, what house we were living in, what we had been talking about that had led me to ask—all that is lost. What stayed with me over the years was her response.

"Your father and his girlfriend Mimi had broken up right before he shipped over to Korea. Your daddy asked me if I would write him while he was over there and I said, yes, of course. When he came back from Korea, we started dating."

That was it; just that short, somewhat unromantic beginning. I carried that story with me for years, into adulthood, through the birth of my own child, through Mother's death.

After Mother died, Daddy and I got even closer. We talked every evening, and visited one another as often as the distance between northern Virginia and southwest Georgia would allow. During one of my visits to Albany to see him, he was reminiscing about his growing up, and I decided to pose to him a question similar to the one I had asked our Mother all those years ago.

"Daddy, how did you and Mother get together? What was your first date?"

"Well, I was home on leave and had been invited to a friend's wedding. I wasn't going to go, you see, because I didn't have a date. But one of my buddies said he bet Becky Gardner would go with me if she was available. I said okay, that would be fine. He checked with your Mother, and she was, so he set the whole thing up. And that was it. After that, we starting going out."

At the time, I didn't think to ask Daddy about Mother's story. I'm not sure why. Maybe I thought the date he was talking about had occurred after he came back from Korea. Maybe I liked Mother's version too much. Maybe I liked that theirs was a love and courtship that was born of letters. I think there is truth in both of the memories. Clearly, the few letters that exist from our father while he was in Korea indicate that he was, well, smitten. He wrote not to the older sister of a classmate, not to someone he'd known most of his life, not to a kind, attractive woman of the community who had agreed to write him while he was off fighting a war, but "to the girl that I love." Perhaps they began writing as friends and it turned into more as they corresponded. None of Mother's letters survived to answer Daddy's questions, but I know without having ever seen them that she answered in the affirmative. Their love and courtship may or may not have necessarily been born of letters, but it was one that flourished through them.

As Mother entered her final year at Guilford in the fall of 1950, then, Daddy was preparing to be shipped overseas to do what he had been trained to do. And while their individual journeys continued on separate continents, a world away from one another, their lives and stories were now joined in a way they had not been before.

3

Korea: 6 Miles from the 38ᵗʰ

March 28, 1951, Korea

Dear Becky,

I just had to write to the girl that I love today and let you know what I am doing and I bet you can guess. That is right. I am sitting in a foxhole and writing to you.

THERE ARE VIRTUALLY NO MEMORIES, NO STORIES to tell of our father's time in Korea. In all the years that Jeff and I had our daddy, he rarely spoke of being there. Mother told me he lost his best friend over there. Jeff told me how iconic the Chosin Reservoir campaign was to Marines. But I seldom heard Daddy talk about it, save to acknowledge that he was there, it was the coldest he'd ever been in his life, and after being wounded spent time recuperating on a hospital ship. His one acknowledgement to being a veteran was the Purple Heart license plate he acquired in his later years, a nod to the medal he received for being wounded in action. He never wore a cap advertising himself as a Korean War vet. Never met up with Marine buddies from his platoon. Never went to any reunions.

In truth, staying mum about war experiences when a warrior returns home is not unusual. Many veterans interviewed for oral history projects confess that they do not speak about it because they don't want to burden their families.

And they probably re-live enough of it in their dreams that, to them, talking about it seems that there is never an escape.

But, though he seldom said anything to us, never wore any kind of overt designation that he was a veteran, Daddy never shied away from acknowledging, when asked, that he fought in Korea, and survived the landing at Inchon and the bitterly cold campaign at the Chosin Reservoir.

In the year or so before he died, he was visiting me in northern Virginia and we made a late morning trip into the District to the Korean War Veterans Memorial. Situated adjacent to the Lincoln Memorial and across from the Vietnam Veterans Wall, the Memorial is a haunting tribute to the 5.8 million American service men and women who participated in that conflict. It consists of two parts: 19 stainless steel statues, nearly seven feet in height, representing the four military branches with an ethnic cross section of America; and a mural wall that honors the various military personnel that supported the ground troops.

We had been before. But it had been a number of years, and Daddy wanted to visit again to take some pictures of the Memorial with his new iPad. That man loved new technology! I decided to drive us in since even the closest Metro station is still a decent hike to the Memorial. At 82, our father was in incredibly good shape, but I didn't want to push it. Amazingly, I found a parking place on Independence Avenue, right across from our destination. As we approached the Memorial, Daddy seemed to become lost in time. As he focused on getting pictures of the statues, I walked along the mural wall, noticing how both of our reflections and those of the other visitors blended in with the soldiers, sailors, airmen, and Marines that were etched in the granite. As we finished up our visit, I asked one of the park rangers if he would take a picture of the two of us. He graciously obliged. We thanked him and turned to walk away but before we could, a woman stopped Daddy and asked if he had been there, had fought in Korea. Without missing a beat, he said that he had, had been with the 1st Marines at the Chosin Reservoir. She thanked him for his service, and we turned to walk back to the car for the 20-minute drive home. How had she known, I wondered at the time. His age? The way he carried himself? The intensity with which he took in the statues and the mural wall? Or was it just a lucky guess?

I know our father was forged deeply into the brotherhood he knew as the Corps, proud to serve wherever called. While he never would have chosen to fight in Korea, I imagine he faced it with the tenacity that defined his life. What I'll never be able to comprehend, particularly after learning more about his time over there, is how he—or anyone, for that matter—endured the horrors of battle that confronted him and yet returned home to anything close to a "normal" life mentally and emotionally.

So it seems fitting that the three letters that survived from Daddy's time in Korea date from the spring of 1951, several months *after* he had survived the brutality of the Chosin Reservoir campaign. That if we were to know what he had endured, it would have to come from some source besides him. It also seems right that the brief bit of insight into our parents' relationship during this time is through only Daddy's letters. For the story of Korea was, at least for our family, our father's story.

May 18, 1951, Korea
Dear Becky,

I bet you think that I have forgotten about you but I have not. I have been moving around so much I have not had time to do much writing. But you know that I would never forget "the girl that I love."

KOREA HAS BEEN DUBBED "the forgotten war." For Marines, it has been anything but. What follows is an unabashedly, not impartial account that valorizes the Corps even while feeling nauseous at the brutality and senselessness of war.

The United States had never had much interest in Korea. But that changed following the surrender of Japan in August 1945 that put a final end to World War II. Almost immediately, Washington politicians and the U.S. military began worrying about Soviet influence in Asia. Korea had been considered part of the Japanese Empire since 1910, an industrialized "colony" of sorts. It was clear that an arrangement similar to occupied Germany, with its division by the Allies to satisfy the increasingly uneasy alliance between the United States, Great Britain, and France on one side and Russia on the other, lay in store for it. The United States proposed dividing the Asian country at the 38th parallel (the horizontal line of latitude at 38 degrees north), with the Soviets occupying north of the division and the United States occupying the south. Such a proposal would conveniently divide the country so that the capital city of Seoul, the best agricultural land, and the majority of the population fell in the south. Incredibly, the Soviet Union readily agreed to the 38th parallel border.

By 1947, the United Nations recognized Korean independence and established a temporary commission whose purpose was to create a unified government. By this time, however, the political situation in occupied Korea had largely devolved into three groups that basically hated and mistrusted one another: the staunch communists, supported in the north by the Soviet Union; the staunch anti-communists, supported in the south largely by the United States; and the domestic nationalists, whose main goal was an independent Korea but who were seen as an enemy by both the communists and anti-communists. The temporary commission had a tough road ahead, one that, in reality, had little hope of succeeding. The communists eventually ceased participating and the domestic nationalists were driven to the north or arrested by those in power in the south. In the late summer of 1948, the anti-communists established the Republic of Korea in Seoul; the communists countered less than a month later by proclaiming the establishment of the Democratic People's Republic of Korea. The United States and the Soviet Union both withdrew their forces at that time. What they left were two virtual police states in each section of the country who saw the other as the very personification of evil and whose primary purpose was to "unite" Korea under their banner and impose their own form of rule throughout the country.

Despite the establishment of a communist government in northern Korea, the communist "threat" in the region was never as real as American perception. Our participation in the war to come largely took place due to a failure to understand that communism was not as monolithic as we envisioned. In truth, there were two communisms at work in the postwar era. The first, which took hold in Soviet Russia and its satellite countries, was a highly centralized organization in which the needs and aims of the Soviet Union became the controlling factor. The second had more to do with anti-colonialism. Those who embraced this brand of communism did so because of its anti-colonial stance, one that stood in opposition to the imperial powers' reluctance to cede power and provide a path to independence for their colonies. This second form was the communism that came to exist in places like Korea and Vietnam. While they may have been armed by Russia, they did not see themselves as controlled by, or part of, the Soviet Union. For these countries, their own national interests took precedent over communism.

This was not a communism the United States understood. We were convinced that the North Korean communists would take no belligerent steps toward the South without approval and orchestration by the Soviet Union, who, in turn, would not want to risk an outbreak of conflict in the region that could lead to WWIII. Interestingly, while the North armed and organized its army with Soviet help, the United States, worried that the southern Republic of Korea would start a war with the North if properly armed, provided only those arms needed to maintain public order and enable self defense. In the end, our own worldview of communism and the military shape in which we left the South almost guaranteed that we would need to intercede in the event of an armed conflict.

On June 25, 1950, North Korea, following some skirmishes with the South and after consulting both the Soviet Union and China but acting on its own accord, crossed the 38th parallel and invaded the South. Washington, based on its faulty worldview, was shocked. Five days later, Truman authorized the use of American ground troops in Korea.

March 28, 1951, Korea

Guess what? I got to shave the other day, and it had been about 40 days since I had shaved, so you can see I had a job. I used 3 blades. I have still got my mustache, and I am going to keep it until I get home and you can see it.

I don't know how long it will be until I get home, but I hope not too long. I sure would like to see you now. I miss you and J.B., and Mr. and Mrs. Gardner.

After the North Korean Army made their own crossing of the 38th, they were rolling toward what appeared to be an easy victory over their southern neighbors, with the intention of reuniting the country under the communist leadership of the North. Their army was better equipped, and at least one third of the troops were battle-hardened veterans, having fought in battles against the Japanese during WWII and with Chinese communists during their civil war. Moreover, the North Korean Army was strongly motivated. They understood their own military campaign as a continuation of these previous wars, viewing the United States and their allies in Korea as imperialists and oppressors, much as the Japanese had been prior to their defeat in WWII. The South Korean Army, in contrast, was young, inexperienced, and poorly equipped, and their closest allies, the U.S. military stationed in Asia, were not at the peak form they had been five years earlier. The focus on atomic over conventional warfare had changed the shape of the American military. Many of the veterans of WWII had left military service and were trying to resume their lives, and many young recruits were yet to be battle tested. American soldiers brought into Korea in the early months of the war did not care for the country and were not sure why they were even there.

The result was that two days following the North Korean invasion, with the South and their U.N. allies offering only ineffective resistance, the President of South Korea evacuated from the capital city of Seoul, located in the northern part of the country not far from the 38th parallel. The capital fell to the North the following day. Throughout the month of July, the North Korean Army continued its relatively easy push and, by the beginning of August, had cornered the South Korean Army and its accompanying U.N. forces into a small southeastern perimeter of the country at the port of Pusan. The Pusan perimeter was an approximately 100-by-50-mile rectangle; the remainder of South Korea lay in the hands of the North Korean Army. Throughout the month of August, U.N. forces hunkered down in this small swath of South Korea. It was due in large measure to steely determination on the part of the soldiers and Marines on the ground, and air superiority disrupting the North's access to supplies, that southern forces held off the opposing army and prevented an early and complete victory by North Korea.

Meanwhile, General Douglas MacArthur, World War II Pacific hero and now commander of the U.N. forces, was planning an amphibious landing at the port of Inchon on the northwestern coast of South Korea, close to the 38th parallel. An amphibious landing meant Marines, and MacArthur had made it clear that he wanted the 1st Marine Division out of Camp Pendleton, California. It was at this point that our father entered the picture.

Daddy was, at the time, a private first class (PFC), serving as a cook with H&S Co, 2dBn, 2dMar, 2dMarDiv, which translated means Headquarters and Service Company, 2nd Battalion, 2nd Marine Regiment (referred to as the 2d Marines), 2nd Marine Division at Camp Lejeune, on the North Carolina coast in Jacksonville, about a four-hour drive from Greensboro. However, this was now wartime, and the 1st Marine Division was in desperate need of shoring up, not with reservists but with veterans and postwar recruits that were well trained. Virtually overnight, then, Daddy found himself in one of the three battalions transferred to the 1st Marines (1st Marine Regiment) of the 1st Marine Division. He also found himself under the command of the legendary Marine Colonel Lewis B. "Chesty" Puller.

Chesty Puller had enlisted in the Marine Corps in 1918, just as World War I was ending. He was trained for battle as an infantryman, cavalryman, artilleryman, aviator, and shipboard officer. Too late to fight in the Great War, he went on to fight in Haiti and Nicaragua, and China, and to command troops in the

Pacific during World War II. At the Battle of Guadalcanal he held off a division of Japanese with a half-strength battalion and an untested Army regiment. The Marines that fought for him on that island were awarded two Medals of Honor, 28 Navy Crosses and Silver Stars, and 264 Purple Hearts. By the time he was called from a career languishing during peacetime to take over command of the 1st Marines in 1950, he himself had been awarded more decorations for valor in combat than any other Marine in Corps history, four of them Navy Crosses, second only to the Medal of Honor. He would add a fifth before he retired.

It was who he was as a Marine and a commander that caused those who served under Puller to revere him. Coming up through the Corps as an enlisted man, his earthiness had a way of making Marines under his command feel like he was one of them. He usually wore old utilities (a combat utility uniform), and, passing among his men, they would often mistake him for a gunnery sergeant if they could not see his insignia. He would just smile and wave. He also stood up for his men, and worked tirelessly to make sure they were ready for combat. The three battalion commanders who arrived from Camp Lejeune—Lt. Col. Allan Sutter, who commanded our father's battalion, being one of them— reported that their weapons were only fair, having been issued no new ones since leaving Lejeune. With the help of an expert gunner, Puller checked every rifle in those three battalions and then every other rifle in the remaining battalions in his regiment. He ended up discarding 67 percent of them as unfit. When the new rifles arrived, he examined and eliminated 37 percent of those, classifying them as in less than perfect condition. After ensuring that every Marine in his regiment had a rifle in good working condition, he spent most of his time at the range where every man in his regiment fired 25 rounds with his new weapon to ensure accuracy, all under the watchful eye of their regimental commander.

Beyond seeing that they were combat ready, he also exhibited genuine concern for his men. As the 1st Marines assembled and trained at Pendleton, Puller stopped one night in the improvised beer hall. Asking for the officer in charge, he told the lieutenant he had heard that they had run out of beer the night before and that the beer they *had* served was warm. When the lieutenant confirmed the rumor, Puller informed him that it would not happen again and asked the lieutenant whether he understood. He responded in the affirmative, but Puller continued. "These boys are going to war, and some of them won't be coming back," he launched in. "They're working like hell all day and half the night to get ready, often 16 hours straight. What they do in their off hours is their own damn business, and, by God, if they want a couple of beers, Lieutenant, they're going to get them." The following evening, Marines could hardly walk for the cans of beer that had been brought in.

The 1st Marines, our father among them, finally departed the States on September 1, bound for Kobe, Japan, a blown boiler on one of the ships having delayed their August 22 departure. Not even Puller knew for sure their final, Korean destination of Inchon until they reached the Japanese port on September 10, although he and the other officers had speculated while on ship that Inchon would be the landing point.

MacArthur was intent that the invasion would be at Inchon. Generally no real friend of the Marines, he felt certain that with the 1st Marine Division he would strike a blow in the northern part of the country to relieve the pressure at Pusan, cutting off and destroying the North Korean army. Peace would be restored and the troops would be home by Christmas. And so went typical, prideful, unrealistic thinking of yet another wartime general.

As a landing site, though, Inchon posed obstacles. There were no traditional beaches along the port city of 250,000 but rather sea walls and jetties that fronted the marshy lowlands and concealed factories and warehouses. The harbor itself was treacherous, becoming a collection of mud flats and reefs at low tide, which differed from high tide by an average of 29 feet. Timing of the landing, both date and time, was critical so that the tide would be at its peak and therefore high enough to support the larger of the landing ships. There were only three possible dates in the coming months, one day each in September, October, and November. The first, September 15, was chosen. The landing would occur precisely at 5:30 p.m., for within six hours of peak tide, the water level in the harbor would fall to six feet.

While the division docked at Kobe waiting for orders to begin making their way to Korea, Puller walked around the port, visiting the Army hospital and the docks, talking to soldiers who had already seen battle. An Army corporal he spoke with at the docks suggested to Puller that he make sure his Marines wear their distinctive yellow leggings. "You see," he told him, "the North Koreans refer to the Marines as the 'Crazy Yellowlegs,' and they never attack them, unless it's by accident or ignorance."

When Puller returned to inspect troops at one of the training camps, he issued one order. "Put the leggings back on the men. We wouldn't want to disappoint anybody when we make landing. Maybe we'll actually throw some business over to the Army."

May 18, 1951, Korea

Well, we had to pull back after awhile and cross the river, and the only way to get across was to wade. It was up to our waists, and it was about dark. Boy, was that water cold. After we got across the river we walked all night, just about all night, until 4:00 in the morning, lay down and slept until 7:30 that morning, and started walking again and walked all day. I never was so tired in all my life.

THIS DESCRIPTION FROM DADDY, written to our mother a full eight months after the landing at Inchon, may not give any insight to that battle, but it does depict the acceptance Marines have with amphibious work. In short, they take the words of the Marines' Hymn seriously: "We fight our country's battles, in the air, on land, at sea." The water is there, you wade through it. The city is on the coast, you approach it from the sea. These kinds of landings are what Marines are trained for.

Puller and his men, including our father, left Kobe on September 12. In transit, the convoy grew until it numbered four carriers, two cruisers, twenty-five destroyers, and many other smaller sea craft. When the landing time of 5:30 p.m. arrived, hundreds of craft took turns entering the port to allow the Marines to disembark and then return to the outer harbor. Inchon was all but masked through a haze of smoke and dust that had come first from the ships and then from the 5th Marines who were landing on the area known as Red Beach.

Daddy's regiment was part of the third wave at Blue Beach, and they ascended the fifteen-foot sea wall that was the barrier, Puller right in the mix with them, using ladders that they improvised while en route on the ship. Once they breached the wall, Daddy's battalion, the 2d, along with the 3d, led the assault. By the time reports were coming into Puller, the battalions were in position on a line that they would defend for the night. Division casualties were mercifully low, and Puller's 1st Marines light. As Puller walked among the troops that night he found the 2d battalion both holding the nearest road intersection and fanned out into some of the surrounding hills. Daddy's battalion commander Sutter reported one dead and 19 wounded.

By early the following morning, Puller was in contact with the commander of the 5th Marines. The two regiments had closed in on the North Korean Army, and a South Korean Marine regiment was working its way through the city to flush out any members of the North Korean Army hiding in homes.

Just a few hours later, around 9:00 a.m., Puller had made a 4000-yard inland drive against mortar and machine gun fire, and by the end of September 16, the day after the late afternoon landing, the assault phase was over. The push for Seoul, 17 miles inland, would begin the following morning on September 17.

The road to Seoul was laid with mines and was treacherous going. Daddy's battalion encountered heavy mortar fire the second night and lost two men, and then beat off two tank attacks over the following two days. They were the first battalion of the 1st Marines to arrive at Yongdong-Po, an industrial suburb just west of Seoul, and after maneuvering a confusing series of dikes and warehouses and a night of heavy fighting, broke through the enemy and secured the town. The remaining obstacle between Puller's regiment and Seoul was the Han River, which Daddy's

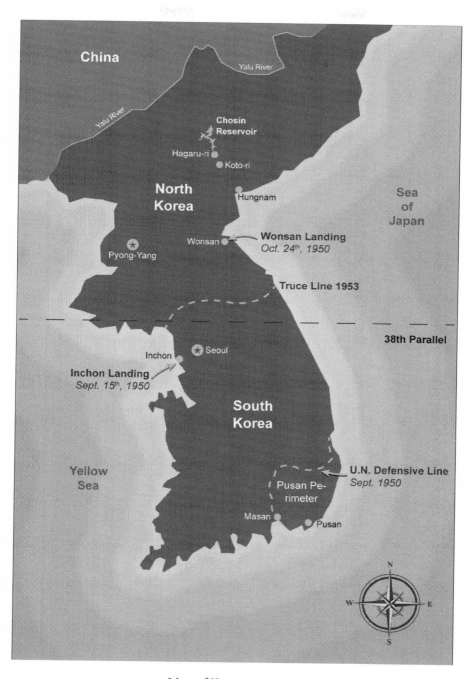

Map of Korea, 1950–51

battalion successfully crossed on the morning of September 24 under sniper fire.

By September 25, the heart of the capital city lay directly in front of Puller, and, while MacArthur had announced that the city had already been secured, much of the most brutal fighting lay ahead, the hardest of which would fall to the 1ˢᵗ Marines.

The North Korean Army would not make capture of the city an easy or bloodless task. As artillery rained down upon a collection of huts on the outskirts of the city, Puller noted with a heavy voice that North Koreans were forcing the U.N. forces to virtually destroy the city in order to recapture it; in doing so, the North Koreans would walk away with a billion dollars of free publicity. In the process, though, it would be the civilians living in those huts, Puller noted from an overlooking hillside, ones that their families had probably lived in for generations, who would be hurt.

Under the command of the U.S. Army's newly formed X Corps, orders were given to begin a street-by-street entry into the city on the night of September 25. The X Corps clung to the conviction that fighting would be light since an airman's report of civilian refugees on the roads convinced them that the North Korean Army was fleeing the city. Yet the commanding general of the 1ˢᵗ Marine Division felt otherwise, thinking that the enemy would not give the city over short of a house-to-house, street-by-street, defense, and so ordered caution as his Marines entered an unfamiliar city in the dark. The following morning, Puller's regrets about what it would take to secure the city were confirmed; that section of Seoul lay in complete ruin, blasted to rubble. It was time for his 1ˢᵗ Marines, along with the 5ᵗʰ, to start their slow, arduous push into the heart of the city.

The 5ᵗʰ Marines came in through a spur while the 1ˢᵗ entered on the main street, finding North Korean soldiers at each intersection behind roadblocks, rice bags, and with snipers in and on top of the houses. Puller urged them to keep the line moving, allowing the South Koreans to come in behind to handle the snipers. Throughout the battle, the legendary Marine seemed to be everywhere, walking among his men and shouting directions and encouragement. He could often be found where the fire was the heaviest, puffing on his pipe, as if there weren't a battle around for miles. It was little wonder that Marines who fought under him, our father included, identified themselves as Puller's ahead of giving their regimental number.

On September 26, for the second time in as many days, the U.S. Army announced most of the city secure, when, in reality, another day of heavy, street-to-street fighting lay ahead of the 1st Marines. But by 11 a.m. on the morning of the 27th, Daddy's battalion raised an American flag over the French consulate and, later that afternoon, at the American Embassy. The race by Marine battalions to raise one at different locations seemed to be in full swing, much to the irritation of the Army, which observed that since Iwo Jima, Marines would rather carry a flag than a weapon. In standard form, Puller countered that having his Marines carry a flag wasn't such a bad idea since any man with a flag in his pack wasn't likely to stray from the objective.

March 28, 1951, Korea

You know what hon? We are just 6 miles from the 38th [parallel] and I sure hope we don't go over again.

WITH THE RECAPTURE AND fortification of Seoul, Daddy and the rest of the Division were transported by truck in early October back to a western port near Inchon. As they boarded ships and prepared to sail for what was anyone's best guess, including Puller's, the Eighth Army was able to break out of where they had been nearly pushed into the sea at Pusan, and fight north to liberate the rest of the country, pushing the fleeing North Korean Army back to the other side of the 38th parallel. The war should have been, essentially, over, and MacArthur's promise to have the troops home by Christmas seemed well within grasp. Indeed, rumors circulated on board the ships that carried the 1st Marine Division that the war was coming to an end and they would head for home. But rumors ran the gamut, with the other extreme being that the Division was headed for a port in North Korea for an invasion of China. The truth lay somewhere in between.

The momentum clearly on the side of the U.N. forces, the temptation to continue and reunite the two Koreas was simply too great to ignore. Washington was clearly afraid of waking the sleeping giant that bordered North Korea, having instructed MacArthur not to cross the 38th if there was any chance of Chinese, or Soviet, intervention. But despite repeated warnings from China, it seemed that there was no one in Washington's political or military sphere willing to think the Chinese serious. Why the United States, which drafted and pushed for the U.N. resolution that called for stabilizing and establishing a "unified, independent, and democratic Korea," thought that China would sit quietly and allow troops to pour into North Korea for those purposes defies present-day imagination. So great was the need to push back against what Washington saw as the creep of Communism that it failed to understand that, to the North Koreans and certainly the Chinese, the American military was understood to be the instrument of a new imperial power.

To complicate matters, the military man in charge on the ground exacerbated all of these larger diplomatic and political issues surrounding the state of the war. MacArthur was the adored American hero of Pacific success in World War II, a role he cherished and sought to cement in Korea. His distaste, even hatred, of civilian oversight and control of the military was life-long, and he routinely chose to dismiss and ignore the civilian chain-of-command. Basically, MacArthur regarded *all* of Korea his in which to wage war until the enemy, the North, capitulated.

There would, then, be no going home for the 1st Marine Division. As they sailed around South Korea and then turned north, most of the Marines merely wanted to disembark anywhere since dysentery had struck widely, making the voyage to who knew where miserable for thousands of men.

As it turned out, the landing was at Wonsan, along the east coast of North Korea, their purpose to open another front for the Eighth Army, which had left Seoul and been marching north along the west coast. As the Chinese had promised, their army had descended, crossing their border with North Korea, and concentrated their forces in the northwestern hills to engage the Eighth Army. Upon learning that the Marines had landed, however, the Chinese began diverting the bulk of their army eastward to the Chosin Reservoir area to drive a wedge between the two U.N. forces and engage both. The 1st Marine Division was on its way to meet *ten* Chinese divisions, over 100,000 men.

The Marines arrived in the region of the Chosin Reservoir to what can only be described as a 100-year blizzard. Temperatures most days hovered around 25°F below zero, made worse by almost constant wind. Canteens had to be carried inside clothing and only dry rations could be used. After ten days, the riflemen in the mountainous regions lost 15 to 20 pounds. Despite being ordered to carry an extra pair of socks next to their skin, many suffered from frostbite.

The short version of what happened next was that, after roughly a month of fighting to push the offensive northward toward the Yalu River—North Korea's border with China—the Marine division, holding three positions in the Chosin region, found themselves surrounded by those ten Chinese divisions. When Puller received the news, he told the messenger, "Those poor bastards. They've got us right where we want 'em. We can shoot in every direction now."

The order was given to extricate the Division from the Chosin Reservoir and head for the sea, but the regiments had been divided up by high command over the protests of the Marine Divisional Commander, General Oliver Smith. The first task, then, was to reunite the Division at the southernmost point of Koto-ri where Puller was with Daddy's battalion. The 5th and 7th Marines, the northernmost regiments, began their trek southward on December 1 facing overwhelming odds, carrying with them 1,500 casualties, and encountering heavy fighting along the way. Once they reached Hagaru-ri, about ten miles northwest of Koto-ri, the Air Force evacuated over 4,000 casualties and offered to fly out every man. General Smith declined, telling the Air Force that the Marines intended to break out on the road so that they could bring with them any salvageable equipment.

By December 7, after heavy fighting at Hagaru-ri, the bulk of the Division with its 10,000 men and 1,000 vehicles was with Puller at Koto-ri. That night, he went through the lines for half the night, going from foxhole to foxhole, checking on as many men as he could.

The following morning, the Division began its breakout from Koto-ri. Puller's 1st Marines became the rearguard at that point, allowing the battle-worn 5th and 7th to get out first. Despite being ordered to destroy equipment, Puller refused, intending to take out everything he came in with that would still move, plus the working equipment the Army had abandoned.

The 1st began their removal from Koto-ri on December 10. What worried Puller most was no longer the Chinese Army but the hoards of North Korean civilians following them to the sea. He ordered Marines to fire over their heads to prevent them from getting too close, knowing that the Chinese troops had disguised themselves as civilians to get close and open fire on the Marines.

Puller's jeep was loaded with wounded, and a few dead Marines were strapped to the bumpers to be carried out with the Division. His seat was left available for him, but he rode very little, choosing instead to walk among and encourage the men. "You're the 1st Marine Division," he shouted as they marched to the sea, "and don't you forget it. We're the greatest military outfit that ever walked this earth. Not all the Communists in hell can stop you."

If he came upon men from his own regiment, he shouted even more proudly. "You're the finest regiment in the finest division in history. We're not retreating! We've made an about-face so we can get at more of those bastards. Be proud you're 1st Marines."

Daddy's battalion, part of the 1st Marines bringing up the rear, walked the last 22 miles of the "about-face" in 20 hours, through enemy attacks, icy roads, and uniforms and packs made heavier from the frozen conditions. By midnight on December 11, the last of the Division was safely ensconced on the North Korean beach. Marine casualties from the time they landed in Wonsan until hitting the beach, from October 26 to December 15, were 718 dead, 3,508 wounded, 192 missing. Communist losses were 25,000 dead, 12,500 wounded. Marines who had survived the ordeal were surprised to hear reporters using the word *defeat*. Morale was as a high as any victory recorded.

May 18, 1951, Korea

Well, we caught up with the Army and waited for the Reds again. Then after that we went back in the rear for a rest, and stayed about two or three weeks, and now we are back on the lines again. Last night the Reds attacked the Army and they fell back some. Boy, that Army just can't fight at all.

Following the departure from Hungnam along the North Korean coast, the Division sailed to and settled in at Masan on the southern coast of South Korea. But there was talk that they would not remain out of the fight for long since the Eighth Army was in retreat again in the northwest.

Puller, having won his fifth Navy Cross for his combat bravery during the Chosin Reservoir campaign, was finally promoted to brigadier general in January and left to become assistant commander for the Division under General Smith. Daddy's battalion commander, Colonel Sutter, took over the 1st Marines as regimental commander. Daddy was promoted to corporal.

Eventually the Division made its way back to the front, rejoining the Army. For roughly six months, various offensives by either the U.N. or Communist forces resulted in a tug-of-war around the 38th parallel, but, by June 1951, the war slowed to a stalemate around the border.

June 7, 1951, Korea

Did I tell you that I hurt my foot and had to go back to a ship at Pusan and have it x-rayed? I stayed there about a week and left there, and I am now in Masan waiting for a way to get back on the lines.

I have some good news at last. I made Sergeant June 4. How do you like that? It took me 3½ years, but I made it. I guess I will have to stay in the Marines now that I made sergeant.

Well, hon, I guess I will close for this time. Don't forget to send me that picture of yourself, will you? Write real, real soon. I am always glad to get mail from you.

I **WAS CURLED UP** with my mother on her bed, luxuriating in her closeness and taking in the scent she was wearing.

"Tell me again how I got my name."

"You could probably tell me, by now, you've heard it enough times."

"I know, but I like hearing it."

It was about me, after all, I was thinking, and I sat up and looked at her as she began, yet again, the story that I knew. I think she enjoyed the telling as much as I relished the listening.

"Okay. Let's see. Daddy had been wounded in the foot when he was in Korea. That was why he received his Purple Heart, you remember. He was taken to a hospital ship for treatment and recovery, and while he was there, the actress Jennifer Jones visited the wounded Marines. Your father remembers that she was dressed very simply, a fitted black skirt and a white blouse, nothing fancy. But, as she walked among them, talking to them and trying to cheer them up, he thought she was the most beautiful woman he had ever seen. He decided then and there that if he ever had a little girl, he wanted to name her Jennifer. I guess it's a good thing that I was okay with it. And that, sweet girl, is how you got your name."

As I nestled back into the crook of her arm, I knew that we both were smiling.

Over forty years later, my brother sat with our father, nursing him as he struggled to fight a staph infection in the hip that had been reconstructed several years before. Jeff and I were playing tag team, thankful for each other and for schedules that allowed us to spell one another. I had left some days before to return to Virginia after flying down when Daddy landed in the hospital, and now here Jeff and Pascale were, holding down the fort and trying to make the best of a Thanksgiving that was far different than any of us had imagined a few weeks before.

As they sat together, one Marine with another, Jeff decided to ask about the specifics of our father being wounded in Korea. If Daddy would talk to anyone about that time, it would be his son, who became first a Marine, then a soldier, and fought another war, one in the desert of Iraq, in the early 1990s.

"You know, Papa George"—Jeff had called our father that ever since his son Jeremy had conferred the title some 25 years before—"you never have talked about how you were wounded in Korea."

Daddy turned to look at the son who had grown to tower over him, who had forged his own path in the military, who he had cut very little slack as he grew but loved with a fierceness and depth that was beyond question.

"Well, we started receiving mortar fire, and a round landed right next to me. I mean, it felt like it was right next to me. When it landed, though, it buried itself in the ground, in the snow, and so it didn't explode with as big a radius as it would have otherwise. When it did explode, some of the shrapnel struck me in the foot, and so I was hauled off to a hospital ship to have it x-rayed and to have it tended to until it healed. I'm here to tell you, Jeffrey, if that mortar round hadn't buried itself in the snow, I would not be here."

"You know, though, when they sent the telegram to Mama, they told her I had been killed in action, rather than wounded. But they realized their mistake pretty quickly, and so the next day, they got me on a call to her. I said, 'Hey, Mama, I'm okay.' She didn't believe it was me though. She said, 'Whoever this is, stop playing around with me. This is just mean. I know my boy is dead.' I chuckled and told her, 'No, Mama, really, it's me. I'm okay. I'm not dead, just wounded.' It took me a while to really convince her."

In war, my brother remembered, the proximity of incoming fire seems much closer than it might be, in reality, and time seems to almost suspend itself. The thing about Daddy's story is that he was wounded during the summer of 1951, months after they had left the Chosin and the snow. So while the mortar round may have buried itself in the ground, it couldn't have buried itself in the snow. And while it may have landed right next to Daddy, it may have just felt like it was right next to him. For our father, there was truth in that story that was more real than whatever actually happened.

The only other record we have of what happened is that June letter he wrote to Mother in which he told her he had "hurt" his foot. Right, Daddy, I thought. The Marine Corps does not award a Purple Heart to someone who "hurts" his foot. It had only taken 62 years and a conversation between father and son Marines to get some semblance of what actually happened.

By July, Daddy was back on the lines with his battalion, back to stalemate. His enlistment had ended in early June but been extended 190 days, convenience of the government.

A couple of months later, following roughly a year of being in the worst of the war, he was finally shipped home and transferred back to the 2nd Marine Division at Camp Lejeune. He had been promoted twice, arriving in Korea as a private first class and leaving as a sergeant. He was one of the "lucky" ones, returning with a mind, body, and spirit that not only survived but also, somehow, found a way to leave behind what he had suffered over there.

There was more fighting after he left, to be sure, but no more significant ground changed hands. It took another two years before the two sides could agree that the situation was not likely to change, definitively establish the border of the two Koreas at the 38th parallel, and declare a ceasefire. As of 2020, a peace treaty to officially end the war has yet to be signed.

4

Newlyweds

June 7, 1951, Korea

Hi Becky:

How is the girl that I love today? Fine, I hope, and I hope I am the man that you love. Am I?

By the time I was in my early teens, it was not uncommon for me to spend my leisure hours wondering about the kind of man I would marry. Would he be tall? I felt certain he would have to be given my height. (While our parents were of fairly average height, Jeff and I were what Mother called "throwbacks to a previous generation," Jeff topping out at 6' 4" and me at 5' 8".) Would this prospective husband of mine have dark hair, be a blonde, or possibly a redhead? I was a bit partial to dark-haired men, but wouldn't rule out the possibility of a blonde. To be honest, though, I really didn't see a redhead in my future. (Of course, that was long before Jamie Fraser, a eighteenth-century highlander, came into my life.) Would he need to have a good sense of humor, or would a more serious man do? While not a deal breaker, a good sense of humor would definitely be a plus since I loved to laugh. Would he be a military man, or a civilian? If he were in the military, he would have to be a Marine, of course. But, I also knew how hard military life could be on families, so he'd better be pretty special if I were to buy into that kind of life.

But the one question that kept rolling around in my mind that I just couldn't seem to answer was, how do you know when someone is *the* one. I decided to seek out a person I considered to be an expert on the subject, and went to talk with Mother. She had found a considerate, thoughtful, faithful man. They clearly were in love after twenty years of marriage. Certainly she would be able to guide me. Her answer? "Well, sweetie, you just know," she responded. Gah, I screamed silently. You have *got* to be kidding me! That's it? That is all I'm going to get from our mother whom I generally considered to be a font of wisdom?

I decided to let that worry rest, and went back to wondering and dreaming, content to put off the issue of "knowing" until closer to the time.

When the time came, more than a decade later, Mother had been right. I just knew.

I'm not sure Daddy was all that thrilled that I had found *the* one; I'm guessing that's the way it is with most fathers and daughters. But I was helped out by the fact that my family had been less than thrilled with my previous boyfriend who was twice divorced and nine years older than me. So, despite the fact that Sam and I had only been dating three months when we got engaged, they recognized him, in the words of my great grandmother, as "good husband material," and gave their blessing.

Sam and I were blissfully happy. While everyone else talked about how difficult the first year of marriage was, ours was lovely. We had no trouble combining our households or our finances, and we reveled in being a couple. In our second year, I took a transfer from New Orleans to Atlanta, and we were happy to be only a little over three-hour drive from my parents. In April of 1991, after three and a half years of marriage, we welcomed a beautiful baby girl to the world and, after a rough start with a premature birth, settled into being a family of three. All seemed good and we started planning for an even larger family.

Eight months later, not long after our fourth wedding anniversary, Sam contracted a viral illness. He was coughing, practically hacking up a lung, when he picked me up from the airport on a Thursday in December as I returned from a business trip, but at least he was mobile. By Friday evening, we were at the emergency room and, after the longest night of our lives while they tried to get his blood pressure back up, they admitted him to the hospital. On Saturday evening, I was by his bedside when he began calling out for our daughter Anna and his mother. The healthcare professionals surrounded him and I backed away as he descended into a coma and was admitted to intensive care. The vigil of friends and family started Sunday morning, lasting all day and well into the night. And then, in the wee hours of Monday morning on December 16, he died at the age of 35 from a virus. I had just turned 31; our daughter was 8½ months. Our family, along with the community we were a part of, was stunned and shattered, and I was left feeling that my world had suddenly cratered. The man that I had known I would spend the rest of my life with was gone.

It took time, an incredible network of family and friends, a healthy dose of therapy, and some good medication, but I eventually moved on from the devastation of losing the man I considered, at the time, to be the love of my life.

There would be another marriage a couple of years later, to a wonderful man that I loved and who helped raise my daughter as his own. He was a widower whose first wife had died of cancer a few years before. A good bit older than me, he had three sons of his own—John and Steve were off on their own, and my John was trying to get his youngest, David, through his teen years. So I became the mother of a fourteen-year-old and two-year-old, and though not as tranquil as my first year with Sam, we blended over those first years into a new family.

Our time together would last 16 years before John succumbed to lung cancer in 2010. Under completely different circumstances, I found myself twice widowed by age 49, steeped in the familiar territory of grief.

Perhaps my own story of loss is one reason I clung to our parents' as I read their letters, that while I would get a taste of what they had in terms of love, the experience of longevity could never be mine. Understanding the fragility and capriciousness of life and the hard work that comes with relationships, I came to admire what they endured all the more.

———

June 7, 1951, Korea

How is J.B. getting along in this Marine Corps? Tell him that if he can get a leave or a weekend when I get home, me and him will have one good time, and you and I will have to go out one night. Is it a date?

WHEN DADDY RETURNED FROM Korea in September 1951, the Marine Corps gave him ten days leave before having to rejoin the 2nd Marine Division at Camp Lejeune. He spent the time at home where he got that date with Mother. She had graduated from Guilford earlier in the year, and, while waiting for a teaching job in music to come open, she worked for Greensboro Music Company and one of the downtown department stores. Regardless of when and how their relationship actually began, by this time, the two were definitely dating.

Back at Camp Lejeune, Daddy linked up with his childhood buddy—Mother's younger brother and our Uncle J.B.—who had enlisted in January 1951 and summarily been sent to Camp Lejeune after completing basic training at Parris Island. The two young Marines, both barely in their twenties, set about having "one good time" whenever they got leave.

When they got a weekend pass, however, they would head for home. They were often joined by another buddy from home, George Elkins, who had enlisted the same time as Uncle J.B. and promptly been stationed, following boot camp, at Camp Lejeune. The threesome would pile in the car as soon as their leave started and drive the almost four hours to Greensboro, where Daddy was spending more and more time over at the Gardners'. After he had kissed his mama and spent some time with his little brother, he would tell them he was going over to see Uncle J.B., or even Mr. Gardner. But as soon as he was gone, Grandmama Mimmie would turn to Uncle Elmer and remark, "Your brother's not fooling anyone. He's going over to see Becky."

After spending as much time at the Gardners' as he could, sometime late on Sunday evening, as late as they dared, the three would take their places in the car for the drive back, Uncle J.B. in the back so he could snooze—he was always too tired to drive, he would announce—with one of the two Georges driving.

That was the routine, that is, until the Sunday evening that our father and George Elkins colluded to force J.B. into the driver's seat. Daddy drove over to pick up J.B., stopping in to say goodbye to the Gardners and kiss our mother, who had become, in a relatively short period of time, not only "the girl I love" but, "his" girl. Only, this time, he took our uncle aside.

"Man, you're going to have to drive back. Becky and I stayed up too late last night. I'll never be able to keep my eyes open."

Uncle J.B. was sure he could get the other George to drive, until they arrived at the Elkins' and that George had a story of his own. "No, man, I can't drive. I had too much to drink this weekend and I'm still a little hung over."

So Uncle J.B. took the wheel, and the two Georges got in the backseat to sleep. About halfway into the drive, our uncle told his buddies they were going to have to pull over for a while because he just couldn't stay awake. Daddy and George Elkins, who had been trying to suppress their laughter since the start of the trip, started laughing so hard tears streamed down their faces. Uncle J.B. realized that it had all been a ruse. "Oh, you two think you're real funny." Daddy, still wiping the tears from his eyes, exchanged seats with his future brother-in-law and drove them the rest of the way back to base. True to form, Uncle J.B. curled up in the back seat and went to sleep.

Greensboro Daily News, June 8, 1952
Rebecca Gardner and Sgt. Hobaugh Engaged to Wed
Mr. and Mrs. Noah S. Gardner, 25 Boren Street, announce the engagement of their daughter, Rebecca Scott, and Sgt. George Francis Hobaugh, Marine Corps, son of Mrs. Samuel Hobaugh, 11 Front Street, and the late Mr. Hobaugh. The wedding is planned for Friday, August 8, in Pomona Friends Church.

For as long as I can remember, I have been a musical theatre buff, loving both the old standards and those that come along to change things up a bit. Growing up, I was especially captured by the movie musicals of the '40s and '50s, with the songs of my parents' generation and the dancing of a smooth Fred Astaire or an athletic Gene Kelly. One of my favorites was *An American in Paris*, built upon memorable songs by the Gershwin brothers, George writing the enchanting melodies and Ira the memorable lyrics.

I think my favorite scene in the movie is when Gene Kelly sings, "Our Love Is Here to Stay," to Leslie Caron, as they walk, and then dance, along the River Seine. It's a short song really, just an intro and two stanzas. But Ira Gershwin's lyrics, especially the last few lines, are timeless—"In time the Rockies may crumble, Gibraltar may tumble, they're only made of clay. But, our love is here to stay"—and it doesn't take much for the melody to earworm itself into my head. Couple that with Kelly's clear, easy voice and his and Caron's lilting dance along the river, and well, it's a classic scene. Pretty easy to see why the musical that began its life as a film won six Oscars, including Best Picture.

Over the years, I think I've come to feel that the lyrics to that song characterized our parents' relationship. It certainly didn't take *them* long to see that the letters, that first date, and Daddy's frequent drives home were leading somewhere. Far different from the extended engagements of today, their courtship, engagement, and wedding all occurred within a year of Daddy's return from Korea. Mother used to say that, despite his being over three years younger than she and only 22 when they married, war had made Daddy far older than the guys she had dated that were closer to her age.

Knowing our father, I can only imagine how he proposed. He was a romantic at heart who adored our mother, surprising her throughout the years with gifts and trips as their slowly expanding family income allowed. Lately I've found myself wondering what the scene was like. Did he get down on one knee? Almost certainly. Did he ask her at her home, where he probably felt more comfortable, or surprise her one evening when they were out to dinner? The only thing I know, besides the fact that they were engaged by May 1952, is what happened when he asked his future father-in-law for Mother's hand, a story that has been an essential part of our family canon.

It is a custom not as strictly followed anymore, one that grew out of our culture's patriarchal underpinnings. The very notion that a woman was being passed from her father to her husband, that she couldn't stand or speak for herself as her own person, rankles me now. But at that time, especially in the South, well, it was how things were done. So as Daddy sat down to speak with Papa Jack, he explained how much he loved the woman who would become our mother, how he would always be true to her and take care of her, how he couldn't imagine spending his life without her. Papa Jack listened respectfully. When Daddy finished, Papa Jack paused for a time, and finally said, "Well, son, if I was interested in giving Becky away, I'd be happy for you to have her. The problem is, I'm just not interested in giving her away."

I think our grandfather was only partially kidding. He and Mother were close and now he was confronted with the realization that another man was stepping in to become, from now on, the most important man in her life. Realistically, though, he must have known this was a done deal. Perhaps he reflected on his own mother-in-law's assessment that George was "good husband material." Grateful that Becky had chosen as fine a man as George Hobaugh, Papa Jack finally relented, and our parents, who had known one another for most of their lives, were now on a path to spend the rest of their lives together.

Greensboro Daily News, August 8, 1952

A lifetime of friendship will resolve as it should tonight when Becky Gardner and Sgt. George Hobaugh, a Camp Lejeuner, pledge an eternity of love at Pomona Friends Church. Things didn't get serious between this pair until the first of September when Becky accepted her first date with the just-back-from-Korea neighbor who never failed to drop by the Gardner home friendly-like whenever he returned from anywhere that could be considered "away."

WHEN I WAS TWELVE or thirteen years old, somewhere in that vicinity, I discovered Mother's wedding dress. It was hanging up in a plastic bag in an extra closet in their bedroom, a house we had moved to just a year or so before.

"Can I try it on," I asked her with pleading eyes and voice.

"*May* I try it on," she corrected, ever the grammarian. Ugh! I thought, giving myself an internal eye roll, and tried again.

"*May* I try it on?"

I was always taller than most of my classmates, having gotten that height of mine early, so it was not out of the realm of possibility that it wouldn't just hang on my prepubescent body.

"Of course," she said through her smile.

We carefully removed the plastic garment bag that "protected" it. The dress was remarkably well preserved for having spent twenty years that way. I stepped into the yards and yards of satin material, and Mother fastened a few of the many buttons that ran in a long row up the back of the dress. We looked in the mirror.

I gasped. "It's so beautiful."

Again, she smiled. "It looks good on you, although you won't need a dress like this for a long time." I was a bit gawky at that age, but Mother always knew the right thing to say.

I looked around a little. "Where's the veil?"

Another smile. "I borrowed the veil. I had already spent enough on the dress, so a friend loaned me her veil."

Curiosity rose in me.

"Where did you find such a beautiful dress? And how did you afford it?" I understood that, while Mother and Uncle J.B. had not grown up poor, there was not a lot of extra cash lying around.

"When Daddy and I were engaged, I was working at a department store downtown, and this dress came in. I fell in love with it immediately, the elegant simplicity of it, but it was a designer dress, and I knew I could never afford it. My boss knew, though, that the display dress, the floor model, would be, after a time, sold at a discount. I knew it was my size, and so we kept our eyes on it, and, the minute it went on sale, I tried it on. It fit perfectly. Between the floor-model and my employee discounts, the price came down enough that I was able to afford it."

My turn to smile. Mother was right. It had an elegant simplicity to it that was beguiling. Very little beadwork, just copious yards of gorgeous satin, with a fitted bodice, and long sleeves that came to a point. Plus, the train was impressive. I remembered the wedding picture of the train swirled around Mother's feet as if to blanket her. Stretched out, it was a good three to four feet. By today's standards, the dress would probably be considered a bit plain. But I knew right then and there that, if I were ever lucky enough to find a man as good as my daddy who I loved and loved me back, I'd found the dress I would wear.

And sure enough, when Sam and I married some 13 to 14 years later, that was the dress I was in.

August 8, 1958, Okinawa
My dearest darling wife:

6 years ago tonight you made me the happiest man in the world. And I still am the happiest man and luckiest man to have a wife as fine as you. If only in some way I could tell you what you mean to me. Baby, you are my everything and I am so glad you are my wife. If I had looked the world over I could never have found anyone as good as you are. You are the one and only one for me.

They married on a Friday evening in August, nighttime really, an 8 p.m. ceremony. In the days before air conditioning was widespread, summer weddings in the South were commonly held in the evenings when it was, at least relatively, cooler. Daddy, and the other Marines who stood with him—Uncle J.B. and George Elkins among them—were in formal uniform, "dress blues" as they are known in the Corps. Mother was in that beautiful, satin wedding gown, attended by her four bridesmaids.

Mother convinced Daddy that the two of them should memorize their vows, no "repeat after me" from the minister. How on earth she convinced him to do this is beyond me. Certainly, he must have been completely smitten. Our father had very little gift for language, so the vows they used that relied on the plain speech of their Quaker ancestors must have seemed a bit awkward to Daddy:

> I, George, take thee Rebecca, to be my wedded wife, to have and
> hold from this day forward. I promise to love thee, to take good
> care of thee, and to be true to thee through all that the future
> holds for us, til death do us part. To thee and before God I make
> this covenant vow.

But Mother insisted if they said them over and over in the weeks leading up to the wedding, all would be fine. She was right of course. While I think Daddy blocked the trauma from his memory, she remembered it as being perfect.

There was no reception. Nana and Papa Jack hosted a cake cutting at their home the evening before the wedding, attended by 50 guests—

Greensboro Daily News, August 8, 1952

Becky Gardner wore a rose faille and lace frock with off-shoulder bodice and was protected from a welcome breeze by a bolero last night, at the cake cutting given by her parents Mr. and Mrs. Noah Gardner at their home on Boren Street. A rhinestone star twinkled brightly on the jacket and teamed up with the white carnations contributed by the hosts. Mood music were love songs that really were unnecessary at that point but pleasant to listen to.

They spent their wedding night at the Robert E. Lee Hotel, a luxury hotel in nearby, downtown Winston-Salem, that had accommodated such famous guests as Mamie and Dwight Eisenhower, baseball player Joe DiMaggio, and celebrities Bob Hope, Frank Sinatra, and Ava Gardner. Daddy always liked to splurge on Mother when he could. The $10 cost of the room for one night seems almost laughable today, but considering Daddy only grossed $160 per month, a night at the Robert E. Lee was an extravagance.

As for a honeymoon, there almost wasn't one. After they were engaged, Daddy sent Mother some money that he intended be set aside for a post-wedding trip. Whether he didn't communicate that point clearly, Mother misunderstood, or she simply thought it a better use of the money, she used it to pay off the last of her college bills.

"I know how much you hate debt," she told him one night on the phone, "and so I thought you wouldn't mind."

"Well, I wouldn't have," Daddy told me years later, "except that I didn't know where else I was going to get money to take your mother on a honeymoon. She felt terrible about it, so I told her not to worry, we would figure something out. As it happened, soon after, I got some additional pay I wasn't expecting, maybe like $40 or so, but it was enough so that we could take a few days and go somewhere."

Caryville, Tennessee, May 14, 1952
Dear Mrs. Gardner:

Thank you very much for your splendid recommendation of our park. We will be happy to hear from Sgt. Habough [sic] concerning a reservation for him during his honeymoon.

Our cabin rates are $5.00 per night for two persons. The cabins are modern, each having a bath, good furniture, etc. Our activities include boating, fishing, hiking and picnicing.

We suggest Sgt. Habough [sic] ask for cabin #11 or 12. Please send a $5.00 deposit with reservation request.

In stepped our Nana to recommend Cove Lake State Park, located about 30 miles northwest of Knoxville. How she knew of the place and whether Daddy asked her to inquire, we'll never know. To an outside observer, it might seem as if our father was entering into a lifetime of dealing with a pushy mother-in-law. But nothing could be further from the truth and he knew it well. He followed up with the park in June, sending his $5.00 deposit to reserve cabin #12 beginning Sunday, August 10, for four nights. Cove Lake *finally* spelled his name correctly on the letter confirming his reservation.

———

March 26, 1954, Camp Lejeune

My Dearest Darling,

Will write you just a few lines this morning before I go to work to let you know that I got back o.k. ... I picked up a Marine just a little ways out of Greensboro and he came all the way back with me.

AFTER THEIR HONEYMOON, DADDY returned to Camp Lejeune and Mother resided, for a time, with her family in Greensboro. At some point, perhaps when married housing became available, she joined Daddy at Camp Lejeune where they began their lives together as a married couple.

But being just four hours by car from Greensboro, it was relatively easy for Mother to visit Nana and Papa Jack. With just one car, though, this meant that Daddy had to take her there on a weekend he had off, and return to pick her up the next time he could get a weekend pass.

Neither of them liked the separation. For Mother, it meant being torn between enjoying time with her parents and wishing she could be with her husband. For Daddy, it meant the loneliness and quiet of an empty house, counting the days until he could head back to Greensboro. But this was the reality of military life. If you had the good fortune to be stationed near an extended family you were close to emotionally, you took advantage of being able to visit when you could because you never knew when orders would come down to transfer you to the other side of the country, or the world. So, at the end of March and beginning of April 1954, Mother spent two weeks in Greensboro. Pregnant with their first child, it must have been an especially sweet visit for her. But for Daddy, there was just work, an occasional dinner with friends, and a quiet house.

March 26, 1954, Camp Lejeune

Honey, I can hardly sleep at night without you here, oh how I love you. I do believe I love you the most.

March 28, 1954, Camp Lejeune

When that "boy" gets here you are not going to leave me again!

I just had to call you last night. I was just about ready to come and get you. If it were not hard on you to ride I would have come and got you. This house seems so lost without you.

April 4, 1954, Camp Lejeune
My Dearest Darling:

I think this has been the loneliest day of my life. I am glad that I don't have to spend another Sunday without you, honey. I am so lonesome here without you. I just don't feel right inside. You know what I mean, don't you sugar?

Mike and Ann had me over for dinner today. I had a nice time, but I would have much clearly been with you sugar. For you see that is where my heart is honey, with you. Baby I love you more than words can ever, ever tell. Take all the words I know and put them together and that still could not tell how much I love and miss you, my darling.

April 5, 1954, Camp Lejeune
Sugar it won't be too long before I can take you in my arms, and kiss and love you, baby. ... I am so lonesome here without you. I sure will be glad when this week comes to an end. I have heard people say you should not wish your time away, but I wish this week away so I can be with you my darling.

In the days before sonograms, Daddy did not know they were having a boy; he just chose to refer to the baby that way. And with no girls in the Hobaugh family for the last two generations, I guess he thought it was a safe bet to expect that his first child would be a boy.

They survived that short time apart, and Daddy drove back to Greensboro on the weekend to retrieve his wife. But as Mother's due date grew nearer, she returned to Greensboro, for they had decided that the baby would be born there rather than at the Camp Lejeune Naval Hospital.

July 5, 1954, Camp Lejeune
My Dearest Darling,

Will write you a few lines, sugar. I got two letters from you and I was so glad to hear from you, baby. I sure was glad to get to talk to you today.... Sure will be glad when the baby gets here, honey, because I know it is hard on you in this hot weather.

WE ENTERED THE CAVERNOUS interior of the Washington National Cathedral on a crisp autumn morning. It was my husband John's favorite place to take visitors. Off the beaten path of the monuments, memorials, and museums, this majestic spiritual place was special to him, in part, because his father had been a major donor during its construction earlier in the twentieth century. It was one of the few places in the District we would sometimes visit even if we weren't showing it off to out-of-town guests.

This time, Mother was visiting, and we had some disposable hours while Anna was in school. We entered the back and looked down the expanse of the nave, the long central aisle, then strolled first down one side aisle, with its bays and chapels, and then up the other, taking in the beauty, the enormity of the kind of spiritual edifice that populated Europe but was rare in the States.

Mother knew about another chapel, though, a tiny one on the lower level of the cathedral, and that was her destination. We found the stone steps that took us underground and wandered through the Resurrection, Bethlehem and St. Joseph of Arimathea Chapels, all lovely but none of them the one she was looking for. As we left the Chapel of St. Joseph, we found another long corridor, and there it was. We entered the petite, unadorned Good Shepherd Chapel, with its four wooden benches and space for only seven. As we did, something in my mother transformed. She became quiet and stood facing the simple, yet touching stone sculpture of Jesus as the good shepherd, holding a sheep, placed in the chapel to give comfort to the suffering and symbolize God as protector. John and I stepped out for a minute to give her some privacy. When I went back in, I could tell she had been gently crying as she stood there dabbing the tears from her eyes. I walked over and put my arm around her, and she leaned her head into the curve of my neck.

"We used the scripture about the good shepherd at your brother's funeral," she told me. "When I read about this chapel in the years since, I always wanted to see it."

I realized, as I stood there comforting my mother, that, for her, the years had rolled away to July 7, 1954, a date that had held the promise of motherhood, a promise that almost immediately turned to overwhelming grief.

His name was Samuel Gardner Hobaugh, the Samuel to honor Daddy's own father that he had lost almost six years earlier. Our mother carried him to term, and then endured the agony of a stillbirth. Why they chose to have the birth in Greensboro rather than at Camp Lejeune, I do not know, not that it would have mattered. The doctors believed that the umbilical cord had somehow wrapped around his neck and he had suffocated. She was inconsolable. She never saw him, never held him. Her doctor told them that it was better that way, it would help her get over the grief faster. And back then, the doctor's word was inviolate. I do not know when Daddy arrived, although I assume that as soon as mother went into labor he made the fastest drive he'd ever made from Camp Lejeune to Greensboro. His last letter to her was dated two days before.

Daddy was devastated. "I remember your daddy come home that night [from the hospital]. I've never seen anyone so brokenhearted as he was" his brother, our Uncle Elmer, told me years later. "He was just so brokenhearted, and he sat down there, and he said, 'I'll not put her through that again. Let somebody else have 'em; I'll adopt.' Of course, he was hurt. Everyone could understand why he was saying it."

Daddy was granted leave for another ten days, through Mother's stay in the hospital, the funeral service and burial—in the same cemetery as his father, the section known heartbreakingly as "babyland"—and through the blessed numbness lifting and the days of the cold reality of grief achingly laying hold. On July 17, he returned to Camp Lejeune while Mother remained to continue her convalescence at Nana and Papa Jack's. Daddy was barely out of sight when Mother penned her thoughts.

July 17, 1954, Greensboro

My Darling,

You just left me—and I'm still warm from your kisses and love. I couldn't go back to sleep because in thoughts I'm making the trip with you.

I've got to try to say on paper what I tried so hard to put into words for the last 10 days. I love you, dear. Not just the empty way the words sound, but with a deep, endless devotion that goes beyond words or time or place. It's a love I'm sure implanted in my heart by God himself. And the strange thing is, I thought I loved you as much as it's possible. I've learned something about love. The more things you experience together, whether happiness or sorrow, just bring you closer together and the deep everlasting roots of genuine love grow still deeper.

You've been wonderful during this leave. So strong and understanding. You had to be strong for both of us and I've only made it by leaning on your strength and love.

I love you—I can never make you know how much. I loved our baby. You and God only know how much I wanted him and how lonely and empty my heart and arms are for a little one.

Goodnight, dear. I still haven't come close to saying what my heart feels. I love you, Darling.

I love you,

Becky

July 22, 1954, Camp Lejeune

My Dearest darling wife,

Will write you a few lines to let you know that I got your letter Wednesday afternoon, and honey, that was the sweetest letter I have ever read in my life. I love you more than words can ever tell, sugar. I am so very, very much in love with you.

July 23, 1954, Camp Lejeune

My Dearest darling,

Will write you a few lines this morning in answer to your 3 letters I got Thurs-

day. I love you, my darling, more than words will ever be able to tell. You mean everything to me, darling. I will be so glad when we can be together again.

Honey, I know it is hard on you when you think about the baby, and it is hard on me too. I don't know any two people that wanted a baby any more than we did, but we must look to God, and I know that he will give us a baby someday.

July 28, 1954, Camp Lejeune

My Dearest darling wife,

Honey, I guess I will be home with you when you get this letter. I will have taken you in my arms and kissed you, and tried to find the words that will tell you how much that I love and have missed you, darling. But I wanted to write you, so I am sitting here at the house, writing you. I just put out [on the clothes line] a [load of] washing so there won't be any clothes that you will have to wash, sugar. Honey, I will help you all I can when we get back home from this weekend with the housework. I want you to take real good care of yourself, baby. You are my everything. I don't want anything to happen to you, honey.

I was hoping we could spend this weekend by ourselves. I know that doesn't sound nice, but I was thinking it anyway.

Sugar, I will never be able to find the words to tell you how I have missed you these last two weeks. I have lay at night and wished that you were in my arms.

Honey, I am sorry I went to that ballgame the last night at home. I wish that I would have stayed at home and took you in my arms. I love you oh so much.

Well, baby, I guess I will come to a close for this time. I will see you before you get this letter. I love you, my darling wife.

All my love always,

George

And that is where the letters end. Daddy returned to Greensboro, stayed the weekend with Mother at Nana and Papa Jack's, and the two of them returned to Camp Lejeune to resume life without the baby they expected to bring home. In seven months, Mother became pregnant again, with my brother, Jeff, who came into the world October 20, 1955, six weeks early. They had been transferred from Camp Lejeune to the Marine Corps Air Station in Miami, Florida, just four months prior. There must have been anxious moments, a fear that things would end as they had with the first birth. He was just a little thing and needed time in an incubator. But he was generally healthy and possessed a fighting spirit—the makings of a fine Marine our father would say—so that he thrived and grew, eventually to all of that 6′4″.

I once asked Mother how she had ever gotten over the loss. Hadn't she longed for things to turn out differently?

"Having you and Jeff helped," she told me. "I came to understand that, if Samuel had lived, we would not have had another baby as soon as we had your brother, but we would have wanted another before we had you. I can't imagine not having both of you in our lives; you are the greatest blessings your father and I could have ever had."

I don't know any two people that wanted a baby any more than we did, Daddy had written. Indeed, not. Or any two people more suited to be parents.

PART II

Okinawa

5

This Island of Okinawa

September 10, 1957, Camp Fuji, Japan

I love you, baby, more than I can find words to tell. I am glad you like the little things I buy and send you. I love you and love to buy and do things for you, sugar.

S<small>OMETIME IN THE MID-1970S, WHEN I WAS IN THE</small> vicinity of fifteen or sixteen, Mother and I took the first of several shopping/theatre trips to Atlanta. Daddy had retired from the Marine Corps by then, and we had remained in Albany—our final duty station—a small city of about 100,000 at the time. Albany was, well, Albany. Atlanta? Now that was mecca. The state capital and only real "big city" that Georgia had, its allure for me included plentiful shopping, fancy hotels, and mostly, the "Fabulous" Fox theatre.

Always just the Fox to us, the Atlanta institution began its life in the late 1920s as mostly a movie theatre. With its red-carpeted entryway and ornate gilt work, it was an impressive, opulent place for Atlantans—well, White Atlantans—to lose themselves for an evening of film entertainment at a time when going to a movie was an event.

With the advent of multiplex theatres in the early 1970s, though, the Fox fell into disrepair. Scheduled for demolition, a "Save the Fox" campaign rallied the city to its plight, and donations came pouring in from the community to save and restore the landmark site. Opening again in 1975, it became the venue for tours of Broadway shows, film festivals, the Atlanta Ballet's performance of *The Nutcracker*, and headlining events through the years like Elvis Presley, Madonna, and Prince.

With the Fox now restored to its former glory, then, here I was about to embark upon a mother/daughter trip to "Hotlanta" for some clothes shopping and a Broadway musical. I was excited about the shopping, of course, but the evening at the theatre was going to be the highlight of the trip, I was sure. It was not just *any* Broadway musical. We were going to see *The King and I* by Rodgers and Hammerstein, that musical theatre power-writing team of the 1940s and '50s. And it was not just *any* production, for playing the king was none other than Yul Brynner himself, the actor who had created and won a Tony for the role in 1951 and landed an Oscar in the 1965 film I had almost memorized. I was pretty sure life couldn't get any better.

As we walked up the red carpet of the newly refurbished Atlanta landmark, I felt princess-like, and I tried my best to assume my most elegant bearing, no small feat for my clumsy self. I felt like I was doing an admirable job of it, too—until we entered the house.

An usher helped us find our seats, center orchestra, about mid-way back, an absolutely wonderful view of the stage. Settling in, I looked around, taking it all in. I was here, I thought, at the *Fox*! Eventually, my eyes wandered up to the ceiling; I gasped and my mouth hung open—okay, not especially regal-like. I motioned for Mother to look up. The ceiling had been made to look like a cobalt blue night sky alight with twinkling stars. We smiled at each other and began looking at our Playbill in anticipation of the show.

And what a show it was. Yul Brynner was completely magnetic, the performance every bit as magnificent as I had imagined it would be. It was, as I remember, a perfect evening.

When we called Daddy the following day, I wore his ear off chattering away about how wonderful it had been and thanking him profusely for the weekend, for he had set up and financed the entire affair. He loved doing things like that and buying gifts for his family; I'm pretty sure, thinking back on it, that his primary love language must have been gift giving.

He couldn't go, of course. Not that he would have necessarily wanted to; musical theatre was not his thing. But even if it had been, my guess is that he wouldn't have been able to take the weekend away from the country club he was managing, the career he had eased into as a civilian. Daddy had never had a nine-to-five job, and weekends are a club's busiest time. It was a good thing that Mother and I were close, for after Jeff left to join the Marine Corps, we spent a lot of time together. I loved our father dearly, but I had learned early in life that, if I wanted to live life and enjoy exciting things, I had better get used to being separated from him.

July 1, 1957, Camp Pendleton, California

Honey, I am going to be so lonesome for the next 14 or 15 months. I love you, more than words can ever, ever tell. You are my everything, baby, and I will always be true to you, my darling. I am so in love with you. You are the best wife and mother in the world, darling. You are my only one, and that is for always.

Sugar, my letter may not be long, but I will write you every night and all my love will be in each letter. Write real, real soon, sugar.
All my love always,
George

By far, the longest separation our family endured began toward the end of June 1957, when the Marine Corps assigned Daddy to fourteen months of duty—most of it on the island of Okinawa off the coast of Japan—without his family. Mother and Jeff, who was a bit over a year and a half at the time and yet to have a younger sister, moved back to Greensboro to live with Nana and Papa Jack for the duration. Daddy was away for two wedding anniversaries, a round of birthdays, two July 4[ths], one Thanksgiving, Christmas, New Year's, Easter, and Mother's and Father's Days. It was clear from his first letters home that this was *not* going to be an easy tour of duty.

For some reason, the vast majority of the letters that survived from this period come from Daddy's hand—we have virtually all of his letters up until about a month before his departure—while only a handful of Mother's letters remain. When I first pondered why this could be, it made some sense to me. Mother was the saver in our family; I can imagine her tucking those precious letters from her husband away somewhere. Plus, Daddy was moving around quite a bit while he was over there, and I'm sure space was often limited. But then, as I was reading through them, I found something Daddy had written in March 1958, a response to a question from our mother: *Yes, Sugar, I am keeping all of your letters till I get home. I have a lot of them, but keep them coming as I like those letters from you.* What happened to those letters, then? Were they lost in transit? Did they make it home but then lost later during one of our other moves? Did Daddy finally decide to clear them out years later on a cleaning purge? I'm grateful for what we have and I'm able to infer a lot of what Mother had written from Daddy's letters alone, but the truth is, I wish there was more of our Mother's voice during these years.

July 2, 1957, Camp Pendleton, California

Honey, you would not like California to live in. I know that you would want to be with me, but this place is so dry, and [has a] high [cost of living] to live in. They sell water to drink out here in the store $1.00 for 5 gal or 24 cents a gallon, about that. The city water tastes so bad you can't drink it. If you have a good well out here you have something.

July 4, 1957, Camp Pendleton

Honey, it sure is hot out here and dry. It was about 100 today. Sure wish that I was back in N.C. with you and Jeff boy.

I sure will be glad when I leave here and get started on my overseas time and out of this place so I can get back to you and Jeff. If I had you all with me it would be o.k. But since I have not I would like to leave California and I hope I don't ever get any duty here. This place has not shown me nothing.

To COMPOUND THE HARDSHIP of the assignment, what counted as Daddy's time overseas did not begin immediately but the separation from Mother and Jeff did, and Daddy was not impressed with his first stop, Camp Pendleton. Our parents had lived their entire lives on the East Coast and much about California was alien to him. The weekend before he had to report to base, he stayed with George Elkins, who had gotten out of the Corps after one enlistment. It was good to see his old buddy, he wrote our mother, his partner in crime who had helped him trick Uncle J.B. on one of their drives back to Camp Lejeune and had stood with him at his wedding. Once on base, though, the monotony of waiting around, particularly on the weekends, was rough, and Daddy struggled with how much to tell Mother. Should he bare all and confess his utter loneliness? Or spare her from all that and deal with it on his own?

July 8, 1957, Camp Pendleton

Honey, I know my letters from over the weekend must have been hard on you. I will try and do better from now on. I know it is hard being away from each other, but if we don't write about it but about other things, it will be better for the both of us.

He was to spend three weeks at Pendleton, two of them at the rifle range in the mornings. Heading out to shoot in the mornings meant getting up between 3:30 and 4:00 a.m. Even for our father, always an early riser, that hour was tough.

The other struggle was that information was often sporadic and fluid, par for the course in the military. When he arrived at Camp Pendleton, he was told he'd be flying out on July 16. But by the end of the first week, he wrote that he did not know for sure when they would be leaving, although he still thought it would be sometime around the 16th. He also didn't know absolutely at that point what the destination was and whether Mother and Jeff would be able to eventually join him. By July 9, he finally got orders that he would be flying over July 18; but what they had suspected all along was finally confirmed: *Honey, I don't guess you will get to come with me, for I know that I am going to Okinawa now.*

July 18, 1957, T. Island (in transit to Okinawa)

My Dearest darling wife,

Will write you a few lines to let you know that I got to T. Island o.k. We left Pendleton this morning at 6:30 and got here at 11:30. Had real good flying weather. From what I can find out here, we will fly out of here and will leave within two or 3 days.

Honey, I don't know just what day I will get overseas, but it takes about 37 hrs. from here to there. I will write you all about the trip when I get there.

The reality of getting "from here to there" turned out to be far different, though. Two to three days passed and Daddy was still on the island off the coast of California, longing to get off: *All I am doing is laying around waiting for a plane out.* With each passing day, his letters were filled with the same—nothing to do, the weather is awful, still waiting to leave, hoping it will be soon, maybe by the weekend.

July 23, 1957, T. Island (still waiting for a plane out)

I still don't know when I will leave here, maybe Thursday. Some of the men that I came here with are leaving Wednesday afternoon. They fly so many out everyday. I sure will be glad when I get overseas, so my time will start. This laying around is about to get to me.

Over the course of the next couple of days, he learned that he'd finally be leaving Friday, July 26, at 7:30 a.m., and on July 27, he let her know that the journey had actually begun. He was in Hawaii, having arrived the night before, expecting to leave that evening.

July 30, 1957, Camp Fuji, Japan

Will write you a few lines to let you know that I got to my new duty station at last. I got here on the 30th of July so I get to count it as a month, so I just have 13 moths to go.

I am stationed at Camp Fuji and I am in D Company, Medical Battalion.

They have a T[echnical] Sgt. as mess Sgt., so I guess I will go to work for him.

Having originally expected to leave July 16 and be in Japan in a couple of days, in the end, it took two weeks to get there, although at least not on a ship. Consider that "military time."

August 5, 1957, Camp Fuji

It is raining here today. They tell me it rains a lot up here. Honey, I don't know if I told you or not but Camp Fuji is right at the [base of] Mt. Fuji. I know you can find that on the map, but I don't know how much longer we will be here. Some of the Marines are leaving this week for Okinawa, and some time this month or next we will be going.

September 15, 1957, Camp Fuji

It is raining here again. That is about all it does here is rain. I never saw it rain so much.

September 21, 1957, Camp Fuji

It is getting cold over here at night. We have to light the stove in the room at night and this morning when I got up Mt. Fuji had snow on top of it.

CAMP FUJI IS, AS Daddy wrote Mother, positioned at the base of Mt. Fuji, Japan's highest peak, an active volcano that last erupted in the early eighteenth century and one of Japan's three holy mountains, sacred to practitioners of the Shinto faith. It is located about 60 miles southwest of Tokyo and, on a clear day, the picturesque and iconic mountaintop can be seen from the city. The Marine base sits on land with a long military history that evokes the culture of its nation, having been the site where the Japanese feudal government trained more than 30,000 Samurai soldiers beginning in the late twelfth century.

For Daddy, though, it was mostly a two-and-a-half-month stopover on his way to Okinawa. While there, he worked hard, including a stint on nights. But he also had some time to explore the area. He had not been there a month when he was writing Mother that he and some buddies had plans to climb Mt. Fuji on Saturday, spend the night at the top, take some pictures, then return Sunday morning. *I will write you all about it when I get back*. But the reality of Mt. Fuji must have been more than they anticipated; for the bold ambition of youthful Marines, one of whom hailed from flat, North Carolina piedmont land, things didn't quite pan out as they had imagined. *I did not spend the night on Mt. Fuji, as we did not get to the top of it. Got about halfway up and then came back down.*

He hoped he would be able to spend some time at the beach, even to the point where he thought he'd need a second bathing suit that he asked Mother to send him. But before long, Daddy let her know that she needn't bother. *I have the one and so far I have not been to the beach here. They are not nice and look too dirty to me. Maybe they will have some nice ones on Okinawa. Hope so. That would give me something to do to pass away the time.*

That was the trick, really. Finding things to do, when not working, to pass away the time. Nowhere was that harder than when on board ship, which is where he found himself by mid-October.

October 13, 1957, On board ship to Okinawa

Well, we are now on ship and on our way to Okinawa. I sure will be glad when this move is over and we get to Okinawa and I get me a good bed again.

October 14, 1957, Aboard ship

Honey, my letters on ship may be short, for all I do all day long is lay around and look at the water and wish that I was home with you and Jeff. There is not anything to write about. We do the same thing every day.

October 18, 1957, Aboard ship

I sure will be glad when I get off of this ship. I am not seasick, but I am sure tired of this ship rocking from side to side. If this letter and the one this morning are hard to read it is because of the ship rocking and it makes it hard to write.

October 19, 1957, Aboard ship

Well, I saw Okinawa for the first time this morning and I am going up after awhile and get a picture of it from the ship. From what I can see from here it is one big rock.

Once on the island, Daddy's company spent four days in the field before heading to the base and that good bed he was ready for. He was impressed with Okinawa; it seemed cleaner to him than Japan had been, and there were other things to impress. The roads were much better, and people drove American-made cars like Dodge and Chevrolet. Seeing the island, some 70 miles long and averaging seven miles in width, was difficult without a car, but Daddy solved that problem eventually. *I am off of duty Friday and me and one of the Army cooks who has a car are going to look this island of Okinawa over and get some pictures of it. I will send them home to you when I get them.*

As at Camp Fuji, the weather was a popular subject of discontent. When there is not much to write about, when letters get held up so that responding to the questions posed from home isn't possible, when the days drag on and day after day seems the same, weather inevitably becomes something to write home about. *I tell you, I don't know about this weather here on Okinawa. The sun shone for a week and then it rained for 2 weeks.* Mostly, it was hot, similar to their previous duty station in Miami, Florida, with a good bit of rain. But occasionally, a bit of a cold snap would sneak in. *It has turned cold here and has been raining for 2 days now. They said it doesn't get cold on Okinawa. I wish someone would tell the weatherman that.* Of course, cold and hot are relative terms when it comes to the weather, and Daddy didn't seem to tolerate the cold well after the Chosin Reservoir.

August 25, 1957, Camp Fuji

Honey, I have a confession to make to you too. When I went to town today I ordered me a pair of pants. I am sending you some of the cloth so you can see what

kind they are. Honey, they cost $11.11, made to order. You can't go wrong for
that, do you think?

THE DIFFICULT DAYS FOLLOWING our mother's death in 2010
we spent doing the things that grieving spouses, children, grandchildren do—
telling stories, making arrangements, receiving visitors, dealing with the mounds
of food people bring, and trying to forget, even for a moment, that she was gone.
Exhausted from it all and having trouble sleeping at night, I often took naps on
her bed, lying in the spot where she had lain.

The house my parents lived in at the time was not where my brother and I
had grown up. I'm not sure if Jeff ever had a house that he felt that attached to,
having moved around more than I had. I always thought of "home" as the house
we moved to when I was in seventh grade, in the subdivision that surrounded
the club and golf course that Daddy managed. By that time, though, Jeff was a
senior in high school so I doubt that the house in Doublegate ever became his.
Not so with me. When my parents moved to the golf villa that they "retired"
to—Daddy stayed retired for about six months before he was scooped up to
manage the new, rival Stonebridge Country Club—I knew the move was right,
but I missed the comfort and memories of a home that had watched me survive
my teen years and grow into a young, married woman with my own daughter.

Still, I took comfort in my parents' new home. They had been there for over
ten years so we had made memories there as well, not growing-up or holiday
memories, but summer visits where my second husband John and Daddy had
enjoyed easy company on the screened-in porch that overlooked the water, and
where we had packed up for the three-hour drive to Panama City, Florida, for
our annual beach vacation with Mother and Daddy.

Their bedroom suite was spacious, with a large sleeping area that opened
onto the screened-in porch, his and hers walk-in closets, and a sizeable bathroom
with the Jacuzzi tub that delighted my daughter. Most summer evenings would
find her taking a bath in Grandmama's tub.

As I awoke from one of those afternoon naps in the wake of Mother's death and climbed out from under the throw, numb with the loss, I felt a shiver from the artificial air being generated to cool the house from the humid, Southwest Georgia July heat. I knew better than to ask Daddy to adjust the temperature in the house. He would do it, with no complaints, but our father never did anything by half measures so that, soon, the entire household would practically be suffering from heat exhaustion from lack of air conditioning due to my "could we turn the temperature up a notch?" (Mother and I used to always give him the look and a decent amount of grief for freezing us out or burning us up with his adjustments to the thermostat.) I also knew that my internal regulator had been out of whack since John had passed away three months earlier; my mother's death had only made things worse. I moved from the bed into Mother's closet where I figured I could find a sweater to put on until my body warmed up to a more natural, July-kind of temperature. Not finding anything that really looked like it would be cozy enough, I turned around and crossed over to Daddy's closet.

I had been in my mother's closet on any number of occasions, retrieving something for her, borrowing a sweater, or, more recently, soaking in her presence. But I had had little reason over the years to venture into Daddy's. I stood there for a moment and looked around the U-shaped interior in mild amazement. I knew our father liked fine clothing, and, in truth, had always been a bit of a clotheshorse. Most club manager compensation packages even include clothing allowances, grease spills being a hazard of the occupation. But I wasn't really astounded by the quality or quantity. It was the immaculate order of it all. To the top left hung his trousers; below them, his golf shirts. Straight-ahead were his suits, with his dress shirts and sweaters completing the wardrobe on the right-hand side.

But that high-level mode of organization was not what made me, in the end, shake my head and laugh out loud. I leaned my head out of the closet door and called for my nineteen-year-old daughter, ensconced in the living room that shared a wall with my parents' bedroom, getting lost in an episode of *Friends* for what was probably the fifty-third time.

"Anna, you have *got* to come in here."

"What is it," she questioned, mild curiosity tinged with a hint of worry in her tone. I stopped her at the entrance to the closet, putting my hands on both shoulders and looking her straight in the eyes. "I am about to show you something that will explain everything."

When Anna was nine, she was diagnosed with a mild case of Obsessive Compulsive Disorder, an anxiety disorder she has thankfully learned to manage. To quell her anxiety, she would arrange things, sometimes for a couple of hours. Her school binders were a work of genius. We walked into the closet together and I ran my hand along the row of some thirty-odd golf shirts. She chuckled and turned to me with a huge smile on her face. "Oh my God," she exclaimed. Her Papa's shirts were not only hung all together, they were arranged by color in a rainbowesque fashion. In fact, the entire closet was. It was just that the golf shirts, with more color options, comprised the most striking section. "Well," I said, "I guess *that* explains some things, huh?"

IT WAS, THEN, THAT, some 53 years prior, Daddy had happened upon a sort of shopping mecca when he landed in Japan, into a country that had experienced something of an economic "miracle" in the years following the war. It turned out to be the perfect place to indulge his desire for an expanding wardrobe. Much of the capitalist world had benefitted from postwar conditions. The same industries that had supported the military complex during the war—iron and steel, as well as shipbuilding, automobiles, and electronics—continued production in peacetime to a postwar economic surge helped along by a more open international trading system. But Japan's growth was on a whole different level. In 1950, the U.S. dollar equivalent of Japan's gross national product was $11 billion. By 1973, it had increased to $320 billion, and Japan's economy ranked the third largest in the world behind the United States and the Soviet Union.

What accounted for such historic growth? For one, the Korean War increased exports at an important moment in Japan's economic recovery, and a favorable yen to dollar exchange rate into the early 1970s further boosted the value of the nation's export market. Moreover, while nations like the United States and Soviet Union and even West Germany taxed and spent to maintain large militaries, the United States' continuing military presence in the region coupled with Japan's constitutional limitation on its military meant the island nation was spared comparable defense costs.

But several domestic factors played a role as well. At the top, a new generation of managers came into their own on the heels of wartime managers who had been forced out during the U.S. occupation. These young Japanese entrepreneurs began competing with the U.S., particularly in the auto industry and consumer electronic goods, as the infant Sony emerged to become a global leader in quality and innovation. These businesses fearlessly took on large debt, and, because of their rapid growth, were able to pay it off without trouble.

At the other end of the spectrum, a well-educated Japanese workforce also aided economic growth. With compulsory education extended through middle school during the occupation, young workers were more educated than their prewar counterparts and happy for the return to a more normal existence. They actively organized themselves into unions and fought hard for better conditions and pay. But they were also committed to hard work and long hours, content to be working for themselves rather than sacrificing everything for the empire.

Both entrepreneurs and workers alike played an important role in the Japanese economy as savers and spenders. As the economy grew, the average percentage of household income saved grew as well—topping 20 percent by the early 1970s—and these savings accounts in commercial banks throughout the country formed the basis for a considerable pool of capital for expanding businesses. But the Japanese not only saved; they spent their salaries on an increasingly wide variety of consumer goods, from household appliances, such as washing and sewing machines and electric rice cookers, to leisure items like radios, record players, and television sets. These were not inexpensive purchases. In the year that Daddy arrived at Camp Fuji, a standard new TV in Japan cost the equivalent of two and a half month's income for an urban family, but by 1963, more than four out of five Japanese households owned one.

The most controversial piece of domestic help Japan's economy received in the postwar era concerned the Japanese government. Japan's postwar economic boom was not based on an exclusively free market system. The Japanese government used something it called *administrative guidance* to encourage some businesses and discourage others. It signaled its interest in the health of the economy by acting as a sort of "economic cheerleader" for certain industries—stepping in to lend capital, facilitate foreign exchange and the acquisition of raw materials and technology licenses, and help rescue companies within favored industries during economic downturns. Such an industrial policy on the part of the Japanese government was the final piece of the nation's postwar economic success story, and it made a distinct difference.

Also fueling the Japanese economy were U.S. servicemen and women stationed there. Though the occupation had ended in 1949, the Korean and Vietnam Wars substantially increased Japanese strategic importance for the United States, creating renewed surges in the numbers of U.S. military personnel stationed on Japan and Okinawa. The United States acutely feared the creep of communism during the period and relied heavily on this new relationship with its former enemy in the postwar era. While the United States was enjoying its own postwar economic upturn, many soldiers and Marines, including our father, took advantage of the favorable exchange rate during their time in Japan to stock up on consumer goods and, in so doing, did their part to help stimulate the Japanese economy.

August 16, 1957, Camp Fuji

Honey, did I tell you that I am having 3 white shirts made? They cost me about $9.00. I am to get them Monday night. Don't you think that is a good price for three (3) shirts made to order?

Daddy was, obviously, engaged in quite a bit of consumer activity while in Japan. He had been there less than two weeks when he wrote Mother not to bother sending some clothes over as they had discussed because he could have them made in Japan for about what it would cost to have his others shipped over. By October, while still at Camp Fuji, he wrote to say that his expanding wardrobe was taking up too much room and he planned to send some of his clothes home once he got to Okinawa. His prize was a suit he had made out of brown doeskin for $36. *I went into town last night and got my suit and, honey, it sure is nice. I wish you could see the way it fits.*

But Daddy's purchases were not limited to clothing. There were practical things, as well—a set of dishes for $31 that would have cost around $125 in the States, and a steam iron that Mother was glad to receive—*I can really keep my Marine sharp now!*

And more than anything, postwar Japan was the perfect place for our father to indulge his penchant for gift giving.

August 25, 1957, Camp Fuji

Sugar, I went to town today and got you and Jeff a little something. I am going to mail it in the morning. It will take about 30 days for it to get to you. Honey, be sure and let me know if these things fit you and Jeff so I will know whether to buy you and him some other things. I love you and him, Sugar, and want to send you and Jeff something each payday if I can.

September 29, 1957, Camp Fuji

I got a letter from Mother today too. I am going down and get her a cup with Mt. Fuji on it and send it to her. And later on I want to get Mrs. Eva a little something. Do you think she would like a nice oil painting on silk?

November 24, 1957, Okinawa

Has Jeff boy got his Marine cap yet and can he wear it? What did he buy with the $2.00 I sent him? Tell him Daddy said hello and for him to be a good boy.

June 16, 1958, Okinawa

My Dearest darling wife,

Baby, I wish you could just see what I got you today. It is just beautiful. I can't tell you what it is for I want to bring it home to you. Sugar, I know you are going to like it.

June 27, 1958, Okinawa

Honey, I got you a ring last night. It is one pearl and looks real good. I think I will send it to you by airmail so you can be wearing it. I think it is real pretty and I do hope you will like it. I am going to get you a pearl and bring home with me so you can put it on a chain. I can get a real nice pearl for $5.00 over here, and that is a nice big one.

July 19, 1958, Okinawa

I went to town [this afternoon] and looked around and I found some helicopters and I got Jeff boy two of them. They are not too strong, but they are right nice. I will send them to him airmail Monday morning.

August 3, 1958, Okinawa

I went to town this afternoon just looking around and I got Jeff boy a car that runs on batteries. It has headlights and taillights. You can turn the wheels and it has a horn on it. I will bring it home with me when I come.

Nothing, however, consumed more of Daddy's time and energy with regard to gifts than the suit he hoped to purchase for Mother while he was in Japan. After he had the doeskin suit made for himself that he wrote her about, he suggested in one of his letters that she should send over a pattern and her measurements and he would have one made for her out of the same material. Two days later, he was reminding her to send the pattern as soon as possible. *Honey, it sure will be nice for us both to have a suit alike, and we could never have one in the States. It would cost us too much money. I only paid $36 for mine and it will cost the same.* And so began a nine-month back-and-forth on "the suit." Mother was worried it wouldn't fit, so Daddy proposed sending the material to her and having her get it made in the States. But a couple of days later, a box arrived for Daddy with the pattern in it.

September 11, 1957, Camp Fuji

I also got the pattern today [in the box you sent] and, honey, since you sent it and the measurements, I am going to have your suit made over here. I know that you wish that I would make up my mind, but after I thought it over, honey, I think I will have it made where I had mine made and send it to you.

Before long, though, Daddy had to delay the purchase because he didn't have enough money. Much of his paycheck was going to Mother for their continuing expenses in the States. *I found out I was not going to get but $23.00 this payday, so I have to wait.* The clock was ticking on how much longer he would be at Camp Fuji, but he heard it might be even cheaper to have it made in Okinawa and so decided to wait and make it her present for her birthday, coming up in early December. Yet unexpected expenses threatened to derail that plan.

October 10, 1957, Camp Fuji

Honey, you said in your letter not to get you anything more [for your birthday]. Don't you want me to get your suit? Or would you rather me pay some bills? Let me know.

Glad the heater works good on the car. I wish there was some way I could help you pay for the heater, but right now I can't. Maybe a little later on I can send you some money.

Our father, who I considered to be a font of wisdom when it came to things financial, definitely had an Achilles' heel when it came to splurging on his family. But in the end, Mother's birthday came and went, and the reality of daily life and the expense of keeping up a household curbed some of Daddy's gift giving. His desire to have Mother a suit made had to be put on a serious hold. After the first of the year, though, it was clear that he had not forgotten about it.

January 25, 1958, Okinawa

Honey, about your suit, I have talked to 3 or 4 people that had their wife a suit made over here and it fit real good. So I would like to have yours made over here.

I think it would be nice to say that we had our suits made in Japan and Okinawa, don't you? So just as soon as we get the settlement for the house, I will get you to send me a little money.

The winter months dragged on and spring arrived, and other financial worries, particularly the sale of their house in Florida, occupied their correspondence. Finally, by early May, Daddy wrote with some good news.

May 5, 1958, Okinawa

Sugar, I got the money order today and I have already gone and ordered your suit and got you something else. I can't tell you what it is. I will bring it home with me when I come.

Toward the end of June, the suit was complete and ready to be picked up. With the time of Daddy's departure from the island so close, he decided to bring the suit home with him rather than have it shipped. It had taken virtually the duration of his time in Japan and Okinawa to accomplish it, but he had finally gotten a quality suit made to bring home to his wife.

I STOOD BEFORE THE mirror at the shoe store, one foot pointed out, gazing down at a lovely pair of shoes on my six-year-old feet. It was time to buy new "Sunday morning" shoes, and I was having a tough time deciding between what I considered to be two equally beautiful pairs. These kinds of decisions could be challenging for a little girl, especially one raised in a culture in which going to church on Sunday mornings meant wearing your best. I asked to try on the other pair in the running and struck the same pose in front of the mirror.

"Well, baby, which one is it going to be?" Daddy had brought me shopping, not an unusual occurrence for the man who loved lavishing gifts on his wife and children and appreciated sharp clothes and shoes.

I turned around and looked up at him. I did my absolute best to look distraught at having to leave behind one of the pairs of shoes. "I just don't know.

I'm having a hard time making up my mind."

"You need to decide. We have other things we need to do today and your Mother is expecting us back home soon."

"Well," I said, dragging the word out and looking up at him with my best, winsome smile, "if I had the money, I'd just get both pairs."

When we got back home, I bounded into the house. "Mother, Mother, look at my new Sunday shoes!" I pulled out the two boxes and showed them off with pride. "I was having trouble deciding so Daddy let me get both pairs."

Mother looked over at Daddy, raised one eyebrow in a look I had definitely seen before, and in a distinctly sonorous voice said, "You did what?!"

"Oh, Sugar, don't be upset. You weren't there. You know how she looks at me. And they both look so good on her."

Mother shook her head and turned away. Two pairs of dress shoes for a six-year-old? She knew that I'd outgrow them long before I had scuffed them up at all. But she also knew the man she had married, his love of fine attire, his generosity, and the adoration he had for his family. She was not going to change him now, nor would she likely, in all truth, want to.

I really have no idea what those suits from Japan and Okinawa looked like, the suits that consumed so much of our father's writing energy. Throughout their married life, though, I witnessed any number of times when he would surprise Mother with a fine suit or dress that he'd seen that he thought would look good on her. It pleased him every bit as much to do it for her, for Jeff, for me, as it did us to be on the receiving end of his giving. That he spent so much of his free time on "this island of Okinawa" indulging his clothing and gifting obsession was in perfect keeping with who he was.

6

Putting Out Good Food

August 2, 1957, Camp Fuji

I started to work today. I am duty mess sgt. for the weekend, but I don't mind, for I am not going out and it will give me something to do.

Well, honey, I will come to a close for tonight and go to bed since I have got to get up at 0500 in the morning. I have to be at the mess hall for all the meals when I have the duty. I will write you again Saturday night, darling.

THE EARLY 1970S WERE MY JUNIOR HIGH YEARS, that time of growing up that can be gangly and awkward and fraught with so much early teen angst. As I was finishing up seventh grade—our father now out of the Marine Corps for five years and doing well in his second career as a club manager—we moved from the house we had lived in on Acker Drive since his retirement from the Corps, to that house I came to think of as home in the subdivision of Doublegate, just a mile and a half from the club.

Jeff was a graduating senior and the move would put us in a different school district, so we waited until the last six weeks of the school year to move—that was the point on the calendar the school system had randomly established at which students would not have to change schools—so that he could graduate from Albany High. That would give us two years to deal with me having to leave my friends at Albany Junior High to attend Westover, for, in its infinite wisdom, the school district had zoned Doublegate to attend the junior high that fed predominately into Albany High, but a high school that was fed largely by a different junior high. Oh well, we had a couple of years to worry about that. No disruption for me at the present.

Why the zoning for Doublegate included Albany Junior is beyond me. It was, at that time, a monstrously long bus ride, at least for the small city of Albany, and not the closest junior high by far. Not that I was complaining. I was happy not to have to leave the friends I had now been in school with since third grade, many of whom had lived near the neighborhood we had moved from and also attended our church.

Mother was still teaching at the time and so I think I rode the bus home most days, although, to be perfectly honest, I have few memories of those rides. I think I've blocked them out of my memory. But on Mondays, unless he was out of town for some reason, Daddy always picked me up from school. In a business where the busiest days were on the weekend, the club was closed on Mondays, so that was his day off. And he spent at least part of it picking me up from school and preparing dinner for the family. I suppose it helped that, with the club closed, he couldn't play golf on that day.

By eighth and ninth grades, I had become an "only child"—Jeff having moved on to a year of college and eventually the Marine Corps—and I relished the weekly ride home with my daddy. I would get in the front seat of the car, unload my book bag in the floorboard, lean across to give him a kiss on the cheek, and settle in for the ride home. Our car conversation didn't vary much from week to week, an exchange of questions and answers we had become comfortable with.

"How was your day in school?"

"It was okay," I'd respond, "but I hate it."

"I don't get it," he said one time. "If you hate it so much, why do you do so well?"

"Because if I failed, then I'd just have to stay there longer," I told him, denying the real truth that, I was, just like him, driven to do everything to the best of my ability. "Plus, you would beat me," I finished off with a smirk. My dark joke and a palpable lie. Our father had never laid a hand on me.

"Right," he deadpanned, as in *sure*.

Next I would turn things around and ask him about his day. It usually consisted of a number of errands to help out Mother, the grocery, cleaners, with sometimes a trip to his favorite men's clothing store mixed in because they had a sale on his favorite brand of suit.

We would finally get to the one question that I never failed to ask. "What are we having for dinner tonight?"

There was no reason for me to ask it. All my life, our father had overseen first the mess hall, then enlisted and officers clubs, and now the fine dining at a country club. He was, at heart, however, a steak and potatoes man. Unless he had recently been away at a food course to work on his certified club manager status, in which case he would return and try out special recipes on us, Monday nights were dedicated to steaks on the grill, baked potatoes, and salad. I knew this, but it was a ritual between us, and both of us would have been disappointed if we had not played it out on those rides home.

"Hog jowls and chit'lins." He always said it with a straight face.

"Daaddy!" I always stretched out the word. "No we're not."

"No," he said as he leaned into a grin. "I'm going to put some steaks on the grill, and we'll have that with baked potatoes and salad."

"Yay," I would exclaim, because, at that time, it was one of my favorite meals as well, a far cry from hog jowls, the stomach lining of a pig, or chit'lins, pig or cow intestines, that, growing up in the South, I had heard of all my life but never tasted, and never cared to.

I settled into the ride home, grateful for time with my daddy, steak and potato, and at least one day of the week that I did not have to be on that blasted bus!

August 22, 1957, In the field outside Camp Fuji

Well, I have fed 2 meals in the field and all the men have come up and told me what good chow it was. Makes me feel good to know that I am putting out good food.

WHAT WAS IT ABOUT Okinawa, this little island in the Pacific some 830 nautical miles from Japan, that was still so important to the U.S. military over a decade after WWII? Okinawa had not always been part of Japan. Okinawans are ethnically distinct from Japanese, and the island chain, known as the Ryukyu Islands, had been a semi-autonomous kingdom ruled from Okinawa. But as the Japanese empire expanded during the late nineteenth century, they brought the islands under their sovereignty. The empire largely ignored the little islands until World War II, when they became strategically important as the U.S. hopped from island to island to beat back what were then, to us, Japanese aggressors. The bloody Battle of Okinawa, waged from April through mid-June 1945, claimed the lives of more Americans than any of the Pacific island battles, and between 150,000 and 200,000 Japanese and Okinawans, a third to a half of them civilians. It is not surprising that many Okinawans remember this as a time when Japan sacrificed their island for the good of the mainland.

In the treaty that concluded the war, Okinawa remained under the control of the United States. Strategically, we considered the islands a sort of barrier in the Cold War, an important safeguard against the Soviet Union's Pacific fleet. The U.S. military quickly appropriated Japanese military installations for their own use and began acquiring land for the construction of new bases. While we paid locals for the land, they often gave it up unwillingly, sometimes only after bulldozers and bayonets "convinced" them. Moreover, during the period of American control—which lasted until 1972 when Okinawa reverted to Japanese sovereignty—Okinawans had no legal means to contest crimes that U.S. servicemen committed, the worst of them handled through court martial. The American soldiers and Marines stationed there did offer a sort of economic boom for the island, but it is not hard to see why the attitude by many Okinawans to the occupation and the U.S. military was, in general, negative.

None of this made it into our father's letters home, however. He surely had a sense of why U.S. servicemen and women were there. As for him, though, he considered his main job to feed these Marines and soldiers—to, as he expressed in one letter home, put out good food. There was never any doubt that our father placed his faith and his family above all else. But there was also no doubt that the Marine Corps and his work in food service came in a close second. In short, Daddy loved his work. I guess it makes sense, then, that the subject took up a lot of space in his letters home—work was where he spent the bulk of his time, and changes in assignment meant there were often new people and routines to write about.

During the fourteen months there, counting the stint working nights and time in the field, Daddy was shifted around ten times. He liked the men he was in the company with at Camp Fuji, D Company of the Medical Battalion, and felt liked by them in return, and, as either chief cook or assistant mess sergeant, thought that he had good cooks working for him. Mostly, what he longed for, though, was his own mess hall, which he thought he might get when he reached Okinawa. *Sure hope so*, he wrote, *and then I can run it like I want to*. For he prided himself on his work, which meant providing the best food he could for the men.

August 19, 1957, Camp Fuji
My Dearest darling wife,

Sugar, I am now sitting here in the mess hall, waiting on some chicken so I can cut them up. I am working nights now. The mess sgt. wanted a staff here at night so I told him I would take it. If I work nights and sleep days my time will go by faster.

When he was on nights by himself, the work could be unrelenting—cut up 70 lbs. of bacon, break three cases of eggs, make 700 sandwiches for 300 box lunches and assemble the box lunches, cook off some meat for chipped beef for breakfast—or, with only some hotcake batter to mix up, some eggs to break, and 80 sandwiches to put together, painfully slow. But while at Camp Fuji, he stayed on nights for almost a month, save the few days in the field. *I like working at nights. There is no one to mess with me. I am my own boss. I know what I have to do and when I get it done, I can sit down and write to you.* But most of all, by working nights, the days seemed to be ticking by at a faster clip. *Right now, time is going fast,* he wrote after having been on nights for three weeks. *I work all night and sleep all day. When I get up and eat it is time to go back to work again. But I like it very much that way.*

When on days, he had the periodic struggle of making sure the meals got out, sometimes when they were down several cooks. *I won't be long out of bed tonight because I am tired. I had to take over chief cook today. We lost 6 men and that left myself and two men so I had to go to work.* With Marines constantly getting rotated in and out, this was a recurring theme while at Camp Fuji. Less than a month later, they had lost four cooks, *and that left me with just two men that don't know too much. I worked all day, and I do mean work.*

November 21, 1957, Okinawa

I will be going up to the Army hospital to work starting next week. The company I am in is going to be working there, and I will be up there cooking for them with the Army. How about that, me working with Army? But it is going to be a good deal for me. I will have my own room up there. I think I am going to like it, as much as I can like anything on this rock. I am just living for the time when I can be with you and Jeff boy again.

After spending about a month on Okinawa as the chief messman at a "nice little mess hall," Daddy was transferred over to the mess hall at Camp Mercy Army Hospital. Here he was in the clutches of the Army, of all things, but, in the end, it turned out to be one of the more stable and enjoyable assignments he had while he was over there. In the days leading up to the move, he approached it with his usual focus and determination.

November 27, 1957, Okinawa

Well, I move to the Army hospital Thursday afternoon and go to work for the Army Friday morning. My C.O. [commanding officer] went down to see them the other day and told them I was one of the best cooks he had ever seen and knew I would do a better job than any other Marine that has ever been down there. I will really have to work to live up to that build up, but I will go down and do my best.

November 28, 1957, Okinawa

I moved today. …These are nice rooms. I could have had one by myself, but I had a sgt. move in with me so I would have someone to talk to. I would get too lonesome in here by myself.

Well, honey, I guess I will have to come to a close for tonight. I have to get my clothes ready to go to work in the morning. First time. Want to look my best.

November 30, 1957, Okinawa

I think I am going to like my new job. I will have to learn how the Army does things and do them that way so I can get along with them.

Our father may have been convinced of the superiority of the Marine Corps and had little use for the Army, but he understood the way to get along in this world. If he had a stint at an Army hospital, then, by God, he would learn how they did things, make the most of it, and, in doing his best, show them how good the Marines really are.

December 3, 1957, Okinawa

I am starting to find out how the Army works, and it is nothing like the Marines, and I like the Marines' way best. I guess it is because I have done it that way so long. But I like my work here. All I have to do is walk around and see that everything goes o.k.

GROWING UP, SUNDAYS MEANT church in the morning—Sunday school followed by worship—and then lunch at "the club." Which club, exactly, changed over time, but from my earliest memories, that is where we went for Sunday dinner.

I understood, at least at some point, that most of my friends went home to a Sunday dinner that their mothers had started early that morning before setting out to church. But for our family, that was not our normal. If we wanted to be with Daddy on Sundays, we ate at the club, either the NCO or (Commissioned) Officers Club on the Marine base, or whatever club he was managing after he retired.

Most of the time we saw him only in passing, walking around to see that everything was going okay. If he had a minute to sit with us, we always reserved the chair that allowed him to look out at the room so he could keep an eye on the operation. He would usually not be seated for long, jumping up to tend to something he saw that needed taking care of, or, more likely, wasn't up to his standards.

At some point, long after he was a civilian and after Jeff had left to start his own military career, Mother and I would wait to eat, going home after church and then coming up to the club right before the serving line closed down so that Daddy could sit and eat with us. Even then, he would inhale his food to Mother's protestations of "George, slow down." But too many years of having to eat when he had a free moment, and often only a moment, were too ingrained in him to change things. Even when he was seated with us, our meal would be routinely interrupted by greetings from other Marines or club members stopping to say hello and tell him how good the meal was.

I was an adult with a child of my own before I realized that our father was an introvert. Seeing him at the club, he appeared to be the biggest extrovert you ever met, shaking hands and greeting virtually everyone. But that was his work persona, and he knew that part of a good food experience was a manager who knew and acknowledged his patrons, even if it interrupted dinner with his family. I really didn't mind. He was my Daddy, and I was proud that he was the one in charge and that everyone seemed to think he was doing such a good job.

Daddy had picked up that strategy of walking around to see that everything was under control long before those Sunday dinners that I remember. From day one, he had received excellent training in the Corps, and he made the most of it. Starting as a cook, he had worked hard and demanded the best of himself, working his way up to assistant mess sergeant. And now, having been at the hospital not even a week, it seemed as if he was on the verge of finally getting his own mess.

December 7, 1957, Okinawa

The mess sgt. that they have here at the Army hospital is going home Tuesday and he told me today he talked to the capt. the other day and told her I was the best man for mess sgt. when he left. I don't know whether I told you or not but we have a woman capt. as mess officer of the Army hospital mess staff.

Unfortunately, it was not to be. He found out a couple of days later that he would continue as assistant mess sergeant, in charge of all the cooking. It was not where he wanted to be and, yet, it was a far cry from a cook.

He repeatedly spoke of liking his work there, particularly as he became more familiar with how they ran things and with how the Army did their paperwork. In fact, the only downside to this assignment was that Mother and Jeff could not be with him, and so, he continued to throw himself into his work. Even though he worked five days a week, he told Mother that he would probably work six *just to make the time go by*. If he had to be away from them, though, he was glad to have a job he liked. He had come a long way from his attitude of the Army in Korea, to be sure. Lest Mother wonder what was happening to her Marine, though, Daddy was clear—*You know I still like the Marine Corps the best.*

December 13, 1957, Okinawa

I am going to work Christmas day so the day will go by faster and by me working maybe someone that works in the mess hall that has their wife and child over here can be with them Christmas morning. I asked the capt. about it today and she said she would see about it a little later on. I told her if my wife and little boy was here I sure would want to be with them Christmas morning and the ones of us that did not have our wife and child over here would work for them.

BESIDES BIRTHDAYS, ANNIVERSARIES, AND days off, the hardest time to be away from family for anyone in the military, whether on temporary assignment or deployment, is around the holidays. The desire to be with family, to live out cultural traditions, is often strongest when we are denied the experience.

The military puts forth a valiant effort at trying to assuage the longing, though, and the Army hospital mess hall, as a central gathering place, did its best to make things look festive. Daddy was part of the decorating committee and, as they began to transform the mess hall and think about the Christmas trees they planned to put up, his thoughts naturally turned to home. *I think we are going to get 4 trees for Christmas for the mess hall, but I wish I could be home and help you and Jeff decorate the tree there. I bet Jeff boy will give you all his help when you start decorating the tree at home.* As the days inched closer to Christmas, he tried to stay busy to avoid thinking about the fact that he wasn't home.

December 19, 1957, Okinawa

We put up our Christmas trees tonight in the mess hall and it sure did make me even more homesick for you and Jeff boy.

December 20, 1957, Okinawa

Honey, I hope you have a real nice Christmas. I am going to work that day so the time will go by faster. I am going to try and call you Christmas night; that will be Christmas morning there.

December 24, 1957, Christmas Eve, Okinawa,

I worked today from 6 o'clock this morning till 9 o'clock tonight, and I am going to work again in the morning at 5 o'clock and work till 6 o'clock Christmas night. That way the time will go by faster.

December 25, 1957, Christmas Day, Okinawa

Well, here it is, another Christmas over with. I can say that I am glad this one is all over.

I went to work this morning at 5 o'clock and worked until about 5 o'clock tonight. That way some of the men that have their wife and babies here could be with them.

Once the new year got underway, the rhythm of the days reestablished itself, and Daddy continued to enjoy his assignment at the Army hospital. He also was getting the opportunity to apply some of what he had learned from the Advanced Cook's Course at Camp Lejeune, a thirteen-week course he had attended and completed during the summer and fall of 1956. Not only did he like the work situation, he was also well liked by the Army staff. *Everyone tells me that the Capt. likes my work*, he wrote Mother after the first of the year. *I just do the best I can.*

But by the end of January, a short round of change was on the horizon, when Daddy received word that they would be sailing in mid-February to the Philippines for training in the field for three to four weeks. Despite his comfortable rhythm at the Army hospital, he embraced the opportunity. He had never been to the Philippines, and he was on board for anything he thought would break up the time there and help him feel like it was going faster. But transporting men via ship from one island to another was not a rapid process, the result generally being an exercise in hurry up, followed by a lot of waiting.

February 18, 1958, On board ship for the Philippines

Well, we got the ship all loaded and then this morning, we had to tie some trucks, and boy did it rain. Myself and all my men got wet.

Did I tell you, honey, that I am not cooking on this trip to the Philippines? I am S.N.C.O. [Supply Non-commissioned Officer] in charge of the trucks. I have myself and 13 men. It sure is nice to go somewhere and not have to cook. But I will be back in the mess hall at Mercy when I get back.

February 20, 1958, Aboard ship

We will leave here and get underway for the Philippines Saturday morning. I don't know whether I told you or not but for the last 4 days we have just been off the coast of Okinawa waiting for the other ships. They will get here Saturday morning and then all the ships leave for the Philippines.

As Daddy predicted, the ships did get underway on Saturday, February 22, and would be sailing for a week to get to the Philippines. There was little to do aboard ship, and the days passed slowly. He looked for anything to do to help pass the time. On Sunday, he joined seven others to attend the worship service. Then in the middle of the week, the Navy offered Bingo, so he went down and played that for a couple of evenings. But mostly, he looked forward to landing. *Honey, I sure will be glad when March the 1st gets here and I can get off this ship. I just don't like this ship life. Sure glad I never joined the Navy.* Once they neared the islands, though, there was more to report—both the beauty of the terrain in the distance and the realities of men crammed aboard a ship.

February 27, 1958, Aboard ship

We are in real close to the Philippines and the hills are big and real green. There sure are a lot of ships in this bay. There are to be over 100 altogether.

Honey, this will be a short letter, as I have to do something I don't like to do, but it has to be done. Some of my men don't like to take a bath, it seems. You see, on a small ship like this they have water hours and ours are two hours a day from 3 to 5 each day. So what I am going to do is stand by the head for the two hours and take the names of the men that take a bath and the ones that don't, and the ones that don't today I am going to march them down Friday to take a bath. I sure hate to do this but I have got to do it.

Despite the unpleasantness of being in charge of men who were not terribly fastidious, new locations and assignments could be exciting. But there was a major downside to them as well—the frustration of mail delays. All the letters that Daddy wrote to Mother while aboard ship, February 18–28, couldn't be posted until they reached the Philippines. With mail taking approximately one week to reach the States, what Daddy experienced and wrote about over those ten days was long over before Mother could read about it. Once they reached shore, with little time for writing, Daddy still did his best. He was not complaining, though, since busy days, for him, were shorter days. As for when Mother would receive the letters, field delays were similar to those aboard ship.

March 5, 1958, In the field in the Philippines

Honey, this is only the 2nd time I have been able to write to you since we hit the Philippines. We have been moving around like mad, playing these war games.

I am writing you this letter, but I will have to keep it for a few days as there will be no more mail leaving till we get back on the ship. I will write you every time I can and mail them all at one time.

March 6, 1958, In the field in the Philippines

Sugar, I may not get to write you but one more time while we are in the Philippines as we will be moving today and there is a lot of work to setting up the hospital in the field. We will be here two more days. Should start back to Okinawa on the evening of the 6th or morning of the 7th. After I get back, I will write you every night again.

Harder still was the waiting for mail on his end. *I will be glad to get on the beach in the morning and get some mail from the best wife in the world*, Daddy wrote the night before they were to make landing. His forced patience was rewarded. He received twelve letters from Mother the first day on the beach.

Each time Daddy was in the field, on ship, or redirected to a new assignment, it took a while for mail to catch up with him. When he left Camp Pendleton around July 16 to start his tour, he did not receive mail until he arrived in Japan, and even that was delayed. He arrived there July 31 but received nothing until

August 9, when a letter dated August 5 from Mother, and a box she had sent him, finally arrived. The letters Mother had written to him after he left Camp Pendleton did not catch up to him until August 26, when he received fifteen letters from her.

September 26, 1957, Camp Fuji
My Dearest darling,

    Honey, I am writing to you again tonight to let you know that I did get a letter from you today. I went by the P.O. this afternoon and they said I didn't get any mail, and I was so blue. So I came down and wrote to you because that helps me when I am blue, to write to you. Well, after I wrote to you and mailed the letter, one of the cooks came down and gave me your letter and said it got misplaced in the P.O. and they found it right after I left. Boy, I sure was happy and now I am not quite so blue. I miss you so much, darling.

Days without mail were, of course, especially difficult, and comments like *I did not get any mail from you today and this has been a long, blue day,* peppered Daddy's correspondence at times. Moreover, without news from home and things to respond to, it was hard to write long letters given the monotony of the days overseas that mostly involved work, writing letters, and maybe a show once a week.

After his mail caught up with him at Camp Fuji, he came to expect almost daily letters. But once on Okinawa, mail came and went only four days a week, and Daddy missed the daily mail. And then, as Christmas approached and the mail service struggled to keep up with the demand, mail call fell off to one to two days a week. Over and over, he expressed the sentiments that were most assuredly shared by all his fellow servicemen and women stationed abroad without their families: *I sure will be glad when mail comes in again. It has been 3 or 4 days since I have gotten any mail, and I sure do miss those letters. For when I can't be with you, darling, mail helps so much.*

———

March 20, 1958, Okinawa

Did I tell you that the Army was moving into a new hospital? Well, it will be ready before long and we will be moving into it. How about that, a new galley to work in? I am not cooking since I am the assistant mess sgt., but it will be a real nice mess to work in.

THE ARMY HOSPITAL AT Camp Mercy where Daddy had been working as assistant mess sergeant was, in reality, a series of Quonset huts, organized during U.S. occupation of Okinawa following WWII that consolidated the isolated military field hospitals previously serving the area. In 1954, the Army began construction on a new 250-bed facility on Camp Kuwae, completed and commissioned in 1958 as the U.S. Army Hospital, Ryukyu Islands.

By mid March, Daddy was back from the Philippines and busy with the move to the new facility. On March 26, he took a tour of the new hospital. *It sure is a nice place*, he wrote Mother that evening. *That galley is out of this world. And just think, I am going to get to work in it for a little while.* But preparing for the move meant long, tiring, fourteen-hour workdays, sometimes working on days off, and Daddy was ready for it all to be behind them.

April 5, 1958, Okinawa

Well, honey, I sure hope these slides come out that I took today. I have never seen so many people in one place. They opened the hospital today for everyone to see, and, man, did the people come out.

The mess staff was in charge of the reception, and provided cookies, cake, and soft drinks—4,000 cookies, a cake large enough to feed 1500–1600 people, along with case after case of drinks. By the end, the cookies and cake were gone.

It would be another month or two before the move to the new hospital, so Daddy would get very little time working in the "out of this world" galley. He had written about it so often in his letters that Mother teased him that she was worried he would get too attached to it. But for him, nothing was more important than getting back home. *Sugar, don't you worry about me getting too attached to that new mess hall. If they told me I could go home now I would be on my way.*

As it turned out, Daddy never made it to the new hospital.

April 9, 1958, Okinawa

Honey, I am leaving D Med. Co. and going to open a mess hall at the rifle range, so I won't be working in the Army mess hall any more. I will have my own mess hall out there. At least, I hope I do. That is what they tell me I will be doing, anyway. They needed a staff sgt. to open it up and they wanted me. Just think, my own mess hall.

While Daddy enjoyed his time at the Army hospital, if there was anything that could get him excited for a change, short of going home, it was the prospect of running his own mess hall. When he got his orders and arrived at the rifle range a couple of days later, he received confirmation that he would be mess sergeant. He also discovered just how different this situation would be.

The rifle range mess hall was, in reality, a tent, and he and his staff lived in tents while there. Daddy saw right away that he had a job on his hands. He had just been put in charge of a mess tent that was, quite literally, a mess. But if he didn't have a healthy enough dose of optimism himself, the Marine Corps had instilled in him a sense that he, along with a few good Marines, could accomplish anything. *I guess it will be o.k. when I get it cleaned up and get my cooks doing things the way I want them done.* And there was, of course, the perennial upside to hard work. *I know one thing. This job will take all my time, all day, 7 days a week, so that will make the time go by faster.* In just two days, he had begun to turn things around, although it meant long, long hours and a struggle to get more help.

April 14, 1958, Okinawa

Honey, I have never seen a mess as this place was in when I got here. It is starting to look like a mess hall a little, and I have had people tell me that the food was good, so I am getting off to a good start. I give them all they want to eat so that way they stay happy. They just eat here one week and then I get 300 new ones for a week.

April 16, 1958, Okinawa

Honey, I will come to a close for now and get some sleep since I have to get up at 0330 in the morning to see that breakfast gets out o.k. I sure hope I get some help out here soon.

April 17, 1958, Okinawa

I am still trying to get some cooks out here to help me. I went to see the C.O. today and he called the capt. in charge of the cooks here on Okinawa and he said he would send two men just as soon as he got them. That could be anytime in the month or two.

April 21, 1958, Okinawa

I got in a sgt. to work for me today so I won't have to get up at 0330 in the mornings now. I have a sgt. as chief cook on each watch now, so I can spend all my time being mess sgt.

With a clean mess, a full staff, and the chance to do things his own way, there seemed to be no end to the compliments he started receiving. *Sugar, everyone tells me what a clean mess and good chow I am putting out. Sure makes me feel good.* Marines started letting him know they were gaining weight the week they were at the rifle range, thanks to the good food he and his staff offered up. And their efforts to maintain cleanliness were recognized as well. *We have a doctor come around every week and this past week I had the cleanest mess here in camp.*

The only thing he was missing at this point was a desk for handling paperwork, but that was soon taken care of. Some former coworkers from the hospital where he had worked had a desk they did not need—presumably surplus in the move—and they brought it up to Daddy for his use. *Now my office is all set up. I have a phone and all. I have your picture on my desk so I can look at you all the time.*

But no sooner had Daddy settled in a bit and gotten things under control when he received word that another change was on the horizon.

May 2, 1958, Okinawa

Well, we close down for a month today, and Monday I am going to start really cleaning this old place up and see if I can get some work done around here so I will have a better place when I start feeding again.

His plan was to work hard around the mess hall getting it cleaned and in his off hours, get in some beach time and work on his tan. But that was not to be. One problem with running a solid operation that served good food was that word got around. Before the week was out, he was tapped to help clean up problems elsewhere.

May 7, 1958, Okinawa

Well, I have got to go over and run the officers' mess for about 3 weeks and see if I can find out what is wrong over there. It seems the colonel doesn't like the way the chow is being cooked, so they told me today I was the mess sgt. of the officers' mess for 3 weeks till the rifle range mess was to open up again.

Within two days, the colonel commented to Daddy that the food was already better, but here he was working long hours again. *I am in the mess hall 3 meals a day, 7 days a week, to see that the col. gets good food and is happy.* Making sure that the colonel was happy meant overseeing things for breakfast, lunch, and dinner, and the workdays stretched from 6:00 in the morning to 6:30 at night. By the end of the first week, though, things were looking up. *I have just about got it like I want it and the colonel is happy now. Maybe I can start working from 8 to 4:30 before long.*

May 22, 1958, Okinawa

I am going to have a lot more paperwork when I open [the rifle range mess] up again than I did before. I have to keep a count of the money it costs to feed and how much plate waste I have and all, and make a report of it every month. All mess halls have to do that now. This division spent $47,000 too much money on food last month.

AS CHILDREN GROWING UP with a father whose career and passion was food service, Jeff and I learned a couple of things pretty quickly. This was no 8 am–5 pm type career, and, once he retired and switched over to club management, it was rare for a chef to stay in one place for very long. The memory of our father coming home from the club and, following greetings and kisses all around, informing us that the chef had given his notice was seared into our family dynamic.

Chefs are always looking for that place to make their mark, to practice their art, to both enjoy artistic freedom and be recognized for it monetarily. Half the time, Daddy admitted that he had seen it coming. After all, having been in food service since the age of 18, he knew the breed.

Interestingly, he often wasn't all that disappointed. Sure, the struggle of being without one for a time was no fun—Daddy would be pulled into the kitchen much more often to keep things under control and running smoothly—and searching for a new chef that would probably come in with grandiose ideas, make his mark in Albany, Georgia, and then decide to move on to bigger and greener pastures, was a hassle. But for all their exquisite culinary talents, many of the chefs that made up the revolving door of the clubs our father managed were either not very good or downright terrible at managing their food cost, a vital part of turning a profit in the restaurant or club business. Which meant that Daddy had a regular battle on his hands over food purchases, both quantity and type, if he was going to keep this aspect of the business under control. And keeping that part of the business under control was the key to profitability.

Daddy had been in food service over fifty years when he finally found someone with the right balance of both. The final club he managed—he was around 70 when the owner pulled him out of retirement to help fix things, and 82 when he finally retired for the final time—eventually brought on a chef by the name of, appropriately, Lance Cook. He was with Daddy at Stonebridge for a number of years, much longer than I can remember any other chef staying put. And, boy, did he cook some delicious meals.

"You really like Lance, don't you Daddy? I mean, as a chef."

I started this conversation with him probably around fifty years after he had written Mother about the increased paperwork that lay before him when he returned to the rifle range mess.

"Yes, I sure do. He's one of the best chefs I've ever had. Not only does he offer a fine menu but the cooking staff likes him. And, he has one of the lowest monthly food costs of anybody who's ever worked for me."

Well, I thought, and it only took you most of your career to find him.

Though I never asked Lance, I'm trusting that, in Daddy, he found a seasoned manager, grounded with years of knowledge and experience that he could tap into, but who, for the most part, let him do his thing in the kitchen. They made a good team.

Toward the end of May, Daddy looked toward the reopening of the rifle range mess tent on the 31st, particularly as a way to, as usual, help the time pass more quickly, not only as they began feeding again but also because of the paperwork that had been added onto his day. They had also restocked the mess with some new things, and he was looking forward to working in a better mess hall than he had left at the beginning of the month. He settled into the routine of feeding a different group of 300–400 men each week and counting the days until he would leave Okinawa to travel home. I'm sure he was hoping that there would be no additional moves and that life in the rifle range mess would run smoothly during his remaining time. But toward the end of his first week back, he found himself in the middle of managing a hazard of the business.

June 6, 1958, Okinawa

Honey, I am going to tell you something but I don't want you to worry about it for I am o.k., but I burned my hand this morning. I heard something in the mess hall and I jumped up and went in there and a field stove was on fire. I had to pull it outside so the tent would not burn and the stove had hot grease in it and some of it got on my hand and arm, but it is not bad. I went to the sick bay with it and they fixed it all up and said it was not too bad.

Now, baby, don't worry. I have told you this because we tell each other everything. But, you see, I had to do it so my mess hall would not burn down. You should have seen me running around in my shorts, no shoes. My shorts were all I had on. That was something to see, haha.

In two weeks, the burn was better, with just a small place where you could still see it. It would leave a scar, a physical remnant and reminder of the fourteen months he spent away from his wife and son.

July 17, 1958, Okinawa
Well, we just got the all clear from one typhoon and two more are on the way. Hope these will miss us too.

HAVING SPENT MOST OF my childhood in landlocked areas, I grew up much more afraid of tornados than hurricanes. But after graduating from college in the early 1980s, I moved to New Orleans for my first job. I had visited there a couple of times with my youth group as a teen, and we had dreamed about how cool it would be if one of us lived there after college. What none of us realized at the time was that living in the "Big Easy" meant developing a whole new understanding of what hurricane season truly meant. Not that it would have changed my mind...here I was, living the dream.

New Orleans is not really coastal, being situated about 40 miles from the Gulf, but it sits in the presence of two other distinct bodies of water, the Mississippi River that snakes around the city, and the 630 square-mile Lake Pontchartrain that sits to its north. The only way to cross the lake by car is to drive around it, or drive the 24-mile long Lake Pontchartrain Causeway, which has the distinction of being the world's longest continuous bridge over water.

As most of the country has known since climate change has become our new reality, a city does not have to sit directly on the coast for storms that come ashore at just the wrong place to cause massive destruction. Hurricane Katrina in 2005 certainly taught us that. But back in the early 1980s, there had not been a direct hit for a while. Still, native New Orleanians often recalled the devastation caused in 1965 by Hurricane Betsy, a Category 4 storm that had come ashore at Grand Isle, Louisiana, then caused widespread flooding in New Orleans when a dangerous storm surge into Lake Pontchartrain caused the lake to breech its levees. It didn't take me long after moving there to start paying attention to the local meteorologists that tracked storms in the Gulf during hurricane season.

I had lived there for three years and my luck was holding—no real threats, no evacuations. But all that changed Labor Day weekend of 1985 when Elena couldn't decide where she wanted to come ashore. She initially approached New Orleans while I was on business with one of my colleagues in Atlanta. By the time we were able to get a flight back home Friday of the holiday weekend, however, the wily storm had travelled east, passing the Florida panhandle, stalling halfway down the Florida Gulf Coast. Worried for the people of Florida, we all breathed a sigh of relief for our section of the Gulf.

I went to bed Sunday night thinking we had skirted another one. Around two o'clock in the morning, however, I was awakened by a loud knock on my apartment door with orders to evacuate. The storm had headed back our direction with a vengeance and it was unclear exactly where it would make landfall, with somewhere between the Biloxi/Gulfport area of Mississippi, or Grand Isle, Louisiana, the likeliest of locations. The governor had ordered a mandatory evacuation. I threw a few things in an overnight bag, hopped in the car, and drove the thirty or so miles from my apartment to my boyfriend's house in Mandeville, Louisiana, traversing the Causeway to the other side of the lake. In the end, it was the poor folks of the Biloxi/Gulfport area that took the direct hit of the Category 3 storm—they had had more than their share of them in the previous few years—but there were enough downed trees and debris in our area for me to see, first hand, the threat of being in a hurricane's path.

That entire weekend, I think Mother wore out the telephone lines with her phone calls. She was fairly glued to the Weather Channel on TV—only in its third year and available through their cable subscription—giving me the latest updates and asking me if I didn't need to get out of there. I assured her that we were getting the most up-to-date information and that I would evacuate if I needed to. At the time, I just thought she was being a typical mother, worried about one of her own situated too far away and seemingly in harm's way. While that was certainly part, maybe most, of it, she had also borne direct witness to a hurricane's power, when, in 1959, the year before I was born, she, Daddy, and Jeff rode out Hurricane Gracie in Beaufort, South Carolina.

Jeff was just shy of four at the time. To this day, he vividly remembers the three of them taking shelter in an interior bathroom in their home as the Category 4 storm with its 130 mph winds and their freight-train noise passed over them. Once the winds and noise died down, he and Daddy went outside to look around. There were downed trees and debris everywhere, but at the same time, the sun was shining and it was eerily still and calm. They walked around the yard a bit, and then Daddy said they better head back inside. No sooner were they back in the house to rejoin Mother when they heard the winds beginning to pick up again. They returned to the bathroom and hunkered down again to wait out the backside of the storm. Jeff squeezed Mother's hand and exclaimed to her in his boldest little voice, "pray, Mama, pray," while Daddy realized that he had just taken his almost four-year-old son out into the eye of a hurricane.

When Daddy was in Okinawa, experiencing Gracie was still a year or two away. But living on an island in the middle of the Pacific meant there were regular typhoon threats, the same weather phenomenon as a hurricane, just referred to by different terms depending on where the tropical cyclone originates. In the thirteen months he was on assignment in Japan, he wrote home about the threat of seven different typhoons, oftentimes one right on top of the other. Most of them bypassed Okinawa, inconveniences that upset the routine of military life since preparations had to be made on a just-in-case basis. In none of Daddy's work assignments did the threat of a typhoon make life more precarious than at the rifle range mess.

June 11, 1958, Okinawa

Well, sugar, we are having a typhoon today but the wind is not strong. But it blew down the mess hall. All we had was a tent, now we don't have that. We will have to put up another one. I will take some pictures of this in the morning and send to you. It sure did make me sick to see that mess hall go down for we sure did have it clean and all. Oh well, we can put up another one. Sugar, don't worry about me, for I have a good, safe place to stay.

It took the better part of three days to get the mess tent back up and running; by June 14, they were feeding supper. But this was typhoon season and most of the typhoon activity that hit Okinawa occurred in August and September, making the final months of Daddy's time at the rifle range spent in a round of preparations for storms that often never hit.

July 3, 1958, Okinawa

My Dearest darling,

Well, we are standing by to take the tents down from the mess hall. There is a typhoon 850 miles away from Okinawa. But it is just a small one. I think the winds are only 80 miles an hour, but it could get bigger.

By July 12, there was another typhoon churning out in the Pacific, and they were on standby to see whether it was coming their way.

July 13, 1958, Okinawa

We are still waiting for the typhoon. They think it might hit Okinawa. We took down the mess hall tent today. If it is going to hit, it should hit Monday or Tuesday.

July 15, 1958, Okinawa

We are still waiting on this typhoon. They don't think it is going to hit Okinawa now. I have not done any work since Saturday [4 days]. When we get a typhoon around they send the shooters back to their base because they have to live in tents out here, and we close the mess hall till we get the all clear.

July 16, 1958, Okinawa
My Dearest darling,

Honey, this will be a short letter as I am tired tonight. We opened the mess hall again today and that meant putting up all those tents. The typhoon is not going to hit here, so we got the people back to fire at the rifle range.

Daddy wrote two paragraphs that night, and that was all. Typhoon threats meant a flurry of activity in advance of the possible storm, with days of boredom as everyone waited to see if the small island lay in the storm's path, followed by long, hard days of reassembly in advance of the Marines returning so the mess could be ready to feed them when they arrived. *I have never been as tired as I was last night,* Daddy wrote when he continued his letter the following morning. By that evening, he was writing about two more typhoons that were on the way and more possible rounds of preparation, the news of which probably reached Mother after the threat was passed but still managed to, I'm sure, scare her half to death on the other side of the world.

May 9, 1958, Okinawa

Well, baby, some good news. I can now tell you where we are going to be stationed. My letter came back today. I bet you would never have guessed where we got stationed. It is Parris Island, S.C. I had rather go there than to the 2ⁿᵈ div [Division] at Camp Lejeune. This way, I won't have to leave you and Jeff. I won't have to go to the field or anything. I talked to some people that just came from there and they say they have good houses for staff and if we wanted to they have nice houses for sale. Honey, I hope you will like it. I know it is not Camp Lejeune, but it is on the east coast and we won't be too far from Greensboro that we can't go up on a weekend.

DURING THE LAST FEW months of Daddy's time on Okinawa, when he wasn't busy preventing the mess tent from burning down, or preparing or waiting for the weekly typhoon threat, his thoughts often turned to his next duty station.

Especially once he had gotten a taste of the west coast at Camp Pendleton, his one wish had been to return to Camp Lejeune. He liked the duty station and it would make trips to Greensboro on the weekends possible. When he found out he would be going to Parris Island, however, he started asking around to see who had been stationed there and could give him some information about what it was like. With a "changing of the guard" of sorts happening as Daddy's time was coming to an end, there were several Marines who had already arrived whose last duty station had been Parris Island and he set about gathering information.

Once he understood the advantages of returning to Parris Island, then, this time as a mess sergeant with a wife and son rather than a recruit, he looked forward to the new assignment. Certainly being within driving distance of Greensboro was a huge plus. But, in truth, he was happiest that he would not have to be going to the field periodically. *I can work at days and be home with you and Jeff boy at nights.*

There was also the prospect of good housing available. Even though selling the house in Miami had been a hassle, they had gotten a taste of home ownership while there and built some equity. This was a period of time in the United States when housing was plenteous, affordable, and available to Americans—well, White Americans, as Blacks were often denied loans that were readily available to Whites—and Daddy, always good with numbers and finances, planned to take advantage of it at every point he could. The Marines he spoke with that had just shipped over from Parris Island described it as "good duty" and said there were some nice houses for sale. *If you want to buy, you can get a nice house for about $500.00 down and $60.00 a month,* so he asked Mother to think about that as an option, particularly if they couldn't get, or didn't like, base housing.

By August 1958, things started to wind down for Daddy as he looked forward to going home the following month.

August 3, 1958, Okinawa

We got in a new staff sgt. Friday and I think he is to take my place. I sure hope so. He will be here just to see how things run for a week and then will take over.

A week after the arrival of the new staff sergeant, Daddy was relieved to learn that he would take his turn at the rifle range. Every Marine, regardless of his or her regular job in the Corps, receives firearm training at boot camp and has to qualify periodically. In other words, every Marine is available, if necessary, to defend the United States. A week spent at the rifle range would, if he were not working full time, help speed the final month along. In the end, he was pleased with his score of 229 out of 250. *Not too bad for me*, he wrote Mother on his last day at the range.

By August 18, the transition was complete. *I have quit working. The new mess sgt. has taken over and all I have to do is lay around and go to the beach.* Having someone come in to take over was a mixed blessing. The typhoons, fires, and other problems would now be someone else's headaches, but throughout his time in Japan and Okinawa, work had been a way to help the days pass more quickly.

But for Daddy, work was about more than passing time, despite how desirable that became while away from his family. It was about doing his best, striving for the precision and perfection that exemplified the Corps. Throughout the sixty-plus years that made up his food service career, he demanded the same from those who worked for him. He exercised good judgment, was fair, being lavish in his praise with those who worked up to his exacting standards and patient with those trying. Those who were just along for the ride usually didn't stick around for long, either by their own choice or his. But he created a work environment that made those who were on board with the program loyal to him and, in his civilian career, often had people follow him from one club to another.

While in Japan, his fitness reports reflected the high standard that he and the service he loved held him to. The captain writing Daddy's final evaluation that covered his time at the rifle range indicated that he had done an outstanding job as mess sergeant, noting that his 94% on the Commanding General's inspection was above most mess halls in the Division. "He is certainly capable of operating a mess hall anywhere within the Marine Corps," Captain Eisenhower concluded.

That was important and welcome recognition, for sure. But perhaps even better was the letter of appreciation and commendation he received from Captain

Louise Stiles, who he worked for at the Army hospital, for he always placed high value on praise that came from another branch of the military, something he was sure confirmed the superiority of the Marine Corps.

April 10, 1958, Okinawa

Upon your transfer from this command, I take this opportunity to commend you for your superior performance of duty as a mess steward, Food Service Division at the Ryukyu Army Hospital.

You have exhibited a high degree of personal interest, leadership and efficiency in discharging your duties and responsibilities. Your outstanding attitude and devotion to duty reflects not only credit to you as an individual but to the military service which you represent.

You have definitely been an asset to the Hospital Food Service Division. You may well be proud of the work you have accomplished for the Army Medical Service.

Personally, I wish to express my sincere appreciation for your cooperation. It has been a pleasure to have you attached to our staff. May you continue to be successful in your military career and may health and happiness be yours throughout life.

The work, although demanding and sometimes exhausting, was the constant for Daddy while he was overseas, for not only did he not have his wife and son but neither did he have the other responsibilities that go with a marriage. In the partnership that Mother and Daddy had forged, his strength with numbers meant that he generally handled the financial end of things. But the paying of bills, car maintenance and repairs, these things did not go away simply because our father wasn't there to see to them. So part of Mother's unending workload was to carry on with them by herself as best she could, with any advice Daddy could provide coming through their correspondence and a two-week delay. For our mother, who struggled every bit as much with math as her own mother did, keeping the household running was a bit of an unwelcome challenge while her husband was on the other side of world.

7

Do What You Think Best

November 16, 1957, Okinawa

Sugar, I know it is hard on you with no more money than you have and don't worry about Christmas gifts. If we don't sell the house before Christmas, we just can't give anything. I am sorry I had to leave when we had so many debts on us, but we will get by some how and we have each other's love. That is more than a lot of people have.

WHEN I WAS FOURTEEN, OR THEREABOUTS, DADDY decided it was time for me to have my own checking account. It was the age of checks, before teenagers were walking around with debit or credit cards, and he thought it would be best if I had some experience with managing a bank account under his tutelage. I had always prided myself on saving, which I achieved even before babysitting age through well-honed techniques of confiscating any money laying around the house to add to my allowance, and conveniently "forgetting" to take my money with me when Daddy took me shopping, this practice always working better on him than Mother. In my late tweens, I had even used this strategy, along with picking up and selling pecans in our yard, to be the first to save the $225 needed to pay my airfare to Hawaii, the condition our parents had set out for Jeff and me to accompany them to the National Club Managers convention in 1973. My brother had a job pumping gas at one of the local gas stations, but I had my airfare in the bank long before him—not that I was competitive or anything. All in all, I was pretty confident I would be good at this checking account thing.

And I was...for a time. Then one afternoon, Daddy arrived home from work and told me we needed to talk. It turns out, I had overdrawn my account. I was incredulous. This *has* to be wrong, I thought. How could the bank embarrass me so?!

"That can't be," I told Daddy. "I have over $200 in my account"—a healthy sum for a fourteen-year-old in the 1970s. "I'm sure the bank must have made a mistake," I announced with teenage bravado.

"Okay," Daddy replied calmly. "Go get your checkbook register and let's take a look."

I bounded up the stairs two at a time to my bedroom, retrieved the checkbook out of my purse, and proudly took it back downstairs to my father, sure that one look at it and I would be vindicated. I opened it to look at the balance, and sure enough, there was plenty there. I handed it to Daddy.

"See. Over $200, just like I thought."

He looked at it and smiled. There *was* a balance of some 200 plus dollars, but there were also a number of check entries I had written down but failed to subtract.

"Sweetie, you didn't subtract these checks out, so you don't really have as much as your balance says."

"Oh, I know that. I was planning on doing it; I just hadn't gotten around to it yet. I figured I had enough to cover it."

He, being a man of numbers, quickly added up the total of the checks in his head, then looked up at me.

"Well, apparently not; the total of these checks is more than your balance. You overdrew your account."

I was mortified, practically on the verge of tears.

"I'm so sorry, Daddy; I didn't mean to. Are you going to take the account away from me? I promise I won't do it again."

"No, I'm not taking the account away from you. But try not to let it happen again."

I'm sure he must have been smiling inside as he said it. The thought that he would close the account for an infraction everyone dealt with sooner or later. This was the very reason he had set the account up, so I could learn while he was still around to prevent serious errors.

"Let me give you some advice, though," he continued. "Unless you have a million dollars in your account, always subtract your checks from your balance when you write them. That's the only way to make sure you know what your actual balance is."

In the years since then, I may have overdrawn my account due to subtraction errors, or, after I got married, because my husband or I forgot to write a check in when the other had the register, but never again because I *failed* to subtract. Lesson learned.

August 31, 1957, Camp Fuji

Honey, if you want to get an apartment, see what you can find and if you need more money, I will try and send you some each month. It won't be much, $25 or $30, or so if you need it, I can have your allotment raised some. I don't really need all the money I am getting each payday. I get about $33 a payday and the only thing I have to pay is the bank and my houseboy. I have to pay him $10.00 a month, so I could send you a little more.

BEFORE THEY LEAVE ON assignment, military men and women who are deployed or stationed in locations without their families can put in for allotment pay for their spouses back home. Daddy had made such arrangements for Mother before he left for Okinawa, allotting the bulk of his pay to her. In the days before direct deposit, this meant that the Marine Corps cut two checks—a larger one that they sent to Mother in Greensboro, and the smaller of the two that came to Daddy wherever he was in Japan or Okinawa.

His regular expenses were pretty minimal. He had agreed to be responsible for sending the bank the monthly payment of $13.53 to cover paying off the stove and refrigerator. And then there was the houseboy he employed, who came at the reasonable sum of $10 for the month. Most Marines of at least staff sergeant grade employed one, which lessened their off-duty chores, and gave teenage boys an entry-level job in the workforce similar to the way American teenage boys of that era would pump gas at a service station or girls would babysit, gender-defined jobs that my brother and I had during our teens. But that was about it for regular, recurring, monthly expenses. Other than that and some stationery and stamps, he spent the rest of his money on clothes, gifts, an occasional movie, and getting pictures developed.

Back in Greensboro, Mother was trying to manage on a fairly tight budget. When Daddy first left, she and Jeff lived with Nana and Papa Jack. She paid them $7 per week in board for her, but they wouldn't take anything for Jeff. It was a small house, though, and things were tight. Mother's foster sister, Jo, whose husband Bill was in the Army, was also living there, so Mother decided, toward the end of August, to see if she could find an apartment within their budget. She and Jeff moved out for a couple of months, but by October, Nana and Papa Jack had moved to a slightly larger home, Jo had rejoined her husband, and Mother decided to move back in with her parents to save money. Daddy was happy that they had moved back for other reasons. *I will feel better about it, just in case you or Jeff would get sick you will be there where someone is.*

The back and forth between them regarding bills, then, took on a loving, comfortable, and familiar pattern. She would write of the latest need, such as a new heater for the car, and the various options. He would offer his opinion, but then often let her know that he trusted her to do what she thought best. She would, at times, worry whether she had done the right thing, spent too much money on something, or not handled things as Daddy would have if he had been there. *Honey, I've tried to do the best I could with the finances,* she wrote in mid-July, less than a month after Daddy had left. He would, at times, suggest that she ask Papa Jack what he thought about a particular situation. He would always reassure her, though, that she had done the right thing, done it just as he would have, and in his absence, was handling the bills just fine. *Honey, you did o.k. with the money,* he wrote in May 1958. *I could not have done any better and I am not disappointed. I think we did o.k.*

September 28, 1957, Camp Fuji

Sugar, I don't think I will be able to get Mother anything while I am in Japan as I only get one more payday and I will only have $2.00 left when I send the bank money, and pay my houseboy, and I have to buy some stamps and get Jeff something for his birthday. I may have to get $5.00 from one of the boys, but I will be o.k. after this payday. Sugar, don't send me any money for I will get along with out it o.k.

Despite Daddy's low monthly expenses, things could be tight on his end as well, thanks in some measure to his generosity with gifts, his penchant for clothing, and his desire to have as much of his pay as possible allotted to Mother. Once in a great while, he would need to borrow a few dollars from "one of the boys" to tie him over until the next payday. This borrowing between Marines was pretty standard, and often as not, he would be the one doing the loaning. Earlier in the month, he wrote that he would send her money to cover the phone call he made while still in California but would have to wait until the following payday. *I loaned out my money to some of the boys in the company and won't get it back until payday the 16th.*

Back home, Mother was also getting requests for money from various family members. Twice while Daddy was gone, she gave one of her first cousins and her husband some money—as much as $100 on one occasion—to help them through some financial difficulties. Daddy reassured her both times that he was fine with her having done it, even glad. *I know they must be having a hard time and I don't think one should put their tithes in just one place. I think they should be put where they are needed the most.* He felt the same way about giving some to his brother-in-law. *Sugar, that was o.k. about sending J.B. the $75.00. He let us have that when we needed it.*

But the strain of living so close to extended family began to take its toll, particularly when family members came to the well too often. Both of Daddy's brothers, along with Elmer's wife and son, were living with their mother. Daddy could be sympathetic, up to a point. *Mother told me Elmer and Mickey are out of work. I guess the people in the States are having a hard time right about now.* Their unemployment may have been linked to an eight-month worldwide economic downturn in 1958, known in the U.S. as the Eisenhower Recession, although, in truth, Uncle Mickey's could just as easily been the result of his alcoholism. But as it started to be a strain on their mother and she had trouble prioritizing, Daddy's tone changed. Mother and Daddy had already given Mimmie some money shortly after he left, and it looked like she would approach them again.

June 9, 1958, Okinawa

I don't mind helping Mother out but she is going to have to stop buying so many things when she needs money for other things.

I guess if Mother comes out and asks you to let her have the money you will have to. I will be so glad when I have my overseas time done and we are together and away by ourselves. I don't see where people think we have such an easy life. Just because we did not run to people when we have hard times they think we have it easy. If only they knew, but they never will for we won't tell them.

The truth is, as Daddy's income increased over the years, our grandmother thought that "Georgie" was flush with cash. I think this was her way of being proud of her middle son and his accomplishments. But Daddy used to say that, if we had as much money as Grandma Mimmie *thought* we had, he would be a millionaire, a situation far from the case.

Sometime in the late fall, Mother decided to return to work, do some substitute teaching, to help alleviate the strain on their financial situation. *I hope you like your job. How does it feel to be teaching again?* This meant, of course, that someone would need to take care of Jeff, since both Nana and Papa Jack worked. *You tell that Jeff boy to be good for the woman that is going to keep him while you work. Tell him Daddy said to be a real good boy.*

But when Mother asked him if he thought she should keep working into the new year, Daddy had a different response.

December 6, 1957, Okinawa

Honey, no, I don't think you should work after Christmas. I think it is nice you can help them out now, but I don't want you to work. I want you to be with Jeff all the time that I am gone.

He recognized how hard this time was on Jeff and, with one parent gone, didn't want the other one working unless it was absolutely necessary. In part, he had the luxury of such a reply because it looked like they would be getting some relief from the biggest financial drain on their income—their house in Miami.

EARLY MEMORIES ARE TRICKY beasts. Are they really our memories, truly glimpses we have of our own past? Or, are they ours because we have been told them by parents and older siblings or seen them in family movies?

I was not even two when we were transferred to Newfoundland, Canada, and four months shy of my fifth birthday when we left, sent on to our next duty station in southwest Georgia. Most of the memories I have of that wickedly cold yet ruggedly beautiful place come from pictures, home movies, and my brother and parents. There are a couple, though, that are just mine, tested against the reality of the event by talking to my favorite keeper of the past, our mother.

One of them is not extensive, but it is clear, like a vivid dream that played itself over and over again in my mind.

I was four and a half, and we were poised to leave the only house I could remember for a place I had never heard of. We lived in base housing, but those words had little meaning for me. This was, for me, *our* house. The house was empty, having been stripped of its contents by the movers who had come to handle the packing and shipping of our household goods to the next place we would live. We stood as a family at the bottom of the stairs, ready to depart, I with one hand in my mother's, the other clasping the stuffed animal that I would trust with no movers, Lady, from the Disney classic, *Lady and the Tramp*.

"Wait! I have to go say goodbye to my bedroom."

I released my mother's hand, and bounded up the staircase, to cries of "Jenny, we need to go," from my parents. Usually I would have obeyed their call, but there is a limit to even my rule following. *This* was important stuff.

My room resided at the top of the stairs, just to the right. It was empty, so it had lost much of its character as *my* room. But it was all I had known. I looked at it with longing.

"Goodbye, room," I whispered.

I walked back downstairs and rejoined my family to set out on our journey, to another duty station, another house, another room. Even my toddler brain knew I would never see this one again.

In the duty stations before Newfoundland, Mother and Daddy had bought homes, Daddy always feeling it was good to gain some equity when they could. In fact, in Beaufort, South Carolina, near Parris Island, they had made the decision to build, certain they would hold onto the home and return after Daddy retired from the Marine Corps, which is why we lived on base in all of our subsequent duty stations. Given the trouble they had finalizing the sale of their house in Miami and the drain on their finances, though, it is a wonder that they took that chance in Beaufort.

In July 1957, Mother sent a handwritten accounting of their monthly expenses in one of her letters to Daddy. The house payment of $69, and another of almost $13 they were paying for the awnings they had added to it separately, made up 30 percent of their monthly expenses. It is no surprise, then, that Daddy's first mention of the house came in his second letter home, from Camp

Pendleton. In what became a familiar refrain, he asked her if she had heard any-thing about the house. *Sure would be nice if we could sell it right away.* But less than a week later, he suggested looking for a renter, despite the fact that doing so would mean additional expense. *Honey, I hope you have heard something about the house by now. If not, I would write the man and see if he could not rent it any-way. If he rents it we may have to have that sink fixed.*

By later that month, a renter had been found. Yet this was not the same as get-ting out from under the mortgage, and things continued to be tight for Mother at home.

August 23, 1957, Camp Pendleton

Mrs. Kunst said that the people that were in our house were about the same age as us, and that the one tree that they gave us was covered with oranges.

Sugar, have you heard anything about the house being sold yet? Sure wish that we could sell it and get our money out of it, and then you could pay the car and other things off. If he [the real estate agent] doesn't hurry up and sell it, maybe we should see about turning it over to someone else, but you do what you think best, honey.

October 6, 1957, Camp Fuji

Honey, I know we owe a lot of money. I wish that I could be there to help you out with it. Maybe we will be able to sell the house real soon and can pay the car off. Hope so.

Finally, in mid-October, Mother wrote that Mr. Cubberly, their real estate agent, had found a buyer who wanted to move in the following month and pay Mother and Daddy rent until the loan went through and settlement could occur.

October 23, 1957, Okinawa

Now, honey, that sure sounds good about the house. I am sure glad it is being sold. That is one worry we won't have and maybe we can get out of the hole a little bit. Now, baby, you do what you think best with the money, but if I were you, I would pay off the loan company and the awnings and any other little bills we have—I can't remember them all—and put the rest of it in the bank. But you do what you think best, honey. I know you will do what's right and best.

But it was another month and a half before she confirmed that the buyers were in the house and the rent payments had been set up.

November 30, 1957, Greensboro
My dearest husband,

I got good news today. Talked with Mr. Cubberly on the phone. The people are in our house and are paying rent—$67.00. They moved in the 15th of November. On Dec. 15, Mr. C. will send me the rent money if settlement hasn't been made. You see, he holds the rent until the month is up because if settlement comes before the rent period is up, he refunds that part of it and sends me the balance. Mr. C. said they were already notified of their set up, payment amount and everything, and to expect settlement right away. Boy, do I feel relieved—I know you do.

By December, the buyers' loan was approved and it looked like settlement would occur before the end of 1957. But then the complexities of having a husband stationed overseas delayed the settlement, and Mother, who had provided another monthly accounting to Daddy, was still struggling to make ends meet.

February 16, 1958, Okinawa
I got a letter from you today and a letter from Mr. Hughes with another power of attorney for me to sign before an officer and return to him at once. He said this was necessary so you could complete the sale of our property in Florida. I thought that the one power of attorney was good for everything, but I will sign this before my C.O. and send it right back to him.

Early February, 1958, Greensboro
Babe, this is one reason I can't go to Florida this month:
$227.10   Allotment Check

67.00   Rent on House
$294.10
-286.35   Monthly Expenses
$ 7.75   left

Now, as you can see, I haven't paid any board out of it nor met the Amoco [gas] bill. Also, no church money, yet. I'm not complaining; I'll get by some way. Just wanted you to know how things are.

Daddy signed the additional power of attorney and returned it, but it was not enough, for the middle of the following month he wrote that he signed the deed to the house and Mother should have it back by the end of the week. When she received it, she shared some good news for a change—they would receive $129 back on their income taxes.

But as the end of March neared, they still had not received their money and the title company continued to require more information from Daddy.

March 26, 1958, Okinawa
My Dearest darling wife,

I got your letter today where you said that the title company wanted my rank and address. I don't know why they should want that because I signed the deed like they told me to do and had 3 officers sign it too. I sure wish they would just give us our money, for I know you need it before you go to Florida. When I left to come overseas I sure thought the house would be sold long before this. Honey, I know it has been hard on you not having the money to pay all the bills. I sure hope we never have to be apart again, but if we do, I am not going to leave you with that many bills.

April 1, 1958, Okinawa
Honey, I feel like you do about that P.O.A. [power of attorney]. It was not good for the deed and no good for the income tax. We might just as well have saved our money and not had it made out for all the good it has been.

April 21, 1958, Okinawa

Sugar, I got two letters from you today and in one of them you said that we got the money out of the house. I sure am glad. And just think, we have $1600.00 more now than we would have if we had rented a house while we were stationed in Florida.

May 6, 1958, Okinawa

Well, we just lack one more payment on our stove and refrigerator, and I am going to make that payday, the 15th of May, and then it will be ours.

Baby, I don't ever want to get where we have to pay out that much money a month again. We will just have to watch ourselves. I know it has been hard on you since I have been gone, trying to meet all those bills, and baby, you have done a good job at it. Maybe we will be able to save some after I get home.

It had taken four months to find a buyer for the house, another month to set up rent payments, another month for the buyers' loan to be approved so settlement could occur, and another four months for final settlement to be made and the check to be cut for their money. In total, they had waited ten months to get their money out of the house. Between securing that money and paying off the stove and refrigerator, things were starting to look up, at least financially.

The somewhat pedestrian topics of finances, income taxes, and the selling of their house were necessary pieces of our parents' correspondence during Daddy's time overseas. In truth, though, even with the months-long saga of the house sale, they were but a small part of their transoceanic back and forth. What consumed the greatest part of their writing hours, what they struggled the most to find words for, was their love and longing for one another, and how they would ever survive fourteen months apart.

Our parents as toddlers. Mother is probably about 18 months; Daddy around three.

Our father, aboard ship in the Mediterranean in 1948, shortly before being sent home for his own father's impending death.

A picture of our 18-year-old Mother
from the scrapbook she kept the year
they lived in Cleveland.

Mother with her loving,
rascal of a brother, our Uncle
J.B., once the family had
moved back to Greensboro.

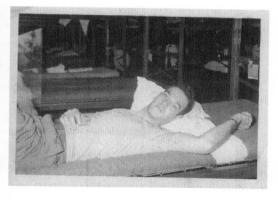

Our father, relaxing on his bunk in the
barracks, as a very young U.S. Marine.

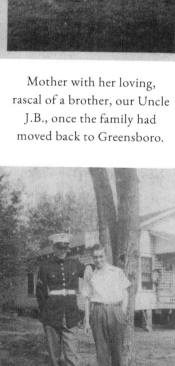

Daddy, newly graduated from
boot camp, with his younger
brother, our Uncle Elmer.

Daddy in a foxhole in Korea, after the war had ground to a stalemate and the temperatures were much warmer than the Chosin. I don't know why, but this was always one of my favorite pictures of our father as a young man when I was growing up.

Daddy (on right), with a fellow Marine, perhaps at Koto-ri.

Daddy in Korea, probably writing a letter to "the girl that I love."

The wedding picture I always admired of
Mother in "the" dress.

Mother and Daddy at the cake cutting,
hosted by Nana and Papa Jack, the
evening before their wedding.

Sergeant and Mrs. George Francis
Hobaugh, newly wed.

Mother holding her son who survived his premature birth, my
brother Jeff, in November 1955.

Our parents' house in Florida,
and them together in the backyard
enjoying my 10-month-old brother
in July 1956, a year before Daddy
left for Okinawa.

Mother, Daddy, and Jeff, soaking up time together in June 1957, the month Daddy left for his TDY in Okinawa.

One of Daddy's photos of Mt. Fuji.

Daddy's first assignment while in Japan/Okinawa was
with the 3rd Medical Battalion of "D" Company.

Catching a bite to eat in the field.
Daddy wrote on the back of the
picture: "Eating dinner the first day.
People in background are C.O. and
two other officers."

Mother (in Greensboro) and Daddy (outside his galley in the field while in Okinawa), keeping up a brave front while separated for fourteen months.

Jeff having fun with his Papa Jack, who became the primary male influence in my brother's life while Daddy was in Okinawa.

A serious Jeff boy in October 1957, the month he turned two.

My precocious brother in February 1958, growing fast, and in a rare moment when he wasn't running around, injuring himself, or making mischief.

Daddy and Jeff outside their house in Florida, a few months before he left for Okinawa. Daddy held onto the dream that his son would not forget him.

Jeff and me with our dog Rusty in Beaufort, November 1961, somewhere in the vicinity of the Great Stroller Accident and my first birthday.

Our father, now the mess sergeant, in his office in Argentia, Newfoundland.

JUNE 1962

Outside our Nana's house in Greensboro, June/July 1962, with Jeff in full protective mode. Those were the steps we launched our "riptide" parachute jump off of.

Happy to be reunited with our daddy in Newfoundland after being separated from him for a couple of months.

Mother, Jeff, and me in November 1963, the month of my third birthday and the assassination of President John F. Kennedy.

A brisk June day in Argentia in 1965, the month before we were transferred to Albany, Georgia.

The official photograph
of Daddy receiving his
lieutenant's bars.

Daddy proudly
showing off the
cake for the Marine
Corps birthday for
MCSC Albany in
1966, and happy
to have overseen
someone else doing
the baking!

Jeff in his little league uniform.

Jeff and me on the first day of school in 1966.

A meal around our Grandma Mimmie's table in Greensboro in the mid1960s.
From left: me, Uncle Elmer, Aunt Peggy, Jeff, Grandma Mimmie, David,
Nana, Mother, and Uncle Mickey. Daddy is taking the picture.

One of our last family photographs before Daddy retired.

8

A Love Like Ours

July 16, 1957, Camp Pendleton
My Dearest darling wife,

Will write you a few lines tonight before I go to bed. Sugar, I love you more than words can ever tell. You are the best thing that ever happened to me. I am so very much in love with you.

Mᴇ BROTHER SAYS THAT WHEN OUR MOTHER DIED, she turned into a saint in Daddy's eyes.

"Have you noticed how since Mother's been gone, according to Daddy, the two of them never argued?" Jeff and I were talking not long after Mother's death when he posed this question to me.

"That's sure not how I remember things," he continued. "They had some spats here and there. He's turned her into a saint."

True enough, I suppose. I would usually just nod my head and mutter an "uh huh" in reply.

That kind of response is not altogether unusual, I expect. I had done the same thing in the wake of my first husband's death years before. I have found that time has a way of course correcting our perspective. Daddy didn't have the luxury of a lot of time after Mother died, but I'm not sure that would have happened in his case anyway. I think he saw their "spats" as disagreements, differences of opinion.

Truth be told, I don't remember that many full-on arguments, any really. Maybe I'm guilty of promoting both of them to "sainthood," as well. Or, as his younger sister by a little over five years, maybe Jeff helped shelter me from some things; he has always taken his role as big brother seriously. He's always had a better memory than me, too, so maybe I've just forgotten—or chosen to forget—some things. I've also had the luxury of reading their letters, and, while the separation and distance they reflect certainly give a different perspective from the day-to-day, lived reality of marriage, there is also a truth to them that gets to the heart of their relationship.

October 19, 1957, Greensboro

O Babe, if you were just here tonight. I'd give all I have to bring you home to me. I sure do love you. I know I say that over and over, but you are the dearest one in all the world. I love you with all my heart.
Yours forever,
Becky

December 23, 1957, Okinawa

Sugar, I love you with all of my heart. If only I could find words to tell you how much that I love you. You mean more to me than life itself, for without you, there would be no life for me.

Goodnight, my darling wife. Always love and need me, for I shall always love and need you, baby.
All my love always,
George

There seemed to be neither one of them without the other. George and Becky. Becky and George. At Mother's funeral, their pastor noted during the eulogy that they simply belonged together, like peanut butter and jelly. An ordinary metaphor for what seemed to those who knew them to be an extraordinary love. And yet that feeling, that knowledge, that they simply belonged together was forged, somehow, over considerable separation at a time when that could have been hard on a relationship.

They stayed connected and their love flourished through letters and the occasional phone call because that was pretty much all they had. *I will be going to the field Wednesday afternoon until Saturday afternoon,* Daddy wrote in mid-August, less than a month after arriving at Camp Fuji. *But I will still write you every night, sugar, for I want to write you every night that I am gone, so you will get a letter from me every day.* Despite trying to deal with handling their finances and raise a rambunctious toddler, Mother was just as steadfast, and while they were not able to live up to the commitment of writing *every* day, the days that each of them missed were few.

This was no small feat for our father, who most definitely was not a man of letters. He was an abysmal speller, something he admitted to—*I sure wish that I would have learned spelling in school*—and his grammar left a lot to be desired, especially the verb tenses that he mixed up constantly. Numbers and working with people were his gifts, and he had left high school before graduation to join the Corps, completing his GED somewhere along the way. At some point I must have noticed Daddy's difficulty with grammar and said something to Mother, she being gifted in the ways of language. I remember her telling me that she knew and accepted this about our father when she married him. He had grown up in a family that had struggled with it as well, and it is hard to learn proper grammar when you don't hear it at home, she suggested. There was so much more to him that grammatical mistakes seemed like a small thing indeed.

And so they both wrote, she with her elegant script and turn of phrase, he often relying on the same phrases to express what he confessed he struggled to find words for. *You are my everything. You are the best wife and mother in the world. I love you with all of my heart. You are the only one for me. I am so much in love with you.* At least one of these, usually more, wound up in every letter he wrote. I'm quite sure our mother did not mind reading the same words over, and over, and over again.

———

August 12, 1957, Camp Fuji

Honey I don't want to write about it every time I write, for it will only make it hard on you, but I miss you so much and I am so lonesome without you. I love you more than words can ever tell. I know that you are lonesome for me and when I write blue letters it makes it hard on you, but I just have to tell you sometimes how lonesome I get for you.

July 13, 1958, Okinawa

Tell Dad I said hello and I sure do want to go fishing when I get home, all of us, for where I go you go when I get home, sugar. I want you with me everywhere. I am the lonesomest boy in the world tonight and every night I am away from you.

BATTLING THE LONELINESS IS one of the hardest things to overcome during separation. From his first letter at Camp Pendleton—*Honey, I am going to be so lonesome for the next 14 or 15* months— to declaring himself *the lonesomest boy in the world* less than two months before going home, Daddy wrote of it. With the time away from each other during Mother's first pregnancy and birth and Daddy's intermittent time in the field at Camp Lejeune, they were no strangers to separation in their married life. But it was nothing compared to this, and Daddy, in particular, struggled to find ways to overcome it. *When [After] I write you, I am going to the show. I have to do something and get out of this room.*

Finding something to do was not always easy, however. At Camp Fuji and while working at the Army Hospital, there was a town to go into with shops and movies. But by the time he was mess sergeant for the rifle range, he was living something more akin to life in the field.

June 3, 1958, Okinawa

Baby, I miss you all the time, but like you missing me most in the evening, I too miss you most that time of the day. When all my work is done and I should be starting home to you, I have to come in this old room and sit around.

He did take advantage of opportunities that came up. *I went to Bible class again tonight. We have it every Tuesday night and I sure do like it. We are now in the Book of Acts.* For an introvert, "getting out" was not always easy since he regularly recharged and drew energy from alone time. But too much alone time reinforced the seemingly unending separation.

For our mother, trying to keep up with a toddler and living with her parents, there was little alone time. When she found some, the reality of the months away from Daddy hung around her like a heavy weight, particularly when she settled down to write him in the evenings.

September 17, 1957, Greensboro

It has rained here all day yesterday and all day today. It's so dreary and I wish I had you here tonight to snuggle up to. I sure do miss you tonight. I always do but seems worse when it rains!

Birthdays, anniversaries, holidays—these could prove even harder than the pattern of ordinary days. Seeing the date on the calendar and having it settle in that another special day had rolled around and you were, once again, apart from one another made the pain of absence especially sharp.

December 1, 1957, Mother's birthday, Okinawa

Honey, I hope you have had a happy birthday today. I wish that I could have been there to take you in my arms and hold you and tell you how much you mean to me. I hope I never have to be away from you on your birthday again.

February 14, 1958, Daddy's birthday, Okinawa

Well, look at what day it is. I am now 28 years old. The captain had the baker bake me a birthday cake, and myself and all the cooks sat down and ate it.

Honey, if I could have been home with you today, it would have been a good birthday, but since I had to be away from you, it is just another day to me. I will be so glad when we can be together again; I am so much in love with you.

Despite being surrounded by family and friends, the situation was little different for Mother. When Jeff's birthday rolled around, Jeanette and Tinker

Cates, close friends who had been attendants in our parents' wedding, invited Mother and Jeff over that afternoon for another round of birthday celebration. As Mother shared with Daddy about the fullness of the day and the joy of having family and good friends to share it with, the reality of Daddy's absence eventually settled in.

October 20, 1957, Jeff's birthday, Greensboro

Honey, I miss you so. At Jeanette and Tinker's today, Tink showed a picture (slide) they had made of us right after Susan was born. You had on your charcoal trousers and sport coat, and I had on that pretty blue taffeta dress you paid $17.00 for at CLNC [Camp Lejeune]. I just let the tears roll. We were sitting on the couch and you had your arm around me. Suddenly, I felt so lonely.

Goodnight, my dearest. You are my everything. I'll be so glad when the time is over and you can put arms around me again. I love you, Baby, more than all the world.

Yours,

Becky

While Mother certainly felt the loss, she also understood that the separation was probably harder on Daddy at these times. In addition to her letters and those of the rest of the family, she did her best to send gifts for those special days and to keep the care packages coming on the ordinary ones. *I sure am happy tonight,* Daddy wrote a couple of days before the Thanksgiving he spent in Okinawa. *This morning, I got 6 letters and a box from you. The banana bread sure is good. You are the best.* It was the second loaf she had sent him since he had been over there. He had raved over the first one she sent the month before and let her know it had arrived in good shape.

In truth, it was pretty amazing the things that she was able to ship over, given the glacial speed of mail between them. Within the first month Daddy was in Japan, while still at Camp Fuji, Mother shipped over some cookies and brownies. *I am sitting here writing you and eating a brownie now. They sure are good,* he attested, a sentiment confirmed by those he chose to share them with. When she asked him in a letter the following day if he needed any canned goods, he couldn't think of any, but praised the brownies again, which were, by that point, all gone.

But of all the things that Mother sent him, nothing was more appreciated, garnered more praise, made him happier, than country ham.

September 25, 1957, Camp Fuji

I did not get a letter from you today but I did get the box with the country ham, and it sure does look good. I am going to have country ham and eggs for breakfast, if I can wait that long. If not, I will go up tonight and have a country ham sandwich. Sugar, you are the best wife in the world and I love you so much.

Country ham is a type of ham produced in the southeastern states that uses a particular method to cure and smoke the meat. It is salt cured for several months, then generally hardwood smoked before being aged anywhere from a few months to up to three years. The result, when cooked, is a chewy, salty ham that is best fried in a pan and topped with red-eye gravy, a "gravy" made from the ham drippings and a little black coffee that forms a dark, reddish "eye" in the center. When served with eggs and biscuits—cheese biscuits if you're lucky—it is a breakfast that is hard to beat. In our family, that very breakfast became a tradition on Christmas mornings that followed the opening of presents.

For our father, country ham was like manna from heaven. Just two days before the package arrived, he had asked Mother in his letter to *tell Dad I sure would like to be there to eat some country ham, for I know he would get one if I were there as well as I like it.* Writing her the evening after the ham arrived, he did not confess if he had been able to wait until that morning to taste it, but he was quick to praise it. *I think that was some of the best ham I have ever had. You are the sweetest wife in the world to think of me like that.* Despite his affinity for the southern staple, he shared some with the other cooks, who all liked it very much. His generosity was no small gesture. For him, that ham was a savory slice of home, a pure delicacy, a precious gift from *the sweetest wife in the world.*

———

December 8, 1957, Okinawa

I got a Christmas card from Mrs. Kunst today with a note in it. She said she had sent me a box for Christmas, and in it she said she had put me a small Christmas tree and other things. There is no telling what all she has in the box.

IT WAS THE CHRISTMAS season in Albany, Georgia, where it was anyone's best guess as to what the temperature would be for the actual day, in the 40s or the 80s, it could run the gamut. More years than not, it swung to the higher end, much to my dismay. Perhaps I still had lingering memories of Christmas when we were stationed in colder climates. More likely, I was just wired to want seasonal temperatures. Albany was definitely the wrong place for that.

But there would be enough time to stew over that later. Tonight, we were decorating the tree, one of my favorite pastimes, and I would be happy no matter what the thermometer read. We had had an artificial tree as long as I could remember, something that would grate on me in later years until, one year in college, I rectified the perceived slight to how Christmas should be. For now, though, I was young enough that the imperfection didn't bother me.

Daddy had assembled the tree and strung the lights, pre-lit trees being a convenience still decades in the future. That was his contribution to the process, unless I could throw enough daughter guilt on him to get him to hang a few ornaments. The rest of us hung the ornaments and garlands or icicles, whatever we decided that year's tree needed, Jeff and Mother handling the top and me the bottom until I grew enough to reach higher up.

As we unpacked the ornaments, I cherished examining each of them, some store-bought, some homemade, some given to us as gifts. I pulled out a small collection of tiny ornaments, ones that the Christmas tree swallowed until they were difficult to see, ones we had had for as long as I could remember. There were little frosted bells and teeny angels. Compared to the more lavish ones we owned, they were simple and spoke of a different era. But we hung them every year, along with the larger, what I considered, more beautiful, ones.

"Remind me where we got these," I said to Mother.

She turned and looked at what I was holding.

"Oh, those. They were the little ornaments on the tiny tree that Mrs. Kunst sent to your daddy the Christmas he spent in Okinawa. You never knew the Kunsts but you've heard us speak of them. They were the older couple that lived next door to us when we were stationed in Hileah where Jeff was born. They adored your brother, thought he was the cutest little thing, treated him like their own grandson, and were such good friends to us while we lived there. Mrs. Kunst insisted that Daddy needed a Christmas tree while he was away from us that Christmas, and so she sent him a little one for his room. These few ornaments are all that we have left of it."

I examined them more carefully. Somebody had cared enough about our daddy to make sure he had a Christmas tree all the way over in Okinawa. Even as the Grinch's heart grew three sizes each Christmas as the Whos began their singing even without any presents, these little, seemingly plain ornaments must have grown three sizes in my eyes that Christmas, and I wished we'd had enough to decorate a little tree of our own.

EVEN A LITTLE TREE of his own could not soften the pain of longing felt over being away from home at Christmas, probably the most difficult of the holidays to be separated from family. Anticipating it was hard enough, but at least the thinking and writing about what to send for gifts, and the shopping and mailing helped ease some of the day-to-day longing that Daddy experienced. Packages took about a month to get to the States unless sent by airmail, which he and Mother saved for food items and urgent needs since it was too expensive.

On the first day of November, he was already mentioning that he planned to do his Christmas shopping the following day so he could get the presents in the mail. True to his word, he went the following morning, and wrote to Mother about it that evening. *I tried to buy everyone something. It is just small, but I give it with love.*

And by mid-month, he was conspiring with Grandma Mimmie for her to get a new purse for his wife there in Greensboro and put it under her tree, so that when Jeff and Mother came over to open presents, she would have something there.

When Mother wrote in October to ask Daddy for Christmas ideas for him, he wrote what I recognized as his standard response. *Honey, about what you all can send me for Christmas, I can't think of anything.* He was, hands down, the hardest person I've ever tried to buy gifts for. He never could "think of anything" if you asked, and, especially in his later years when he had more disposable income, he would often go out in the weeks leading up to Christmas and buy it for himself, spoiling whatever inspiration one of us had come up with, and then responding to, "Daddy, you did again!" with an, "Oh, I'm sorry," and a sheepish grin. Somehow, Mother responded to the challenge. By December 8, she wrote Daddy that she still had not bought any Christmas gifts for the family, waiting to see if the Miami house would settle, *except I've sent you one small box and another is on the way now.*

Food, however, now that was a different matter altogether, particularly those treats that reminded him of the holidays, and Daddy was not leaving that to chance.

December 1, 1957, Okinawa

You know what, honey? I was just sitting here thinking the other day that I was hoping you would send me a date nut cake for Christmas. But if you send it early I will keep it for Christmas.

And as if she had read his mind ...

December 2, 1957, Okinawa

I got the date nut cake today and, honey, it sure is good. You are the best. I was going to save it for Christmas, but I just had to eat some of it today when I got it. I bet I have it all gone by Christmas. It sure is good.

Apparently, when it came to food, our father was not so great at delayed gratification.

As he began to receive boxes from home laden with gifts, he would try, he wrote one mid-December day, to make believe he was home with Mother and Jeff when he opened them on Christmas Day. And, of course, he planned to work on Christmas Eve and Christmas Day so that the days would go by faster and to allow those who had families with them to have some of the day at home. But, in the end, all of this was just trying to put a great big mask over the truth that he wouldn't be home for Christmas.

December 2, 1957, Okinawa

Well, honey, it won't be long till Christmas now. I know this will be a lonesome and blue Christmas for me, for I won't be with you and Jeff boy.

December 23, 1957, Okinawa

I will be glad when Christmas is over, for it is so lonesome at Christmas time without you and Jeff boy. I am lonesome for you and him all the time, but Christmas, being here, doesn't help any.

December 24, 1957, Christmas Eve, Okinawa

Merry Christmas, darling. It will be Christmas in 2 more hours, and I am sure lonesome here without you and Jeff boy. I hope this is the only Christmas I will ever have to spend without you and him, darling.

December 25, 1957, Christmas Day, Okinawa

My Dearest darling wife,

Well, here it is, another Christmas over with. I can say that I am glad this one is all over.

Honey, thank everyone for the things they sent me. I opened them, and all I got I needed. I sure do like the date nut cake. That mother-in-law of mine is the best.

I hope you and Jeff boy had a nice Christmas. I wish that I could have sent you and him more, but I did not have the money.

One of the Okinawa boys that works in the mess hall asked me to come out to his house tonight and have coffee, so I think I will go out. Him and his wife just had a new baby and I want to see it and maybe I will be able to hold it a few minutes.

Honey, I hope I never have to be away from you and Jeff another Christmas.

By the end of the year, Daddy had received a letter from Mother describing their Christmas Day—Jeff's excitement, all the presents, going to his mother's house, and most of all, missing him. The purse that Daddy and Grandma Mimmie had conspired to get for Mother was a successful surprise. *I am glad you like your handbag,* Daddy wrote after receiving Mother's letter. *Sorry that it made you cry.* To be fair, it did not take a lot to make our mother cry; something tells me, though, that it was not really the handbag she was crying over.

August 30, 1957, Camp Fuji

Baby, I sure am in love with you. I know that I say this a lot in every letter, but I mean it with all of my heart, sugar. You are the only one for me. I will always be true to you and I know that you will be true to me, honey. That is one thing we don't have to worry about because we trust each other.

I WAS SEVEN WHEN Daddy retired from the Marine Corps, Jeff twelve. In my seven-year-old brain, it made perfect sense that Daddy was retiring; that is what a person did when they were "old," and had worked for a long time, the 20 years he had been in the Corps. He was 38 years old. I laugh now to think of how young he was when he made this transition.

While our parents had always intended for us to return to Beaufort, South Carolina, where they still owned a home, Daddy took a job managing the Elks Club there in Albany, and soon, at Doublegate Country Club, and so we stayed, and stayed, and stayed. It took Mother a while to come to terms with remaining, but for Daddy, he always felt that the good Lord had placed what was known as the "Good Life City" on the face of the earth just for him.

With retirement, we moved from the Marine base in East Albany—the military and "blue collar" section of the city—to the western, predominantly "white collar" side. It was like being transferred to another duty station. I left behind my friends that I had known for three whole years, an eternity to a seven-year-old, and spent the beginning of third grade crying quietly at my desk, the tears leaving great big circular splotches on my penmanship papers. We were learning cursive, and it was my luck to get the oldest, strictest, meanest teacher in all of third grade at Sherwood Elementary. She would hold our papers up to the light to see whether any marks, loops, or swirls had gone past the right-hand margin, and, if they had, we had to rewrite the *entire* paper. I liked to follow the rules but even I could see that this was insane! Basically, the fall of 1968 was not a good time for me. When I left third grade, I decided that, just to spite Mrs. Mitchell, rather than observing a right-hand margin I would spend the rest of my life writing all the way to the edge of the paper. And so I have. In the end, I got my revenge on that woman.

By the time I made this lifelong vow, I had made some friends, both at school and church. In truth, it was pretty much the same set. The church we went to was situated just across the street from my school—we lived half a block away from both—and my friends lived in neighborhoods that surrounded the church and school. This became Jeff's and my group, for many of my friends had older siblings that were Jeff's age.

When I graduated from college, I couldn't wait to land somewhere besides Albany, Georgia, which was too flat, hot, and humid for my taste. Even then, though, I recognized it as a pretty decent place to grow up, at least if you were White and middle or upper class. It was a horrible time for Blacks to be in Albany, and racism and White privilege still haunt the area. But as I reflect back on those years for me, I think what made it special was that group of friends. Despite the fact that they remained in Georgia and I have long since resided just outside Washington, D.C., I still get together with a small corps of women from that set of friends twice a year. We get out yearbooks and church directories, laugh about good memories, but mostly make new ones that turn into stories that are funny to no one but us.

When we played together in those carefree days of our youth, the thing that I think we took for granted was that, when we went to each other's houses, it was to a two-parent household. None of my friends' parents were divorced. This is not to say that everyone's home was idyllic; we each had typical, and maybe not so typical, family dynamics, things that we wanted to hide from the world. But there was always a Mr. *and* Mrs. Hatcher, a Mr. *and* Mrs. Sawyer to say hello to. Most of us have lost one, or both, parents. The marriage tally comes in, in each case, at 50, sometimes 60, plus years.

Such extraordinary marital stability was not the case in the world we had left. Not long after we moved from the Marine base, the parents of my best friends on the base announced they were splitting up. I'm sure there were couples that surrendered to divorce that I did not even know about.

Military life is hard on a family. Frequent relocation, war, PTSD, and long periods of separation, even in peacetime, can make it seem like a third party of loneliness, despair, and distrust has moved into the home, disrupting the already delicate balance of relationships that exists. It takes a heavy dose of love, commitment to be "true" to one another, and, as our parents wisely knew even at their young ages, basic trust.

October 1, 1957, Camp Fuji

Honey, I too need you, more than I can ever tell, but it is you I need and no one else. I could never love anyone else but you, baby. Sugar, I trust you. I know that you need me too, but me alone and I know that you will be a worthy wife and mother while I am gone and I will be a worthy husband and father too. Baby, I am so much in love with you, my darling wife.

Over and over, Daddy wrote of being true, of saving his love for her, of his commitment to being "a worthy husband and father." Not being true to one another was something they didn't have to worry about, like other people, he assured her.

They wrote to each other about people all around them that they knew who were separating, getting divorced. When Mother wrote Daddy about one set of friends getting divorced, he assured her that she did not have to worry about the two of them, for *each day that I live I love you more and more. I just don't understand people,* he continued. *All I can say is that they don't have a love like ours, but don't many people do.*

Daddy was completely incredulous over the news of good friends of theirs from Camp Lejeune who were talking of splitting up. *I don't see how people can live with each other and just up and say "I don't love you anymore." All I can say is they don't have a love like ours. I love you with all my heart.* A few weeks later, Mother wrote that the husband had put in for a transfer over to Okinawa. *I don't see how anyone could put in for this place and leave their wife and baby. I would never put in to leave you and Jeff boy.* He knew of another Marine in his company who, despite being married, had put in to come over to Okinawa, and he couldn't imagine choosing to leave someone you love. *I will never leave you if they wait for me to put in for it, for I love you and want to be with you always. The only reason I am over here now is because they sent me.*

A month later, Mother wrote that these same friends from Camp Lejeune were expecting a baby, and Daddy hoped that they would be able to work things out to stay together. Daddy was able to hook up with the husband when he was in Okinawa and learned that they had had a baby boy, but their letters are silent on whether the friends managed to, in the end, make their marriage work.

TRUST WAS ALSO ABOUT bringing up difficult topics in their letters to one another, waiting over the long weeks for a reply, and trusting that the other person would be honest in his or her response.

At some point when I was growing up, I learned that our father had stopped smoking when Jeff was born. I knew that he had smoked at one point. I had heard stories about how he and Uncle Elmer used to go behind the steps of the house to sneak a smoke when they were just boys. One of the few pictures of him in Korea that I liked to look at as a little girl showed him looking up from a bunker with a cigarette between his fingers.

But growing up in a non-smoking household, it was beyond my imagination that, when he and Mother married, Daddy was a smoker. Having seen his father die at a young age from what was emphysema or perhaps lung cancer, struggling to draw breath, I am sure that Mother longed for Daddy to quit. I asked her at some point when he did.

"When Jeff was born and he came into the hospital room to see me after the birth, he was chewing gum, chomping on it with abandon. He never chewed gum. I asked him what was going on, and he told me that he had quit smoking."

Just like that. Cold turkey. He stopped.

January 23, 1958, Okinawa
My Dearest darling wife,

Sugar, I wish that there was some way I could get this letter to you faster, but it will take four or five days. I just got your letter where you asked me if I had started smoking again. No, baby, I have not started smoking again. I would never smoke again. I looked at the picture. I don't know what is in my hand, but it is not a cigarette. I can understand your letter, honey. It does look like a cigarette but believe me, sugar, it is not.

Sugar, when I stopped smoking that day in the hospital, it was for good. There are two reasons I will never smoke again, and they are, I told you I would stop when Jeff boy was born. I would never start again for that reason. And the other one is I told the Lord if he would let Jeff boy live, I would never again smoke another cigarette, and I would never go back on that, sugar.

Honey, don't ever worry about anything making me love you less. I love you with all of my heart and that is for always. Oh, how I love and miss and need you, sugar. Honey, you keep right on telling Jeff boy that his mommy and daddy don't smoke, for they never will. I don't even want a cigarette any more and I am so glad that I stopped smoking.

I cannot imagine the anxiety our mother felt over writing the letter that prompted Daddy's reply; the anguish as she waited for the letter that would answer her question; the self-doubt over whether bringing the subject up reflected a lack of trust on her part; the letters she wrote as she waited; the relief and tears that accompanied the reading of Daddy's January 23 letter. But just to erase any doubts she might have about whether she should have written, Daddy brought the subject up again two days later.

January 25, 1958, Okinawa

Honey, don't you worry about that letter you wrote me, asking me if I had started smoking. I understand, and I can see why. When you look at the picture it did look like a cigarette. But like I said, it was not. Now don't you worry about that letter any more.

As far as I know, she didn't. As for our father, after Jeff was born, he never picked up another cigarette.

October 31, 1957, Okinawa

Honey, I am going down in the morning and see about calling you. I will write you in the morning and let you know what day and about what time it will be. The way that they do it is that the ham radio operator gets a ham radio operator in the States, and he gets the phone operator. Then I say what I have to say and then say, "over," and then you talk to me. But now, here on this end, what you say comes through a loud speaker, but I don't care. At least I will be able to talk to you, my darling.

WHEN DADDY WROTE THESE lines, he had been gone for four months. During that time, they had talked once, back in July when he was still in California. Other than that, they had to rely on letters and photographs to sustain them during their separation. Regular, frequent phone calls were beyond a staff sergeant's pay. Eventually, though, he found a way to get a call through that wouldn't be as expensive.

But placing phone calls from one side of the globe to the other in the late 1950s was not an easy, reliable proposition. Often, when a call was put in, the reception would be so bad that no connection could be made to the States. And then there was the issue of how many Marines wanted to call home. When Daddy went to talk to the ham operator the following morning, he was told he would have to put his name on the list. The time he was given was Monday afternoon at 4 pm. It was Friday morning, and while he wrote Mother with the information, little good he thought it would do, since the time for the call would come before the letter reached her.

That Monday morning, November 4, Daddy could hardly contain himself, as he finished up a letter from the night before. *I sure will be glad when 4 o'clock gets here today for that is the time my call goes in to you. I want to talk to you so much, darling.*

But it was not to be. *Sugar, as you know, I did not get to call you tonight. The place was all closed up. But I am going back in the morning and see what happened, and maybe I can [call] Wednesday night.* As it turned out, though, it didn't look like he would have to wait until then, for he had been able to work out a time to call Tuesday evening.

Tuesday, November 5, 1957, Okinawa
My Dearest darling wife,

Will write you a few lines tonight. I am going to play bingo for a while, and then I am going to call the best wife in the world.
Next Morning [November 6]

Honey, I could not call you last night because they could not get the States. I am to go back Friday. Sure hope I can talk to you then.

It had been a week since Daddy had set about trying to place the call to Mother, with no luck. Into week two, both he and Mother were anxious for success.

Thursday, November 7, 1957, Okinawa

Baby, I sure hope I can talk to you Friday night. I want to hear you speak to me so badly, and I know you want to hear me.

Thursday, November 7, 1957, Greensboro

My darling George,

I'm sitting here wishing I could hear your voice. I do wish you would call. I've been on needles and pins ever since I got your letter.

Next morning, [November 8]

You should hear Jeff say all the things he's going to tell "Daddy" when he calls. That he's got cowboy boots, and what he wants Santa Claus to bring for Christmas. I do hope he'll say something.

Friday, November 8, 1957, Okinawa

I did not get to call again tonight. I went down, but they could not get the States, so they told me to come by Tuesday afternoon and they would try again.

Tuesday, November 12, 1957, Okinawa

I went down to call you again this afternoon, but they could not get the States again, so I am to go back Wednesday night at 11 o'clock and they are going to try again. I sure hope they can get them this time so you and I can talk together.

Wednesday, November 13, 1957, Okinawa

I was to call you tonight, but we are waiting on a typhoon to hit, which I don't think it will, but we have to get ready for it so they are not calling the States. I guess I will get to try another day this week.

Thursday, November 14, 1957, Okinawa

We are still waiting on this typhoon to see if it is going to hit Okinawa or not. I don't think it will.

Honey, I am to call you Wednesday night. Now, that will be Wednesday morning your time. I don't know whether you will get this letter before then or not, and I may not be able to call then if they can't get the States. I have been trying to call you for over two weeks, now.

Sunday, November 17, 1957, Okinawa

I got your letter today with the man that is the ham operator. I don't think these people here will try and get hold of him, for they call one place in the States, and from there, they get hold of you by phone. But I am going to ask them when I go down, and I am going to give them his call code and see if they can get hold of him, or if they will.

Monday, November 18, 1957, Okinawa

Sugar, I just got back from calling you and Jeff and it sure was good to hear you and him talk. There was so much I wanted to tell you, but I just could not think of them. It was good to hear you again. I wish I could talk to you and Jeff boy every day.

Sunday, November 24, 1957, Okinawa

I got your letter tonight, the one you wrote right after I called. I sure was glad to hear from you. That was the first letter I have had from you in 5 or 6 days.

Honey, I was "shook" [up] when I first started talking to you, for I was talking to the one that I love most of all. It had been a long time since I had talked to you and I got all weak inside. I love you more than words can ever tell, baby. You know what? You always could get me "shook up." You are the only one for me.

In the end, it took two and a half weeks for Daddy to place the call that he had first written Mother about on October 31.

As Christmas approached, he made plans to place a call for the holiday. But when he arrived at the office, there were so many Marines trying to call home that the radio operator couldn't make Daddy's, and so he settled for an alternate plan. *I am off the weekend after New Year's. I am going to try and call you that weekend, or I will say, I am going to call you that weekend if I have to stay over there the whole weekend.*

January 3, 1958, Friday night, Okinawa

Sugar, I just got back from calling you, and it sure was nice to hear you and Jeff boy talk to me again.

Honey, there was so many things I wanted to tell you, but when I start talking to you all I can think about is how much that I love and miss you. I wanted to talk to you longer tonight, but there were a lot of other boys waiting to talk to their people and they only have the States on at one hour at night.

I could hear Jeff say Happy New Year and for me to hurry home. Could you hear me o.k.?

January 3, 1958, Friday morning, Greensboro

Babe, I just talked with you on the phone and it sure was nice to hear your voice. That's all Jeff has talked about since. "I talk my daddy; Daddy come home soon." It just excited him so. And it doesn't make me feel too calm!

Babe, I do love you. O, I'll be glad when you get home. I'll keep the letters coming, and you too.

When Daddy was transferred to the rifle range, he was 23 miles from the nearest phone or ham radio operator that could reach the States, which made calling home even more difficult. But just five days after writing Mother that being out at the Range made him too far from a phone, he found a way to do it.

May 20, 1958, Okinawa

Honey when I call there are so many things I want to tell you and when I start to talk all I can say is how I love you and miss you. Now, honey, if you get that phone bill and don't have the money to pay it take it out of the bank, for I would rather talk to you than to have money.

That would be their last time to talk to one another while he was in Okinawa. In mid-August 1958, less than a month before he was to leave for home and after his replacement had taken over the mess tent at the Rifle Range, he made the long trek to place a call several more times, with no luck. With the bus trip taking two hours each way—*I left there at 10 o'clock and it is now 12 o'clock, so you can see how long it takes a bus over here to go 23 miles*—he resigned himself to waiting until he got to California on his trip home to call her again. In the meantime, their letters would have to continue to hold them.

March 19, 1958, Okinawa

I dreamt last night that I was home with you and Jeff boy. I sure did hate to wake up and find out that I was still on Okinawa.

There was one other thing that sustained Daddy during his time in Okinawa—dreaming of home, and the day he would be reunited with Mother and Jeff. Particularly during times of loss or absence, dreams are powerful connectors to those we miss or have lost, continuing to remain with us long after we wake. Certain dreams have the power to strip away in some fashion the layer that separates us from those we love who are not near. They can comfort; they can also lay bare the seemingly unending absence that stretches before us.

While still at Camp Fuji, before ever getting to Okinawa, Daddy was writing Mother about seeing her in his dreams. *Honey, I have dreamed about you for the last three nights, but I like to dream about you. You are the one, even in my dreams. You are the only one for me,* Daddy had written over and over again. And, so, he confessed, his dream state was no different. Coming back to reality, though, could be depressing. *I lay down this afternoon and went to sleep and dreamed that I was home with you. Sure was blue when I woke up.*

There was one dream, though, that recurred time and again. From early September 1957 until he came home a year later, he wrote Mother describing his dream about the day he would arrive home. *I dreamed last night that I was coming home and you had come to meet me and when we got home Jeff saw me and said, "Daddy," and came running to me.* I know it was a dream they shared.

October 13, 1957, Greensboro
My Dearest George,

This has been one more day! I did better with my Sunday school class, but they still wear me out.

I miss you so much and love you very dearly. These 10 months [we have left] will go by slowly but that sounds a lot better than 14, doesn't it? O, I wish you were here with me.

DADDY HAD WORK, SOMETIMES unrelenting, to keep him occupied and fill up the empty spaces of missing Mother and Jeff. Mother, too, found ways to keep busy, since during the bulk of Daddy's time away she did not work outside the home. Faith was central to her life and the life of the community, so it was natural that the various opportunities she found were connected to the church. Daddy had been happy when she wrote in October that she would begin teaching a Sunday school class at Hunter Hills Friends. *Glad you got the Sunday school class. Like you said, it will give you something to do.*

After the New Year, when Mother was no longer substitute teaching, she decided to apply for a job as a church choir director. Daddy hoped she would get it for many reasons—he thought she would enjoy it, she was good at it, and, of course, because it would help the time pass more quickly for her. By February 23, she was in the position, and Daddy, aboard ship bound for the Philippines, was inquiring how she liked it. *I know you will get along o.k., for like I said before, you can sing and you know how to get other people to sing.*

Over the summer, Mother found another volunteer opportunity to keep busy, and her enthusiasm poured from the page.

June 18, 1958, Greensboro

I've been teaching the teenage class in the Vacation Bible School. The church decided to have it at night so we could have better teachers. It's from 7 o'clock until 9 o'clock. It sure has worked out well. Everyone was surprised at the number of teenagers I've had in my class. I've had 12–14 every night. They have been so quiet and attentive and said they really enjoy being in the class. After the lesson we are painting plaques out of plaster Paris. Then we're working on a couple of choir numbers. And they are interested in singing! Honey, there are kids up to 19 years old and they haven't given me a bit of trouble.

When Daddy replied to her letter a week later, he was glad she was enjoying the experience, especially since it would make *her* time go by faster!

Outside of volunteering at the church, keeping up with the bills, and helping out around the house, there were other things to keep Mother busy. Short trips to see family and friends, backyard dinners with the family, going over to visit with her mother-in-law, and even taking on repainting a bedroom in her parents' house with one of her cousins. But nothing took up her time like caring for, and keeping Daddy updated on, the growth and antics of their toddler son, my brother Jeff.

9

Jeff Boy

July 7, 1957, Camp Pendleton

Honey, every time you write, be sure and tell me all about you and Jeff. I have never been so lonesome in my life. You and him are my whole life and I love you both more than words can ever tell.

In our house on Doublegate, the one we moved to six weeks before my brother graduated from high school and that I associated the most as home, all of the bedrooms except one were upstairs. The lone bedroom downstairs became Jeff's. As a soon-to-be-graduated 17-year-old, I'm sure he appreciated the privacy. My upstairs bedroom was at the opposite end of the short hall, across from my parents'. Even as a preteen, I appreciated the closeness.

On the walls just outside my bedroom door hung two sets of professional collage photographs, one of Jeff and one of me, made when each of us were toddlers. I never asked where the photographs had been taken, but given their similarity to one another at a time when we were never in one place for more than three years, my guess is they were both done at times while we were visiting family in Greensboro.

I'm sure the walls of many homes of the late fifties and early sixties proudly displayed similar collages. The photographs had been done in black and white, with color added after. The collage was set up quite simply, with a picture in the middle staring out at the camera, and "action" shots in each of the four corners, me using an ironing board, Jeff playing with a train, a similar one of each of us on a toy telephone.

No matter what house my parents were in, those pictures went on the walls somewhere. When we cleaned out their last home after Daddy's death, Jeff took his, and I took mine, which now resides in a guest room of my home.

It was right that we each have our own, but I miss getting to look at my brother's. Those pictures greeted me every time I walked out of my bedroom as a teenager. When my parents moved to the golf villa where they spent their final years, the pictures resided in the guest room that my daughter insisted was "her" room at Grandmama's house. They were always there for me to look at as a pair, each of us captured at similar ages that occurred five years apart.

I enjoyed looking at the photos of me, but my favorite of the two was Jeff's. When my friends would come over, I would stop and often remark what an adorable little boy he had been. They agreed. No surprise. He had turned into a strikingly handsome teenager and most of them had crushes on him. But there was something else that called to me in those pictures, something that eluded me. Eluded me, that is, until I read our parents' letters. In those pictures, I saw the delightful, precocious, gregarious little boy I had never known, the one who was born five years ahead of me and who I would know affectionately as my big bubba.

JEFF WAS TWENTY MONTHS old when Daddy left for his assignments in Okinawa. He was, to put it mildly, into everything. To say that he wore our mother out is understatement writ large. But he was also a bright, talkative, loving little boy who reveled in having his grandparents right at hand but who also missed his Daddy. A full two months after Daddy had left, Mother was still having trouble getting Jeff to settle and sleep through the night. *The only thing you can do is just let Jeff boy cry it out,* Daddy suggested from Camp Fuji. *It was me that made him like that when we were on leave, but I wanted to hold him all I could while I was there.* Mother didn't know at the time that Jeff would be five years old before he really slept through the night. As a toddler, she would hear something in the night and get up to check on him. No tears. He would just be sitting in the bed, playing in his imaginary world. When he saw our mother, he would look up, smile, and say, "Hi Mommy, want to play?" At three o'clock in the morning, it was the furthest thing from her mind.

In Daddy's absence, family stepped in to help, keeping Mother from having to be the sole parent. Grandma Mimmie lived close by and Mother made frequent visits over there. Writing to her own son about his, our grandmother worked to keep Daddy alive in Jeff's memory—*George, you will love him to death if you could see and hear him talk. I always ask him whose boy he is. He says, "my daddy's boy."*

Of course, Mother lived for the majority of the time with her parents, our Nana and Papa Jack. And there were aunts, uncles, and cousins all around. Mother's Aunt Bill and Uncle Wade lived next door, and Wade would take Jeff for rides in his pick-up truck. Jeff also adored their youngest, our cousin Ruthie, who was just around eleven. As a special treat every so often, Uncle Wade and Ruthie would take Jeff to the airport to watch the planes take off and land. And our Nana and Aunt Bill were full of poems, stories, and songs.

But no one, outside of Mother, was more important to Jeff during Daddy's absence than Papa Jack.

November 1957, Greensboro

Son, I am writing you with your son on my lap, and he is saying, "my daddy." Wish you could see him. He is a darling and is growing like a weed. He is into everything. I have bought him everything I see until he has toys all over the floor.

Son, I am looking out for your family the best I can but that is not like having you here. You will soon be home again. Don't forget I am praying for you. Love from all,
Dad

Jeff trailed around after Papa Jack, and the man who had deemed it a privilege to stay home with his own children while his wife worked on her college degree at nights set about helping to raise the next generation. He held him, read to him, played with him. Pictures testify to the closeness, with Papa Jack having fun sitting Jeff up on the hood of the car, or pushing him in the swing at the playground. When our grandfather had to be out of town working on a bridge construction project, Jeff missed the closest thing he had to a father while our own was overseas. *Daddy came home tonight,* Mother wrote in August 1958 during one such absence, *and Jeffrey was thrilled to death to see him. He really loves him.*

Papa Jack seemed to be Jeff's go-to for sharing interesting things. One night when the family all went out to eat, they went past a glass case with some cooked lobsters on ice on the way to their seats, and Jeff had a fit over the "big bugs," something he kept exclaiming to Papa Jack. *All thro' supper he said, "Papa, big bugs!"*

And, at a time when people remained in their cars while a service station attendant pumped gas, no one could play "service station" like our grandfather.

August 22, 1958, Greensboro

You should hear Jeff and Daddy play "service-station." He rides his tricycle right up to the back steps. Dad sits there and he's the station-man. Jeff always has his wagon hooked on to the back and he says, "I want 5 gallons (or a half-gallon, or whatever enters his mind). Here's my Amoco card." They are really a pair.

Jeff followed Papa Jack around everywhere and was not happy when he wasn't around: *He cries after Daddy if he has to leave him too often.* And whatever he saw his grandfather do, Jeff had to try it. If Papa Jack was stretched out in his canvas cot in the backyard, then Jeff was bound and determined to do the same, even if it meant waiting until nightfall.

August 22, 1958, Greensboro
My darling husband,

Today Daddy had his canvas cot out in the yard and Jeff decided he would sleep out in the yard tonight. Well, we just forgot about it and after I got Jeff all ready for bed, he went into his room, got his pillow and started out the back door. I said, "Jeff, where are you going?" He turned around and said, "Well, I'm going to sleep outdoors tonight. Mommy will you tuck me in?" Well, we took him out and situated him on the cot and I told him I'd turn the light out as I went back in the house. Jeff said, let's leave the light on. As I turned off the porch light his feet hit the ground and started for the house. He heard a bird and he said he didn't think he would stay out cause it might rain. We nearly died laughing! That's your son's first "camping out."

When Jeff's second birthday rolled around a few months after Daddy left, our extended family did their best to make up for Daddy's absence. But our father wasn't the only one who felt the pain of loss from missing out on these kinds of celebrations.

October 19, 1957, Greensboro
My dearest darling,

Two years ago tonight I remember us getting into bed and saying, "only 1 more month"—and the very next day our little Jeff was born. O baby, I'm sure sorry you can't be here for his birthday. Mrs. Emma made him a cake, plain, with white icing and "Happy Birthday, Cowboy" written on it. Just before the words was a little candy cowboy on a horse. It sure is cute and Jeff has stuck his little fingers all over it. He is so excited about it.

Jeff certainly didn't lack for attention on his special day. There was a myriad of gifts—two flannel shirts and grey trousers from Grandma Mimmie, a striped polo shirt and suspenders from Aunt Jo, and a pair of corduroy overalls, a blue shirt, and a toy helicopter from Nana and Papa Jack. And those were just the ones Mother allowed him to open early. There were more gifts from Mother and Daddy and our great aunts that would be saved for the following day of celebration, his actual birthday, along with a whirlwind of events.

October 20, 1957, Greensboro

My dearest George,

This has really been a day! Jeff really knows what "bur'day" is! I have never seen a little boy so excited. This morning, when I was getting him ready for Sunday school, he was really a-wiggling. He kept saying "deep-wide." (He sings that most of the time). Then he said "burday, burday" over and over. At S.S. he put his pennies in pretty good and afterwards went to the airport with Ruth and Wade to watch the planes. Then Wade brought him on over to the Battleground Club house for [Aunt] Mary's party. It was real nice and we ate til we nearly popped! Then the nicest thing of all happened. Jeff and Mrs. Emma and I took Jeff's birthday presents and cake over to Jeannette and Tinker's [Cates]. Tinker took some slides—which he is giving to us—of Jeff and his gifts and cake. Then some of Susan and Mary Jayne [Cates] and Jeff eating cake and [drinking] Pepsi. They are just going to be darling. As soon as he gets them back I'm going to send them to you. It's the nicest gift I could have (at Jeff's burday!).

Despite those pictures of the children at the Cates's being *the nicest thing of all* for Mother, it was that same visit where she had *let the tears just roll* upon seeing the slide of her and Daddy. Mother may have had an abundance of family and friends to help out, but her husband was still on the other side of the world.

July 18, 1957, T. Island, off the coast of California

Honey, I sure was sorry to hear about Jeff being so sick. Be sure and let me know how he gets along and what the Doc said about him.

MOTHER SPENT A GOOD bit of the time Daddy was overseas in and out of doctors' offices, dealing with a sick child. Perhaps there was little surprise to this. He had been born a "premie" and probably had a compromised immune system to start with. And at a time before the benefits of breastfeeding were touted, the formula he was fed did nothing to boost his antibodies. Yet how much to tell Daddy about Jeff's illnesses? After all, he wasn't there, so he couldn't do anything about it. And by the time a letter arrived describing the latest round of doctor visits, Jeff would probably be better.

One of the hard things about holding a marriage together through letters is, in truth, knowing how much to write. Neither Mother nor Daddy wanted to burden the other. But their relationship was based on openness and trust and so early on they opted for that in their letters as well.

July 16, 1957, Greensboro
My Darling,

I do not want to fill your letters with bad news, but you are Jeff's father and I believe you want to know all that happens. Jeff has been real sick. He had gotten over his nasal drainage pretty well. Last night he went to sleep as usual. Then, about 11 o'clock, he woke up screaming. For 2 solid hours he cried and screamed. Nothing would stop him—I rocked, played with him, put him on the big bed— nothing worked. Finally, I called Dr. Smith. He said he thought he had had a nightmare and called the Wesley Long Hospital and Jo and I took him down. They gave him something to put him to sleep. It calmed him down but he didn't sleep much. Today, Dr. Smith had me bring him in and the little fellow had an ear infection and a sore throat. He has been a mighty cross little boy.

Dr. Smith was so nice. He said anytime I need to call him, day or night, to do so. And he told me not to worry about the bill, that the important thing was Jeff. In all, I owed him $24.00. I paid him $5.00 today and $5.00 the last time. Babe, I have to take him back Thursday. Dr. Smith is so nice and really interested in Jeff.

Certainly this episode must have been hard on our mother. Having lost her first child, was every illness visited upon Jeff a reminder of how vulnerable life was even once a baby made it through birth? But I am also struck by the vast change in doctoral care since my brother and I were young. Mother didn't seem to be at all angry that the doctor had thought it a nightmare at first and merely prescribed him something to sleep, which meant a trip to the hospital in the middle of the night that offered little relief. No, at a time when physicians were revered and their word often went unquestioned, Mother had nothing but praise for Dr. Smith and his interest in, and care of, Jeff. But there was a relationship there, too. He was "so nice," she had written, and encouraged her to call whenever she needed to. And when she worried over the bill, she spoke with *him*—not someone in a billing department that she did not know— and he reassured her about her need to spread payment out over some weeks.

By the end of the year, it seemed that Mother had gotten comfortable writing to Daddy about Jeff's, and everyone else's, illnesses.

December 31, 1957, Greensboro

We had a good trip down to Plymouth [to see family] and Monty and Naomi were real glad to see us. We talked til about 8:30. Then when I started to put Jeffrey to bed he wouldn't stay in that strange room without me. Poor little guy, he coughed all night and Monday we took him to the doctor. He was real nice. Showed Jeffrey a little white rat (a toy he held in his hand) and gave him a stick of chewing gum. He said it was a good thing I brought him 'cause he really had a bad throat. He gave him a shot of penicillin (at Jeff's request!). The doctor laughed at the nurse and said, "Here's a miracle, a little boy who wants a shot."

Then, on top of everything else, Dad came down with such a bad cold. He was real sick and couldn't talk he was so hoarse. Mother had to spend all day Monday in bed. In fact, I was the only well one. So instead of going on to Chester to see Sister today, we loaded up and came home.

I can only imagine how difficult Daddy's fourteen-month absence must have been for our mother—keeping track of the bills, chasing after a rambunctious toddler, worrying over rounds of illnesses, helping out with the housework, trying to find a measure of enrichment for herself through church and friends—all without her husband. She must have been bone weary at the end of each day. I had a taste of it the two years between my husband Sam's death and my second marriage to John as I tried to juggle a career, a reduced income, a baby, and the seemingly unending work of grief. I know there were tears; she admitted to those in her letters. But what about the anger at having to deal with all of these things for fourteen long months? She had to have experienced some, but she never mentioned it to our father in her correspondence. That really wasn't our mother's way. Oh, she could lose her temper, all right, but not often, which made it all the scarier (and more effective!) when she did. And her anger was often reserved for perceived injustices or when Jeff and/or I had pushed her way too far. No, the fact that she had to live without her husband for fourteen months would have made her sad and lonely but wouldn't have gotten her riled up. Of the several pearls of wisdom our mother left us with, "life isn't fair; get over it," was one of her most instilled. Whatever anger she might have felt off and on would have been private, living beneath the surface.

Sometimes I think people who did not know her well thought that our mother was, with her gracious Southern hospitality and charm, a bit of a shrinking violet. However, nothing was *further* from the truth. She lived in a time when she liked to be treated like a lady, expecting a gentleman to open a door for her, but she never shied from speaking her mind—at home, at work, in church, it didn't matter. That bit about a woman being quiet and subject to her husband that resides in the New Testament did not faze her in the least, having obviously been written for a different culture. Moreover, a strong woman—our Nana— had raised Mother to be a strong woman, and she definitely had the fortitude to stand up against and survive whatever the military could throw at her. If I had ever thought otherwise, or wondered where she got the strength to make it through those fourteen months, an incident many years later answered all questions.

Jeff was about sixteen, deep in the throes of his teen years. It must have been summer or a Saturday because Mother was sitting at the table trying to finish her lunch and probably working on a crossword puzzle. To this day, I can't imagine what possessed my brother to hassle our mother, but who really understands the mind of a teenager. He began annoying her, kind of poking her on the shoulder. She told him to stop, but did he listen? I could see that very little good was going to come of this interchange, but knew enough to keep my mouth shut. Let Jeff dig his own grave.

By this point in his life, Jeff towered physically over Mother, and he just kept at it. "Come on, Mama, you know I can take you. Come on, come on."

What? I thought. Has he gone *completely* insane? Maybe he was having an ADD moment. She'll be kind, to him, I reasoned.

Mother tried again, a bit more insistent and stretching the words out for effect. "Jeff, I said, that's enough!" But did he stop? Of course not. He was sixteen, for God's sake; definitely not in his right mind.

What happened next occurred so quickly I couldn't even be sure I was witnessing it. Mother looked around the table, saw an empty Coke bottle, picked it up above her head, held it there, and said in an eerily firm, yet quiet, voice, "I. Said. Stop."

Jeff, with eyes as big as I had ever seen them, recoiled, and intoned, rather hurt, "Mama, you wouldn't!"

"Son," she said, "when you're out-sized and out-classed, you fight dirty."

Never for a minute would she have struck either one of us, but she had sure made her point. So, our mother...a shrinking violet? You have got to be kidding me.

June 14, 1958, Okinawa

Tell Jeff boy that Daddy said hello and for him not to be running out the back door and falling down like that, that it was hard on the head and Daddy doesn't want his Jeff boy to hurt himself.

BESIDES LOOKING QUITE A bit like him, Jeff took after our father in one essential way. Mother used to say that Daddy had two speeds—full speed ahead, and asleep. As a little boy, I am told, my brother was much the same way. This did not change after I came along.

It was sometime after I was born, and many of my baby teeth had come in. They came in early I was told, and Jeff remembers that we were living in Beaufort, South Carolina, on Woodward Avenue at the time when Daddy was stationed at Parris Island—Lord, what a memory that brother of mine has always had. As a very young toddler, I was still a bit of a novelty to my older brother and he liked to help keep me entertained.

We were outside on a warm summer day, and Jeff was pushing me around the yard in my stroller. At some point, no longer content to take things slow, he decided to pick up some speed. Sensing from my squeals of glee that I liked it, he accelerated again. In his six- or seven-year-old brain, my stroller had suddenly turned into a racecar, the yard his own Nascar circuit. We were having a grand time, as he recalls, except he had to slow down for the sidewalk, which was higher than the grass. Troubleshooting on the fly, he decided that hitting the sidewalk without slowing down would probably work. What he failed to factor in to the plan was the need to raise the front wheels of the stroller to adjust for the change in height. The result was that the stroller pitched forward. I have no memory of any of this, it being part of family lore told again and again and most recently corroborated by the stroller driver himself. But I imagine it in my mind in a sort of a slow-motion sequence in which we both saw the horror of what lay ahead.

I was not seriously hurt in the Great Stroller Accident of 1961, although my two front baby teeth would remain chipped until they eventually fell out, but, following that split second of "what just happened" silence, my joyful squeals morphed to a less pleasant sound, and Jeff rushed me inside to our mother.

"Mama, Mama, I'm so sorry. I'm so sorry. I didn't mean to. Is she okay? Is Jenny going to be okay?"

As Mother calmed me and ascertained that I would be little worse for the wear, she also calmed Jeff, also crying by this time, and then gathered together the story. Seeing that he was already heaping enough hot coals on his head for what had happened, she gently admonished her son for going too fast, suggesting that, next time, he take things a bit slower with my stroller.

"Okay," he responded sheepishly. "But she liked it."

"That well may be," Mother replied, "but she doesn't like it now, does she?" There were no more stroller accidents.

IN ADDITION TO THE rounds of illnesses that Mother had to cope with while Daddy was in Okinawa, she also had to keep up with an active toddler who was always on the move. The concrete steps out of the back door of our grandparents' house and into the backyard could be tricky to navigate for a two-year-old, and Jeff always wanted to be outside.

May 25, 1958, Greensboro

Babe, Jeffrey is the dearest little boy. The very minute he wakes up, he wants to go out in the yard. He just loves to play out and he does it most of the day.

Even the weather did not deter him. *I have had quite a time with Jeff today,* Mother wrote on a dreary, rainy September day. *He has wanted to go out and "whing (swing) in the wain (rain)."* Instead, Mother made him stay inside. At least he got to watch "Mickey Mouse" when it came on the television, and then proceeded to go around the house singing "Mick Mou" all the time. *Boy, he keeps Jo and I on the move.* I'm sure Daddy's comment regarding Jeff falling down the back steps was far from an isolated incident.

If it wasn't enough to care for the wounds Jeff inflicted upon his little two-year-old body, there were other injuries that occurred, partly because things just always seemed to happen to my brother. Mother's account of it is lost, but the implication from Daddy's letter is that Jeff had to get rabies shots from an altercation with a dog. *How is Jeff boy? I hope his shots did not hurt him too much. Tell him Daddy said for him to leave those dogs alone.*

There were also the times Mother had to "clean up" after Jeff had been playing with something that he shouldn't have.

May 25, 1958, Greensboro

My dearest darling,

This morning when I came out of church our car wouldn't start. Then, I noticed the lights were on—had been on since before S[unday] school. Your son has a very bad habit—turning on the lights, radio, heater and windshield wiper.

Fortunately, Jeff and Mother were able to ride home with Nana and Papa Jack, and, after Sunday dinner, Nana called a garage in town and had them come out to jump start the car. *You see, she did it on her AAA plan. They just run it through as her car and it doesn't cost anything.* Perhaps that is why Mother was able to write *Babe, Jeffrey is the dearest little boy,* in the very next paragraph.

September 17, 1957, Greensboro

When Jeffrey first wakes up he crawls out of his crib and gets in bed with me. Then he hugs and kisses me over and over and says, "my mama." Then he takes your picture off the head of the bed and kisses it and says, "my daddy" and "Daddy's baby," "Daddy's man," and Daddy's b-o-y." He spells it out. Then the main thing comes. He grabs me and tries to pull me out of bed and says "down," and then "eat, eat." Then he starts naming what he wants—"ham, aigs (eggs), milk, and cereal." I sure wish you could hear him and see him.

THROUGH ALL THE DESCRIPTIONS of his birthday, illnesses, accidents, dog bites, antics, and general weariness of chasing after a rambunctious toddler, Mother mostly just tried to describe to Daddy how quickly their son was growing and changing during these fourteen months. *Honey, I do wish you could see Jeffrey "pixing" things (fixing). He has a little plastic tool set, a real nice one he got for Christmas, and he "fixes" everything in the house,* she described as 1957 came to a close. *This whole letter has been about Jeff and I could write more,* she concluded another time. Many of her letters that survived were that way, in part because she struggled to put on paper what she was experiencing everyday with him. *There's just no way to tell you how cute and sweet he is,* she wrote at the first of the year before she went on to describe his independent, yet helpful streak. *He doesn't want anyone to help him do anything. He says, "I'll do it by myself." But if I start to do anything he says, "I help Mommy." I could do very well without his help most of the time*, she confessed.

As with any parent, she glowed with pride over others' reactions to their pre-cocious, gregarious son.

October 13, 1957, Greensboro

Honey, everyone around thinks our son is brilliant. The way he knows the nursery rhymes and stuff. Bill Flinchum thinks I ought to have him tested in the psychology department at Guilford College. He thinks he is a little genius. You can tell him a story (for the first time). Then ask him questions about it and he can answer them. He remembers places. One night we went to "Harold's" at Friendly Road Shopping Center for supper. So now, every time we pass the center Jeff wants to go eat. Before we even get close enough to see it he remembers and starts saying, "Eat, Mommy, eat."

January 2, 1958, Greensboro

J.B. is just amazed at Jeffrey. Jeff has about 2 dozen books, and he can tell you the name of everyone. You can pick up anyone of them and begin reading, then stop or leave out any word and Jeffrey will start right in and tell you the word or even sentences. He wants someone to read from the minute he wakes up until he goes to bed at night. J.B. just can't understand how he remembers so much.

To them, he was special, of course, but beyond that, who knew. *I don't know,* Mother wrote regarding the suggestion by their friend that they have him tested. *I think he's pretty smart, but then, I'm his mother.* And when she wrote that Jeff wanted to play with older boys, it worried them both. *Honey, I feel the same as you do about Jeff playing with older boys,* Daddy wrote in reply. *He should just play with boys and girls his own age.* He was, after all, simply, and not so simply, their "Jeff boy."

November 7, 1957, Greensboro

You should hear Jeff say all the things he's going to tell "Daddy" when he calls. That he's got cowboy boots. What he wants Santa Claus to bring for Christmas.

I do hope he'll say something to you. Right now he's pestering me to "write" to Daddy. So here it is—

Jeff says— "I want Marine cap, airplane. I love Daddy 2 pounds."

Well, that's about all for Jeff-boy and Mommy. I love you a good deal more than 2 pounds.

December 4, 1957, Okinawa

Tell Jeff boy that Daddy said hello and that I could hear him real good over the phone, and it sure was good to hear him.

Among my brother's many gifts, there are two that have always amazed me—his memory, and his gift for language. Okay, and his eyesight, which used to frustrate the dickens out of me when we played the alphabet game on road trips and he could always find the next letter on some billboard way in the distance. I just knew it couldn't be, but drat him, we would get close enough for me to see it and there it would be. I didn't stand a chance.

But it was his gift for language that was on full display one night as the four of us, my little nuclear family, sat gathered in the living room of the base house where we lived in Albany. A thunderstorm had caused the electricity to go out and we resorted to the ancient art of candle power to provide a little light to the evening. I was probably six, Jeff eleven. I was not quite as interesting to him as I had been as a toddler but not altogether annoying, at least not yet, and he had not quite arrived at the stupid teenager stage. But let's be realistic. With five years separating us, we didn't have just a whole lot in common.

It was the age before powered-up laptops, tablets, or smartphones could animate a lightless house with Netflix and turn what might otherwise be a dull evening into family movie night. No, on a dank, humid night in Southwest Georgia when the weekly thunderstorm had knocked out the power, our parents were left to their own devices to create entertainment for the family.

Our mother, the teacher and woman of words whose own mother was a reciter of poems and stories, suggested that we sit by candlelight and tell an add-on story. I see this now for the ingenuity that it was. It was not easy to find games that interested both a six and eleven year old. I was not of the age yet where reading captivated me for long stretches at the time and our dad, at that time, was not much of a reader. With little to do on a dark night and bedtime still a ways off, she knew that things could quickly spiral out of control as boredom descended. An add-on story put us on a fairly level playing field and engaged us as a family.

I don't remember who began the story. I don't even remember what the story was about. Perhaps there were multiple stories we told that night. I'm sure Mother admonished Jeff to keep his contributions tame, not too scary, for my benefit. Besides the sounds of the storm and our voices, the house was quiet, save for the ticking of the German coo-coo clock that hung on the living room wall.

We were well into the story when it came around to Jeff's turn again.

"... And then the clock struck midnight," Jeff intoned, somewhat mysteriously.

At that very instant, our coo-coo clock chimed the hour. We looked at each other. Mother, Daddy, and Jeff broke up into laughter. My eyes got wide as saucers. I already thought my big brother could do just about anything, but this was truly extraordinary.

"Do it again, Jeff," I squealed. "Do it again!"

To which my parents and big brother chuckled, and we continued with the story. I'm not sure they even tried to explain to me why that wasn't possible. They just let me revel in my six-year-old world of wonder and mystery, and the awesome ability of my big brother to choose the right words at the right time.

WHEREAS MY KINDERGARTEN TEACHER asked Mother what they did to get me to talk, talking had never been a problem for my brother. Our father used to joke that Jeff came out of the womb talking. When my own daughter came along and we were thrown into the world of first words, I asked Mother about Jeff and me.

"Jeff practically started talking in complete sentences," she told me.

"Really," I asked her, not altogether surprised, but still somewhat amazed.

"Well, not anything complicated, but from the first he would often connect a noun and verb together."

Given that Jeff was just twenty months old when our father went to Okinawa, Daddy was naturally curious about his son's verbal progress. *How is Jeff boy getting along with his talking*, Daddy asked in August, shortly after he shipped over. *I bet he can say about anything he wants to now.* Mother often wrote about what Jeff had said, confirming Daddy's suspicion. *New words*, Mother reported the following month: *"towel, hotdog, corn"—O he can say almost anything*.

And say it he would. Whereas I was painfully shy as a child, Jeff would talk to almost anyone. *He tells everyone his name is "Jeff-boy Ho-maugh" and that he's two*, Mother wrote the following month. *Then he'll grin and say, "I'm a cool cat." Boy, what a show-off.* I'm sure our mother smiled broadly as she wrote her amused assessment. By the New Year, Jeff could *say his prayers and return thanks by himself. And [he] always says, "God bless Daddy."*

The talking fairly quickly turned into singing. *He can sing "Mickey Mouse," "Wyatt Earp," and "Jim Bowie," lots of Sunday school songs, "I'm a Little Teapot," and "Jim Dandy to the Rescue." You'd laugh your head off to hear him.* But Daddy was doing anything but laughing. He was thrilled. *How about him singing? Must take that after his mother, for he sure did not get it from his Daddy. Sure would be nice if he could sing when he gets big.* Shortly before Daddy was to come home, Mother wrote in a postscript that Daddy should hear Jeff sing the entire first verse of the Marines' Hymn.

As with most children that age, though, not all of the words came out like they were supposed to, and Mother, who loved it, was loathe for Jeff to grow up too fast and correct himself before Daddy could return.

August 22, 1958, Greensboro

I sure am glad you'll be here soon because he is learning so fast and talks so well. I don't want him to say all his words just right til you can hear some of the cute ways he mixes them up. The one mistake that he can't say right is "L." He says "yord" for "Lord," and "yove" for "love." It's just adorable.

She needn't have worried. He would still be having trouble with his L's long after Daddy returned and after our family had been transferred to the next duty station, repeatedly referring to our neighbor Lewis Young's lumber business as "Yewis Young's Yumber Yard."

September 24, 1957, Camp Fuji

I love you and Jeff so much, honey. I sure hope he doesn't forget me before I get back. I know that 14 months is a long time and he is a little boy.

MORE THAN ANY WORK challenge or threat of impending typhoon, Daddy's biggest worry while he was in Okinawa was that his son would forget him while he was away. As his rational mind reasoned that it would be natural, his subconscious hoped for a different outcome.

Everyone in Greensboro worked to make that dream a reality. Mother kept Daddy's picture in the bedroom where Jeff would wake up to it and kiss it every morning, referring to himself as "Daddy's b-o-y." Early on, Jeff would tell everyone that his daddy was a 'rine (Marine) and that he went on an airplane to Japan.

Papa Jack wrote letters to Daddy with Jeff sitting on his lap, saying, "my daddy." Grandma Mimmie reassured her own son that Jeff was not likely to forget him. *Jeff is really learning to talk good,* she wrote one night after Mother and Jeff had been over for supper. *He can say [Uncle] Mickey real plain. Becky showed me the slides you sent and he let me know which one was his daddy, so I really don't believe he will forget you.* And back at Nana's, Jeff repeatedly asked to see the pictures and slides that Daddy sent from Okinawa. *I had to show Jeffrey the slides again today,* Mother wrote the month before Daddy was scheduled to come home. *That boy would look at them every day. And, boy, he never misses on picking you out. He knows his daddy.*

April 3, 1958, Okinawa

I dreamed last night that I was on my way home and I saw you and Jeff in the doorway and you ran out and kissed me and then Jeff came out to me. It was so real I woke up this morning and had to look around, and when I saw I was still on Okinawa I wanted to go back to sleep. Oh, Baby, I am just living for the day when I can take you in my arms again and hold and love and kiss you.

May 11, 1958, Okinawa

Well, I just have a little over 100 days to do on Okinawa and believe me I will be glad when they pass and I am home with you, darling.

As the time drew nearer for Daddy's dreams of being reunited with Mother and Jeff to become reality, he talked increasingly of counting down the days and of the specifics of getting home. Toward the end of May, he heard that, after July, the Marine Corps would not be flying any more people home, in which case he would leave by ship sometime between September 1st and 5th. *That seems like a lifetime from now,* he wrote. Even so, he held out hope that he would still get to fly home.

June 20, 1958, Okinawa

My Dearest darling wife,

I heard some good news today. I am going to be flying home, and the way things are now I will leave Okinawa on the first of Sept. or right close to that date.

He knew the method of transport though not the exact date, although that did not keep him from finding various ways to mark the time. Five more pay-days. Another month gone. Sixty-eight, now fifty-seven days until September 1.

On July 19, he went to check on making arrangements for his flights once he reached California. Buying the ticket in Okinawa would save some money and mean he could fly nonstop from San Francisco to Washington, D.C., and then hopefully on to Greensboro. There was still no word, however, as to the exact date he would leave the island. Despite Mother's worries that his departure would be delayed, he assured her that he would be home sometime in September.

July 24, 1958, Okinawa

My Dearest darling wife,

Well, they called me up today and said they had my orders in the Battalion office and I will leave Okinawa on the 10ᵗʰ of September. That leaves me 47 more days from Friday. Honey, that will be the longest 47 days of my life, but at least I know what day I am leaving and that sure makes me feel good.

The date was now set but the plans were not. Mother wrote that she was thinking about driving up to D.C. to meet Daddy's plane, what was then at least a six-hour drive from Greensboro. But in the age of no cell phones and expensive phone calls, there were any number of things that could make such a hook-up difficult. Daddy now knew he was supposed to leave Okinawa on September 10, but there was no guarantee that would actually happen. From Okinawa, he was to fly back to Camp Fuji before flying to Hawaii. However, if a Marine in food service had to go on unexpected leave due to something like a death in the family, then Daddy may have to fill in there for a day or two. The same thing, he suggested, could happen once he got to Hawaii. Perhaps if Mother could plan to stay for a week with friends they had up there, then that would work.

August 15, 1958, Okinawa
My Dearest darling wife,
Today was payday and I only have one more before I come home to you. I will more than gladly give it to them if I could leave now.

Well into August, the countdown and back and forth on details for the trip home continued. Twenty-nine more days. One more payday. With so many variables, Mother gave up on her plan to drive to D.C. and asked how she would know which plane to meet at the Greensboro airport. *I've promised Jeffrey he could go with Mommy to see Daddy get off the plane and that's all he talks about.*

Once Daddy found out he would have a six-hour layover in D.C. before leaving for Greensboro, though, he started looking around for another option. By late August, he wrote Mother that he would be flying into Raleigh, North Carolina, and for her not to worry if she couldn't meet him there, for he could always just take the bus home. *I just could not see waiting around D.C. for 6 hours before I left to come home to you.*

August 28, 1958, Greensboro
My dearest husband,

I got your letter today saying you would arrive in Raleigh at 10:28 on Friday, Sept. 12 and we're thrilled to death! I don't mind a trip that far, but to drive all the way to D.C.—340 miles. Whew! Really, Babe, I was a little afraid to attempt a trip that long with Jeff alone. But Raleigh! We're thrilled to pieces!

I'm not bringing anyone with me, just Jeff and me. Isn't that grand? We can stop by the Capitol and you'd get a chance to watch Jeffrey go wild feeding the pigeons. Every time we go thro' Raleigh that's a must.

Jeffrey told me to tell you that he's been a good boy—but that's a matter of opinion! I may as well warn you. He's thrilled over your homecoming and he says, "When my daddy comes, I can climb on him and roll in the floor and we can box and fight! And I can ride on his back and we can wash the car and go to the milkshake dairy." (He always says the milkshake dairy, not Guilford Dairy.)

By this time, there was little for Daddy to do but go to the beach, and, as he put it so many times, lay around missing Mother and Jeff and dreaming of the day he would get off the plane and take his wife in his arms and have his son come running to him. After almost fourteen months of separation, the days were approaching when they would be together again. He could write of little else.

September 5, 1958, Okinawa
My Dearest darling wife,

I got your letter today where you said that you and Jeff boy would meet me at Raleigh. I am glad that only you and Jeff boy are coming. But, honey, be real careful on the way down. Start so you won't have to drive fast and give yourself a lot of time.

Sugar, I am so in love you. Oh, think, one week from now I will be with you. It seems that these last five days will never pass.

Baby, I am so lonesome when I am not with you. I am just living for the day I get home to you and Jeff boy.

Sugar, I know that this is a short letter, but I just can't think of but one thing anymore and that is my coming home to you.

Goodnight, Sugar, and just think, next Friday night I can go to bed with you. Oh, I love you, sugar, with all of my heart. You are the only one for me.
All my love always,
George

Seven days later, at the Raleigh Airport, Jeff boy spotted a twenty-eight-year old Marine staff sergeant descending the steps of an airplane, let go of Mother's hand, and raced into our father's arms—exactly like Daddy had dreamed.

PART III

Military Life

10

A Few Lines from My New Duty Station

I HAVE NO MEMORIES OF BEAUFORT, SOUTH Carolina, but have always been proud to mark it as my birthplace. No memories, that is, from when we lived there, only the times we would return to visit the lifelong friends we had made at the time, the Marsdens. It is a beautiful coastal town in the South Carolina low country that lies along one of the myriad inlets, marshy land strewn with Southern live oak trees laden with Spanish moss, perhaps best known as the setting for such films as *Forrest Gump, The Prince of Tides,* and *The Big Chill*. It is also situated just about ten miles north of the Marine Corps Recruiting Depot at Parris Island, the new duty station Daddy had written Mother about from the rifle range in Okinawa.

Beaufort was an idyllic location for Mother, Daddy, and Jeff to take up residence, and Parris Island was a good duty station. They were on the east coast, close enough to family in Greensboro without being too close, and it was warm, something our father always prized in a location. And, as Daddy had noted in his letters from Okinawa, he didn't have to worry about time spent in the field since this was a recruiting depot. Most importantly, though, there were good friends.

It was the first place that Jeff has any real memories of, turning three around the time of the move and living there until a few months before his seventh birthday. He started school there, and, from the time we met the family, he was inseparable from Doug Marsden, the youngest of three boys in a family of two Navy parents.

Daddy's first position at Parris Island was that of meat cutter, something I watched him do at home with expertise and ease throughout his life; I miss him every time I *attempt* to carve a roasted chicken or turkey. I wonder, though, if he felt like he was taking a step backward. The rifle range mess in Okinawa had been a small one, but at least he had been in charge. Regardless of how he felt, he continued to work hard, do his best, undertake a self-study course, and receive the highest marks on his fitness reports, acting as "an example for others with his cordial personality and adaptability."

Mother settled into a teaching job and Jeff still kept her on the run, although at least now she had help from Daddy in the evenings and on weekends. There was no Quaker meeting to be found in Beaufort, so they visited around at some different denominations. It just so happened that one of the Baptist churches in the area needed a choir director, and their charismatic pastor wanted Mother for the job. So our parents were "dunked," as baptism is affectionately known in the Baptist church, they joined the church, Mother became the choir director, and that, in a nutshell, is how our family became associated with the Southern Baptists.

In March 1960, having been at Parris Island for almost a year and a half, Daddy was promoted to Assistant Manager of the Staff NCO (Staff Non-Commissioned Officer) Club. His days as meat cutter, at least for the Marine Corps, were over, and he entered a position that began laying the groundwork for his later career as a club manager after retirement from the Corps.

Jeff turned five in October of that year and finally began sleeping through the night. And just in time, for 22 days later on November 11, the day after the Marine Corps birthday, Mother delivered a healthy, five-pound, fourteen-ounce baby girl with "Marine Corps green eyes," and Jeff boy Hobaugh found himself with a new baby sister. I had the distinction of being the first Hobaugh girl in three generations.

The polar opposite of my extrovert, high-charged brother, I was sleeping through the night by three months. Mother was grateful for the good fortune but continued to awaken in the night, not from noise, but silence. This was not normal, she thought, and rose to check on me, thinking that surely I must be dead if I wasn't crying. After living through the first three months of sleepless nights with my own daughter, I always thought that it bordered on miraculous that our parents ever had another child after my brother's early sleep patterns.

While living in Beaufort, we employed a maid, a Black woman by the name of Hilda, who did housework and took care of me after Mother returned to work, whom our parents revered as a paragon of child-raising wisdom. I have no memory of Hilda. And, yet, I sensed early on from the reverence in our parents' voices when they spoke of her that she was part of who I was and am.

To our father's great joy, his position at the SNCO Club afforded him the luxury of coming home some days after lunch had been served at the club. My naptime would come up shortly before he had to leave to return to work, and he delighted in rocking me and then putting me down for my nap before he left. (Even as an infant, I was working on securing my place as "Daddy's girl.")

I usually went down for a nap quite well for Hilda. But with Daddy, I would often cry just as he laid me in the crib. One day, he decided to tap into Hilda's wisdom.

"Hilda, how come it is that when you put Jenny down for her nap, she goes right down without so much as a peep, but when I put her down, she cries?"

Hilda shook her head at this Marine, who could manage an operation like the Staff NCO Club but was being hoodwinked by his infant daughter.

"It's simple, Mr. Hobaugh. That's because Jenny has learned that I'm not going to pick her up again, but she knows her Daddy will."

Generally speaking, though, I was much quieter than my brother, preferring to take in the world from my perch before choosing to say much. This did not prevent me from doing my best to keep up with him after I became mobile, however. As for Jeff, I think he considered me his personal live-action doll, as evidenced by the Great Stroller Accident of 1961. So I suffered some bumps and bruises here and there, along with those chipped baby teeth, but, all in all, I managed to survive infancy and babyhood just fine.

When Daddy wasn't trying to get me down for a nap, he was busy working to improve club operations and lower food cost at the SNCO Club, improvements indicated in his first fitness report in the position. Each successive report attested to his knowledge, diligence, and excellent growth potential. By the time he had been in the job for a year and a half and we had celebrated my first birthday, he had been evaluated by three different colonels, all who wrote in similarly glowing terms as Colonel Stewart: *Staff Sergeant Hobaugh's keen sense of business management is reflected in the improved services and financial status of the SNCO Club. His attention to duty and diligence in the details of club work have substantially benefitted the staff non-commissioned officers of this depot. His growth potential for the future is excellent.*

That, however, was to be the last fitness report he received from Parris Island. In April 1962, when I was eighteen months, Daddy received orders for the Marine Barracks of the United States Naval Station in Argentia, Newfoundland, Canada. Jeff remembers all of us thinking, where is this "Argentina" place in Canada? He would get to take his family with him for this out-of-the-country duty station, but, for a short time, there would again be separation as he assumed his new position, arranged for housing and transportation, and we remained behind until it was time to join him. Our little family, now as big as it would ever get, was on the cusp of an adventure to a new land.

June 13, 1962, Argentia, Newfoundland

My Dearest darling,

I will write you a few lines from my new duty station.

I love you, baby, with all of my heart. You are the only one for me. I wish you were here with me now.

We got here today at 1400, or 2 o'clock in the afternoon, the sun was out and it was 50° outside. They tell me this was the best day this year, and I believe them, for now it must be about 40° or 35° outside and the fog is coming in.

NEWFOUNDLAND. IN TRUTH, IT is really the province of New-foundland/Labrador, but we never called it that. It is the easternmost and newest Canadian province, with only the territory of Nunavut added more recently. By the time we arrived in 1962, it had been a part of Canada for only thirteen years, having been under British rule until March of 1949.

The richness of its culture stems from a diversity of influences. Its indigenous population dates back thousands of years before Vikings made their way there around 1001. Once John Cabot claimed the island for England in 1497, a flood of British and eventually French settlers brought in more variety during the sixteenth and seventeenth centuries. But the influence we found most pronounced in Argentia, which sits on Placentia Bay in the southwest, was the blend of Scots and Irish that peppered the language and gave its culture richness and warmth.

The warmth of the people was needed to counteract a clime that was going to take some serious getting used to, as Daddy described early on. Moving from the eighties and nineties of the South Carolina low country to brisk, breezy temps some thirty plus degrees cooler was a serious adjustment. *If you would you could send me some of my winter clothes, just 2 or 3 pairs of pants and some long sleeve shirts. You have to have warm clothes here*, Daddy added into that June 13 letter. By early July, he was asking Mother to bring one of his winter suits when we joined him because the summer suit was just not warm enough for high temperatures that hovered around 60. A week or so later, Daddy's own barometer for what was acceptable was beginning to shift: *It is real nice now, sun out and warm, if you call 55 or 60 warm. It is warm for here.*

The thing that was most difficult about the Newfoundland climate was not the temperature, which did not tend to extremes, but the winds that blew in off the Atlantic Ocean, and, in Argentia, Placentia Bay. They were fairly constant at around 20 mph, although regular wind gusts could reach much higher. Not long after we moved there, a wind gust caught the screen door at the back of our house at the same time that my hand was on the handle, and Mother observed me flying across the yard and into a grassy ditch. When she reached me, I was no worse for the wear save for the scare, a few bumps and bruises, and a gush of tears; according to her, she never again had to tell me to leave the screen door handle alone. I often wondered how embellished that story became over time, but that is how I always remember it being told. Suffice it to say that, particularly along the coast, Argentia, Newfoundland, was a windy place to live.

It was also a wet place to live, with substantial rain during the summer months and snow during the winter that could come upon the island suddenly. Years later, Daddy and I were reminiscing about our family's time there, and he recalled an Easter Sunday when we entered church with the sun shining and exited with eight inches of snow on the ground. Suffice it to say that the unpredictable weather was a popular subject of conversation among the locals.

June 13, 1962, Argentia

Oh, by the way I am the mess sgt. How about that? At last, I have my own mess, work from 8 till 5 o'clock, 5 days a week. I have to stand O.D. (Officer of the day) about every ten (10) days and that is all the duty I have besides being mess sgt.

At last, I have my own mess. He had had a taste of it while in Okinawa, but that had been a small mess tent operation. This, this would be the real thing, and he had a promotion to go with it, E-6, still listed as staff sergeant because of a change in rank structure in 1958, but a grade increase nonetheless.

The duty station in Argentia wasn't a Marine base at all but a naval air station that dated back to the early days of World War II. Argentia had predominately been a fishing village when the British granted the land to the United States in September 1940 in exchange for 50 old naval destroyers; England overnight increased its naval inventory and the U.S. acquired strategic land for a base meant to defend the North Atlantic region from a possible Nazi invasion should Britain fall. The U.S. military wasted no time beginning construction on the base and runways; on February 13 of the following year, the Marines, ever the flag raisers, raised the American flag for the first time in Argentia. Later that year, in August 1941, the historic meeting of U.S. President Franklin Roosevelt and

British Prime Minister Winston Churchill to draft the Atlantic Charter took place aboard a warship anchored in Placentia Bay off the coast of Argentia. While the treaty was never formally signed, it set forth an agreement on how to maintain peace in a postwar world that served as the basis for what would become the United Nations Charter. In late 1944 toward the end of the war, the base became the site of internment for German POWs, most of them survivors of bombed submarines.

By the time we arrived in 1962, the strategic importance of the base had shifted to the Cold War and was being used predominately as a detection site for Soviet nuclear submarines. The Marines stationed at the naval air station provided security for the base; it was our father's job to see that they got fed.

As he had discovered in Okinawa, being in charge of the mess meant doing whatever was necessary to make the operation run smoothly. *I am sleepy tonight*, he wrote Mother in early July. *I got up at 5 this morning and went on cooks' watch because one of my cooks is on leave.* It would be one of those nights when he apologized for the "short note." His day didn't stop after the cooking was over, for there was paperwork to do afterward. A week later, he was relieved that his cook was back. *Now I can be just the mess sgt. and no more cooking.*

There was not much more to report home about his work. Daddy's office was a room in the back of the mess, and he gave Mother the phone number in case she needed to call as they continued to make the arrangements for the rest of us to join him. *We are getting a new C.O. [commanding officer] on the 18th of this month*, he wrote in July. There had been a party for the outgoing C.O. but Daddy had been unable to attend. He had been standing duty, his every ten-day stint as "officer of the day," a responsibility that Jeff and I would refer to as "the dirty duty" throughout Daddy's military career since it took our father away from us overnight.

As for his off-hours, life was looking a bit different than his stint on Okinawa. It had only been five years earlier, but while in Japan, shopping or going out for a show had been his main form of off-duty entertainment. But by 1962, television had become much more ubiquitous. *I think I will go watch some T.V. tonight*, he wrote in July. *They have a T.V. in the barracks here. [Only] get one station, but they have some good things on, Ben Casey, and some other ones we used to watch.*

It was no surprise that Daddy singled out *Ben Casey* in his letter. That 1960s show was to become a staple in our household. A few years later, when I was five years old and somewhat sophisticated in my home viewing tastes, it became my favorite television show.

We had moved to Albany during the summer and Mother had reverted to being a stay-at-home mom our first year there to help Jeff and me adjust to the move, a new school for Jeff, and my subsequent entry into the expanded world of kindergarten.

Ah, kindergarten! What blissfully beautiful days of a time when the grade was much more loosely structured—of playing inside with books and puzzles, and out, exerting my ability to run faster and jump higher than most of the boys in my class. I'm not sure what happened to my coordination and gross motor skills just a few years later, but, well, those were the days. Sometimes Mother would arrive early to pick me up, just to look in and observe. If I weren't working a jigsaw puzzle by myself, then I was "assisting" some classmate by calmly finding the correct puzzle piece as substitution for the one he was furiously trying to cram into a location that would never fit. Can't he see how ridiculous his choice is?! That piece isn't remotely shaped like the hole in the puzzle!—but I wisely kept these thoughts to myself. No use shaming the poor lad whose skills clearly lay elsewhere.

When the kindergarten half day was officially over, we would gather up my belongings and head home. Jeff was in fifth grade; I would have Mother all to myself until he got home from school.

Our dog Rusty was waiting in the kitchen for my arrival home. He had a bed in the corner and somehow, we who were never really schooled in dog training got that dog, without any barrier, to remain in the kitchen and never venture to any other part of the house. He was, without a doubt, the best dog we ever had. I loved on him and then settled in to have some lunch, sharing with Mother my various exploits of another exciting morning of kindergarten.

After lunch came my favorite part of the day, when Mother would turn on the television to ABC, which was running daytime repeats of its popular night-time medical drama, *Ben Casey*. Dr. Ben Casey was a young, idealistic, intense neurosurgeon at County General Hospital, played by the dark-haired, dreamy Vince Edwards. Let me tell you, for anyone who has drooled over the doctors in *Grey's Anatomy*, Vince Edwards was the original McDreamy! He dealt seriously with medical issues, but had a bedside manner that melted hearts. Plus, he had an especially tender spot for his pediatric patients, a quality that endeared him to me. We owned a Ben Casey jigsaw puzzle depicting him at the bedside of a little girl; it was my favorite of our collection.

Mother and I settled onto the couch, both of us lying on our sides, me nestled in front and her with her arm around me, cuddled up to watch whatever medical dilemma Dr. Casey would solve. Sometimes, after the episode had concluded, we would remain right there and end up taking a nap, which, I realized once I became a mother, was one of *her* favorite times of the day. Besides some snuggle time whose days she well knew were numbered, this break gave her time to rest from the rigors of being a Marine wife and the mother of two children. For me, it gave me one of the best memories of my life and, though I didn't realize it for years, modeled the importance of taking time out to just be with your children.

But that memory was still some years in my future. For now, what I knew was that Daddy was gone, living in a place we had never heard of and were struggling to remember was Argentia, *not* Argentina.

THE MAIN THING THAT occupied Daddy during his off hours was fi-nalizing the details to reunite his family. Despite receiving orders for Newfound-land in April, he did not arrive until mid-June. A delay between receiving orders and reporting to a new duty station is fairly standard, since the wheels of military bureaucracy grind slowly and Marines will often put in for leave, anticipating that, depending on the post, there may be some period of time without their family during the transition. There was also travel time, which, from Beaufort, South Carolina, to Argentia, Newfoundland, in 1962, was no small matter.

There are two main things that have to be handled during a military move—housing and transportation. With both of these, families are at the mercy of the military. Each duty station has its own character about it, and some are easier than others, so it is important to get the lay of the land as quickly as possible. The sooner plans are in place, the sooner families can be reunited. Since we're talking about our father, here, he wasted no time in gathering information and trying to move things along. But at this particular duty station, finding available housing was a real issue. Not only did base housing stay constantly full, but off-base options that would pass military inspection were limited.

June 13, 1962, Argentia

I will tell you what I have found out so far.

I had a long talk with 1ˢᵗ Sgt. Crist when I got here today and he said if we started looking for a house (him and me) now, it would be the end of July before we could find one. He said he knows a lot of people here and he is going to try and find me a place.

There are not any houses that are not full now. What you have to do is find someone that is moving on the base and get the house they are living in and when your name comes up on the housing list the same thing happens. You just don't go out and find a house that no one is living in around here.

By the end of June, Daddy had found an apartment, and Mother began inquiring about things like whether it had shades or blinds for the windows so she would know whether to bring the curtains. School was out for her and Jeff in Beaufort so we were splitting our time between there and Greensboro. Mostly, though, Mother just wanted to be in Newfoundland with her husband.

June 30, 1962, Greensboro

Honey, I'm glad you found us a roomy, clean place, but I would have come to you to live in anything. I love you so much I can hardly stand being away from you.

July 10, 1962, Argentia

I went out to the apt. this afternoon to see if it would be ready and it will be ready on the 11th of July. So I will have to be there in the morning and let the people from the base look it over, but it will pass o.k., for it is a new place.

I checked on the shades today too for the apartment and it comes with shades, so that will help. We can look around for curtains, or wait till ours get here.

The following day, "the people from the base" inspected the apartment and it passed, Daddy paid the first month's rent, and the apartment was ours. He planned to start moving some things in from the barracks so that *I will have everything all fixed up when you get here.*

Each new duty station was a bit of an unknown, but this change felt especially adventuresome. *You never did tell me how you like it in Argentia, or, how long the flight is,* Mother wrote from Greensboro. Daddy had written about the weather and happiness over finally having his own mess, but what did the area look like, had he had a chance to check out the base chapel, were the people friendly? There was also the issue of whether Mother would work, and, if so, doing what.

July 1, 1962, Greensboro

Sweetie, if I can't get a teaching job, is there anything I could do up there to help out financially if we need it? Perhaps we won't but I'll be glad to work if it's necessary.

Life was not as tight financially as it had been when Daddy was overseas, partly because Mother had worked while we were in Beaufort. But preparing for the move and the vagaries of life itself had eaten into the income—$17.00 for a dental bill for Jeff that was only the beginning, $3.85 to get one of the tire tubes on the car fixed. There were also clothes for active and growing children—Mother considered our current wardrobe *in a sorry state*— but she only bought two polo shirts for Jeff to replace ones he had split and a couple of outfits for me. For the rest, she would wait until we arrived in Newfoundland, for we'd all need a much different wardrobe there.

As they did with one another, Mother shared everything and worried about all of these expenses. *Babe, I'm sorry, but it really is taking the money. I'm doing the best I can.* And Daddy was always quick to reassure her that he trusted her judgment and knew she was doing her best. Plus, with the exchange rate in our favor and Daddy's promotion, the situation in Canada looked like it would lighten the financial burden.

July 10, 1962, Argentia

I went to the bank today and changed our money into Canadian money to pay the rent. You have to pay in Canadian money, and $90.00 Canadian money only cost me $84.12 in our money, so rent will be $84.12 in our money.

Honey, the only thing you could do up here would be teach, but I don't think you will have to unless you want to. I got $35.00 raise when I made E-6. I get $20.00 overseas pay and we get $13.50 off-station housing. So that is $68.50 more than I was getting and I get $36.00 for not eating in the mess hall. So I don't think you will have to work. You can stay home with Jeff and Jenny and just love me, o.k. baby.

Mother was also anxious about all of the specifics related to the move, and these questions peppered her letters...would she need to wait for authorization from Daddy to ship the furniture, would she need mine and Jeff's birth certificates on the trip up, should she sell my crib and have Daddy get a single bed in Argentia, and most urgently, when and where would we drop off the car and catch the transport to bring us up to join him. So she waited, and queried, and continued the busy life of a young military wife raising children.

June 27, 1962, Greensboro
My Darling,

I just miss you so I can hardly stand it. We had a light cold wave and I've been so blue and lonesome I don't know what to do with myself. I know what you mean about us needing to be together. I'm just not happy unless we are. I love you, Babe and need you more than you know.

WHEN DADDY WAS IN the Marine Corps, every summer and most Thanksgivings our family would travel to Greensboro to visit our grandmothers, aunts, uncles, and cousins. At least once while we were there but oftentimes more, Mother would give Jeff and me money to walk up to Merritt Drug, a short block or two up Clifton Road and then a right at the intersection, where the drugstore, complete with ice cream/soda shop, resided on the well-traveled Merritt Drive. I have a vague memory of holding my brother's hand, he being the dutiful older brother tasked with looking out for me, although as the years passed, neither of us was much interested in that level of closeness anymore.

Whoever was working behind the counter would often remember us from the summer or fall before, or relate us as George Hobaugh and Becky Gardner's kids, with a "You up visiting your grandmothers?" and "How are your parents doing?" to go along with our order. Jeff would do the talking, of course—"Yes, sir; just fine, sir"—as I sat quietly and took in the surroundings with big eyes. Sometimes we would sit at the counter, other times a walk back to Nana's with our summer treats was in order, depending on what we ordered and how hot the day was. No use having the sumptuous ice cream melt down our arms on the way home.

Jeff's order would generally be more extravagant than mine. He was the culinary adventurer; I the one of simple, some would say picky, tastes. He might do a root beer or Coke float—gross!—or, if we had the money, a banana split, with its trifecta of ice creams topped with bananas and hot fudge, too many flavors assaulting the senses for me. My needs were simple. Give me a chocolate ice cream cone or milk shake and I was a happy little girl. At one point in my childhood, I hoped to compare chocolate ice creams in as many locations in the eastern United States and Canada as possible. It never hurt to be on the hunt for the best one out there.

Once our summer afternoon treats were consumed, or with them well in hand, we would begin the short walk back to Nana's where I would proclaim to Mother and Daddy with great excitement and satisfaction how wonderful the outing had been and proceed to have my sticky hands and chocolate covered mouth cleaned up. Not having any kind of similar all-purpose drug store within walking distance of where we lived, it was, in my young eyes, a novelty and adventure, a memory for just Jeff and me gifted to us by our parents.

For the first several weeks after Daddy went up to Newfoundland to begin his new job as mess sergeant, adapt to the local climate, try to find housing, and work out the specifics for his family and belongings to make their way up to Argentia, Mother, Jeff, and I stayed in Greensboro with Nana. Papa Jack had passed away suddenly sixteen months earlier in February 1961, just three months after I was born, from a massive stroke, in the days long before bypass surgery could have given him some more years. We originally planned to stay with Nana until June 28, when she would depart for the summer camp where she served as the speech therapist. But then Mother decided to take a two-week childhood education course there in Greensboro that began on June 25, which extended our stay even after Nana left for camp. Although Mother's degree from Guildford was in music education, she quickly discovered that there were fewer positions for music than classroom teachers, particularly moving around the country every three years or so with a Marine, so she had switched over to elementary education once in Beaufort. The two-week course, attended by 124 members of the N.C. Association for Childhood Education, probably earned her some continuing education credits.

June 24, 1962, Greensboro

My Dearest,

I didn't write you last night. Please forgive me. I won't let it happen again, even if it's only a note. I start to school tomorrow, and Saturday I tried to get all our washing and ironing and cleaning done. Aunt Bill sang in a recital at the church at 4:30, so I went to that. I had promised Mrs. Tesh on Friday that I would teach her S.S. class (ages 16–20), so I stayed up till 2 o'clock studying the lesson. So tonight I'm pretty bushed.

Needless to say, these were busy days for our mother as we re-entered the life of the extended family and community where she had grown up and where she and Jeff had spent fourteen months just five years earlier. Once the course started, Jeff and I stayed home with a babysitter during Mother's 9 a.m.–3 p.m. class time. Then she arrived home to children who had missed her and wanted her attention—*Jenny behaved well for Mary Sue today. She really cuts a shine when I come home though. Jeff isn't too excited over the idea of my leaving him but he's doing pretty well.* At night there were books to read and papers to write, and once Nana left for camp, the house felt empty and there was no backup in the evenings to help out with two tired children.

June 28, 1962, Greensboro

My Darling George,

Mother left today at 3 o'clock and it sure is lonesome around here tonight. Peggy and Elmer invited us down to supper and everything was really good.

Babe, after tomorrow my class will be half over. It really has been enjoyable. Under other circumstances it would be wonderful, but at times I find my mind wandering and going clean to Newfoundland in no time at all!

The beauty of extended family living close by, though, was that other family members pitched in. The week that Nana left, Grandma Mimmie invited us over to have supper with her every night. And the night that we went over to our aunt and uncle's for supper afforded us some time with our cousin David, just a year younger than Jeff. After supper, Mother agreed to watch the children so Aunt Peggy and Uncle Elmer could try to make a final decision on a new car they were looking to buy. We returned to Nana's so Mother could put me to bed, and Jeff and David continued to play for the next three hours. Jeff had been invited for a sleepover with David a couple of weeks before—*I sure do feel sorry for Peggy, but she asked for it!*—so I imagine Mother felt like it was her turn to watch over the little rascals.

For two children who were the part of the family that had left the Greensboro area, being there for several weeks in the summer gave us the chance to play with cousins we only saw during visits. Besides David, our first cousin on Daddy's side, our Mother's first cousin Wadena had a little boy, Jay, our second cousin whose birthday fell in between Jeff's and mine, and he was a constant presence and playmate for us that summer. One of Jeff and Jay's favorite outdoor games was to imitate the skydivers Ted McKeever and Jim Buckley in the popular TV series *Ripcord*, an adventure drama in which the two characters chased criminals and performed daring skydiving rescues. Since I spent my early years trying to imitate and keep up with my older brother, I did not see any reason why, at the mature age of nineteen months, I could not participate in whatever games he and Jay might devise.

June 24, 1962, Greensboro

Honey, Jenny is a rough one! She tries to do everything Jeff and Jay do and almost makes it. She'll jump off the bottom step and yell "rip cord." She tried to jump off the top one but I caught her in time and spanked her legs! She is a cutie pie!

Early in our stay, Jeff attended Vacation Bible School at the Friends church in the evenings. I was not old enough, so Aunt Bill or Aunt Peggy would take him and Mother would stay home with me. He really enjoyed it, Mother related to Daddy, as they learned the Ten Commandments and worked on making a pencil holder, standard fare for Bible school of that era, and the first of many pencil holders we were to make and bring home. There was a program at the end of the week and Mother proudly wrote about Jeff's participation: *Jeffrey was in the Bible School program at church tonight. He took part in the singing and all and then said the 5th commandment—he learned them all. He is some cute boy.* It was probably random that Jeff was assigned the fifth commandment to recite, but the fact that it's the one about honoring your father and mother seemed somehow fitting for my rambunctious brother.

As for me, Mother updated Daddy on my almost daily changes and growth, just as she had for "Jeff boy" five years earlier when Daddy was in Okinawa. Reports such as, *Jenny is a pure mess! She is really chatting now and really is into things*, and *Your daughter is a gal! She says, "I love Daddy," "Daddy gone bye-bye" and "pair pane" (airplane) and lots more. She's a real cutie pie*, frequented her letters up to Newfoundland.

Sometimes Mother would take me along to places that were surely against her better judgment when there weren't other options. *Babe, I sang at church tonight and took Jenny. I just knew she'd be a mess, but she was real good.* She was yet to fully grasp my introverted, quiet, rule-following personality, and who could blame her. I was still a few months shy of two, and her only other experience to date had been the exact opposite. My brother, with considerable energy and a precocious vocabulary, had always had some trouble sitting still and remaining quiet. Despite my own propensity for silence, there were a couple of little blips that evening at church. *She did say "Mommy" a time or two, but she really surprised me by behaving so well.*

But, in truth, when Mother wrote about Jeff and me it was often to tell Daddy how much we missed him. I was roughly the same age Jeff had been when Daddy left for Okinawa, and, Jeff, who was now six, well, Mother thought that he missed our father more than he ever had.

June 14, 1962, Greensboro
Dearest Babe,

We were thrilled to get your letter today. Jeff met the postman and came in screaming, "I got a letter from my daddy." I believe Jeff misses you more than he ever has. 'Course, he's older. After the bus left Sunday and we went back to the car he just went to pieces. He cried and said, "Now my daddy won't be home when we get back." About once or twice each day he has a little crying spell 'cause he misses you so.

Jenny's doing fine except for missing you. And the trains wake her up. She called you all day Monday and cried so hard at naptime, but she's doing better. Today she talked to you on the "telephone" all day. She says "Daddy bye bye" constantly.

July 1, 1962, Greensboro

Jeff's getting awfully anxious to come to his daddy. He informed me that he loves me very much but that a boy just needs his daddy!

Despite the fact that we were getting to see our grandmothers and play with our cousins, the days until we could head for Newfoundland seemed interminably long, and Mother had to continue to deal not only with her own longing but ours as well.

June 30,1962, Greensboro

I love you so much I can hardly stand being away from you. The kids are missing you mighty bad too. Night before last Jeff had a real crying spell for his daddy. And this morning for about ½ hour Jenny cried and fussed for Daddy— banged on her telephone 'cause she couldn't get Daddy to talk to her on it.

Now old enough to compose his own letters, Jeff wrote to Daddy as well, sometimes short ones in his own hand, other times longer ones that he dictated to Mother.

June 16, 1962, Greensboro

Dear Father,

We miss you. We are going to call you for Father's Day. I went to the dentist and I have a loose tooth.

Love,

Jeffrey H.

June 30, 1962, Greensboro

Dear Daddy,

I love you. I'm glad that you found a house. I'm glad that we can come up there soon, and I miss you, and I want to come up there. Daddy, where shall I go to school?

Daddy, I know I'm saying this over again, but I want to, I love you! Jenny loves you, too. Daddy, if you could see Jenny now you would give her a great big

kiss and Jenny is a cute little girl. I caught the ice cream man today. Jenny keeps
playing like she is calling you.
Jeff and Jenny
P.S. Can we send my bicycle?

By the start of the second and final week of Mother's class, we were all more than ready to be on our way to Newfoundland, the days made harder by Nana's absence and Mother's long days at school followed by an afternoon and evening of single parenting and homework. In the midst of what was turning into a busy last couple weeks in Greensboro, she managed to fit in doctors' visits for the shots and physicals that were necessary before we left. By June 22, I had gotten my second of three typhoid shots, Jeff was all finished, and she still had one more tetanus to go; a week later, shots and physicals for all of us were complete.

In addition to Mother's already full plate, she and Daddy were busy trying to work out the plans for wrapping up things in the States and getting us up to Newfoundland. Daddy had written when he first arrived that, when we came, we would fly out of an air base in New Jersey, the precise one to be identified later, but probably about 60 miles from where we would drop off the car to be shipped up to Newfoundland. By the end of June, there was still a good bit to be worked out, but at least we had a probable timeframe.

June 30, 1962, Greensboro

I got the letters from you telling me the things to ship and the possible depar-
ture date from the States. The 25th [of July] sounds wonderful. At first I thought
it would be best earlier. But by the time I tie up things in Beaufort, come by here
[Nana's] and rest a few days, it will probably take that long. I'm so thrilled and I
can hardly wait to get there with you.

All of the arrangements were complicated once again by a house. Back in late February/early March, about thirty days before Daddy received orders, we had moved into a new house. And not just any house but one that Mother and Daddy had had built, since they had decided to make Beaufort our civilian home once Daddy retired from the Marine Corps. This was all so recent that settlement on the house had not even taken place. *The problem now*, Mother wrote as she recapped the plan as she knew it on June 25, *is getting the house settled.*

Besides settling on the house, Mother was also trying to find a couple or family to rent it. Located across Narcissus Lane from our friends the Marsdens, they had agreed to look after our home and act as sort of onsite landlords in our absence. By the end of June, it looked as if all was falling into place. The closing date for the house was set for July 12 or 13, and it looked as if a renter was in hand. A woman whose husband was due back on August 1 and would be stationed at the air station had driven up from Charleston to see it and written to let Mother know she was impressed and interested in it for their family of four—a boy 17 and a girl 13—and hoped to speak with Mother once we returned to Beaufort.

But for some reason the promising lead did not work out. Once back in Beaufort, Mother continued searching, but by July 16, just two days before we were to leave, we were still without a renter.

July 16, 1962, Beaufort

So far I have not rented the house but I talked with Jim Rentz yesterday and he said not to worry, he'll help me find someone and send them to Everett [Marsden]. Our first payment is not due until September 1. Everett suggested that I withdraw $100.00 and let him start a separate account at Beaufort Bank (so he won't confuse it with his account at Peoples). Then if anything should ever happen we'll have enough for a payment. Also, if we rent it right away and the 1ˢᵗ payment isn't due til the 1ˢᵗ of Sept., that will be another payment ahead.

While a renter for the house was not panning out like our parents hoped, things continued to move along to wrap up in Beaufort so we could begin the journey to join Daddy in Newfoundland. On July 11, Mother got word that the movers would be out to our house the following morning to load up our furniture and belongings. That Thursday morning, she penned the following brief note...

July 12, 1962, Beaufort
Darling,

   They should come for the furniture in a few minutes. I decided to sell Jenny's bathinette and crib so please arrange for a cot or something for her to sleep on.
   Must go—lots to do. I love you and hope to be with you soon.
Becky

   We weren't set to start out on our journey for another few days, but the Marsdens had offered to let us stay with them in the interim. Mr. Marsden sent Daddy a short note after checking on us the morning of the move saying he would write a longer letter after we left—*Becky will keep you up to date until then*—and assuring him that they would *keep Beck and children squared away, so don't worry about them.* Until we left, then, there were last lovely days with friends. Doug was ecstatic to have Jeff back—*Doug sure misses Jeff. Hardly knows what to do with himself,* Mrs. Marsden had written Mother during our time in Greensboro. As for me, I was happy to be back with my "Brucey," their middle son who babysat some for me and always held a special place in my heart.

July 14, 1962, Beaufort

   I took Jeff, Jenny, Bruce and Doug to the beach today. We had a pretty good time. We only stayed in the water 1 hour 'cause it was near noon. Then we found a shaded table and ate a picnic lunch.

   When we arrived home from the beach, Mother had received the letter authorizing us to be on the flight on July 25 from McGuire Air Force Base. We were instructed to be at McGuire before 0600 on the 25th. With two small children and not willing to leave anything to chance, Mother planned for us to be there on the 24th.

July 16, 1962, Beaufort
Dearest Darling,

   1 week and 1 day and I'll be with you. I sure was glad to get those papers

authorizing me to be on that flight on the 25ᵗʰ! I love you so and I just long for the
time when we'll be together again.

    Honey, I have worked it out like this so far. Everett is going to ride with me
to Greensboro and catch the bus right back. We will leave this Wednesday night
about 11 o'clock so he can catch the Thursday morning 8 o'clock bus back. Then
Mother is going to go with me to Washington. That leaves only 170 miles and
I'm sure Murray will probably drive with me the rest of the way to Bayonne. (You
remember Murray was at Dad's funeral.)

    Babe, I don't guess there's any need for you to write me anymore; it will just
have to be sent back. I'll write every chance I get.

    Goodnight, my darling. I love you with all my heart. The children are fine
and send you kisses.
Becky

Two days later we began the long journey to finally join Daddy at this new, somewhat exotic duty station, making our stop in Greensboro for a few days so Mother could rest up and we could see family one last time before leaving the country. For Jeff, the trip in and of itself would be an adventure because we would get to ride a *real* airplane! I know Mother was grateful for the friends and family who joined in to accompany us as we made our way up to New Jersey to drop off the car and catch the early morning flight at McGuire.

    The *real airplane* we boarded took us to St. John's, the capital of Newfoundland. From there, we took a helicopter—"hoppy coppy" in my toddler language—to Argentia. The constant island winds made that helicopter ride a bit dicey, and I threw up on the last leg of the journey, all over Mother and the stuffed animal that I had along for security. Welcome to Argentia!

    And so we joined our father for what became some of the happiest years of our time in the Marine Corps. We soon learned that the proper way to pronounce Newfoundland has been a subject of great debate among the locals over the years, but, whether stressing the first or last syllable, the pronunciation should rhyme with *understand*, and never, ever, under any circumstances, be reduced to noo´-fun-lund, robbing the last syllable of its "land" status. The New-foundlanders, or Newfs as they are called if you know them well, are made of sturdy stuff to weather that clime, but they are also gracious and accepting. And so they welcomed us into their world, warming us even as we adapted to weather far different from what we were used to. Even Daddy, who after Korea and the Chosin Reservoir was content to keep venturing south and away from the cold, adapted. In the end, we put in for the extra year there, postponing the inevitable move as we delighted in the rugged beauty of this island and the genuine hospitality of its people.

11

———

Quartermaster School

I DO NOT HAVE MUCH MEMORY OF THE MARINE
Corps taking our father away. It helped that I was not even born when he went
to Okinawa and only seven when he retired.

What I do recall is that if Mother wanted to spend any extended time in
Greensboro in the summer, then she would pile Jeff and me in the car and brave
the eight-hour car trip, leaving Daddy behind to work. Much more seared into my
childhood are the years following our father's retirement from the Marine Corps,
when he entered club management and a seemingly continuous cycle of working
long hours because he was in between chefs or did not have an evening hostess.

At some point, Mother understood that this is whom she had married...a
man dedicated to doing the best he could, whether for the USMC or Doublegate Country Club. It is not everyone who finds what they love to do early on
and is blessed to do it most of their lives.

When he was there, he was the best of dads, attending Jeff's little league games,
encouraging him in scouting, and sitting through what was, for him, achingly
long piano recitals. The time he would spend with us at home jokingly became
known as "quality time." There may not be as much of it as we wanted, but
when we were with him it was a treasure. For me, from the time I can remember,
that meant sitting on his lap and watching a baseball game. "Come over here,
baby," he'd say, patting his lap, "and let's spend some quality time together."

I'm not sure why this became our version of "quality time." Perhaps the slower pace of the sport with its in-game intricacies appealed to my personality. The truth was probably closer to the fact that, as a Daddy's girl, I wanted to be where he was from the time I was little. On a Saturday afternoon in the springs and summers of my formative years, that meant watching NBC's Game of the Week, at a time before we had the luxury of watching all the Atlanta Braves' games on TBS.

Together, we sat in "his" chair, me positioned in his lap, nestled against his chest. It is there, in that happiest of places, that he taught me the game of baseball. I learned about balls and strikes, that circling the bases to arrive home was the goal, and that most of the umpires were blind when the calls went against our pitcher or batter. We rooted for the Braves even though in the 1960s and '70s they were terrible, and I learned lessons of loyalty and patience as one long season after another ended in disappointment, encouraged every year by the additional forty or so home runs Hank Aaron had added to his career total as he chased down the legend that was Babe Ruth.

As I grew, there was always more to learn since baseball is a game grounded in rules and statistics, writ large. I still remember the day he taught me what a balk is.

"Daddy, why did the batter get to go to second base? The count wasn't full and the pitcher didn't even throw the ball."

"The pitcher balked," Daddy began, always keeping the explanations simple.

"The pitcher walked? Do you mean he walked him? How could that be?" I asked, already having explained that I knew the count and was keeping track of the game. I prided myself in a fairly thorough knowledge of the game even though I was still under double digits in age.

"No, he balked," Daddy replied, "with a *b*."

"What's that?" I asked. This is a wonderful day, I said only to myself. I was, in Southern parlance, "fixin' to" learn a new baseball term.

"The pitcher can't interrupt his delivery once he starts his pitch, Daddy explained. See how he started his pitch but then stopped to try to fake out the runner on first and keep him close to the bag?"

We were watching the replay.

"When that happens," Daddy continued, "the runners on base are all award-ed the next base."

"It's hard to tell," I confessed.

"Yes, it can be. But you'll get better at noticing now that you know what to look for."

I settled back in and we continued watching the game. Neither of us had to say a lot when we were watching. It was quality time, and it was enough to be together enjoying the game we both loved.

OUR TIME IN NEWFOUNDLAND was wonderful. As mess sergeant of a small mess, Daddy, true to his prediction, had one of the most stable, 8 a.m.–5 p.m. assignments he was to ever have. By early 1963, he had taken on the additional duty of NCO in charge of the Enlisted Club, and he quickly set about making it, according to one of his fitness reports, "a highly successful and unsurpassed recreation facility aboard the Naval Station."

Later that year, eleven days after my third birthday, our parents watched and listened in horror at the news that President Kennedy had been shot. We grieved with our nation, and the Canadians we lived among grieved with us, shocked and saddened at the death of a U.S. president they had come to admire.

Kennedy's assassination made its indelible, grievous mark on our time in Newfoundland, as it did for Americans everywhere. But the rest of our duty there was joyous. Eventually, we traded out the apartment Daddy had found and moved into base housing, which finally became available. As happened at each duty station, we got involved in the base chapel, where Mother sang in the choir. Over time, we adapted our wardrobe to fit the bitter cold of this Cana-dian province, learning the value of wool and down. There was sledding and snowmen and, for Jeff, snow forts, that filled our winters in ways we had never experienced. Mostly, though, we made good friends, some stationed there with either the Marine Corps or Navy, and some, those enchanting, friendly Newfs.

In the summers, Nana would come to visit, both to enjoy time with these grandchildren now stationed so far away and to explore the rocky climes that are part of the rustic beauty of Argentia. When Daddy got leave, we would make the long trip back to Greensboro so we could see both grandmothers and all the aunts, uncles, and cousins who had settled in Greensboro or the surrounding area. While we were in the States, we would also make our way down to Beaufort to stay with the Marsdens and enjoy time with good friends, visit our dog Rusty who was camped out with them while we were in Newfoundland, and look across the street at the house that belonged to us and that we one day planned to actually live in for more than a month or two.

And so life took on a rhythm, a cold, but good one, until, in late spring 1965, after having spent our additional year in Newfoundland, Daddy received orders for the Marine Corps Supply Center (MCSC) in Albany, Georgia. In July, we moved from a place where Mother had trouble keeping Jeff and me out of the pool if the temperatures reached the 50s, to a place where, when the temps reached 50, the native Albanians were thinking about pulling out their heavy coats. There would be no chance of 50-degree weather in July as we readjusted to the heat and humidity of the Deep South.

Daddy's assignment in Albany was as Assistant Manager of the Staff NCO Club, familiar terrain for him. At a much larger base than the Marine Barracks in Newfoundland, he had the opportunity to make an even bigger impact on base morale. His first fitness report, after just six months on the job, indicated that he had "contributed greatly to increased patronage at the Club."

Things continued this way for a year, with repeated high marks and a notation from his reporting officer that he had the necessary skills for "advancement to the next higher grade," until in May 1966, he was awarded the next higher grade when he was promoted to gunnery sergeant and put in charge of the mess at MCSC, Albany.

Just two months into his new position and grade, a different reporting officer observed the following:

> GySgt Hobaugh is a strong, capable leader who always seeks the
> highest possible degree of performance from his subordinates

as well as himself. He has the capacity to handle assignments of increased responsibility. His growth potential is excellent to outstanding. GySgt Hobaugh has the necessary qualifications for selection to Master Sergeant.

That evaluation would be Daddy's last *noncommissioned* officer fitness report, and he would never make master sergeant. Just two months later, he received his first *officer* fitness report by the lieutenant colonel that was commanding officer of Headquarters Battalion. Daddy had received a commission; as 2nd Lieutenant Hobaugh, he was now the mess administrator overseeing all mess operations.

It was not unheard of for an enlisted Marine to earn a commission as an officer, but it usually occurred when an NCO that had distinguished him or herself was selected for and successfully completed Officer Candidates School (OCS). However, Daddy never attended OCS, being a bit on the "old" side by this point. Rather, he benefitted from something known as the Limited Duty Officer program that had been authorized by the Personnel Act of 1947. First implemented during the Korean War, a time of increased need for officers as well as specialists and technicians, the program provided a way for enlisted Marines to become officers and advance within their area of specialty up to the rank of lieutenant colonel. To be selected for the program, an enlisted Marine had to be in the top two pay grades, have at least ten years active service, and be less than 37 years old. There were only certain fields in which a Marine might be commissioned through the program; fortunately, food service was one of them. When the program was reinstituted in 1966 with President Johnson's commitment of ground troops to Vietnam a year earlier, Daddy's recent promotion to gunnery sergeant was the final criteria to make him eligible. With eighteen years in, he easily surpassed the ten years of active service requirement, and, at 36, he just scraped by on age.

Eligibility gave him the opportunity, but it was his hard work and dedication to excellence over the years that earned him the commission. It was a recognition well deserved and gave him status he had only ever dreamed of. Years later when

Jeff was an enlisted Marine being enticed to re-enlist with the dangling carrot of Officer Candidates School, our father was fond of telling him that his worst day as an officer was still better than his best day as an enlisted man.

I was only five at the time and don't remember the commissioning ceremony itself, although an official photograph captures our family as Mother and the commanding officer pin Daddy's 2nd lieutenant's bars on his shoulders. But I used to thrill when we would re-enter the main gate of the base and, after waving us through, the MP would snap to a smart salute as our car passed through.

Some years later I asked Daddy why the MP salutes even when Mother was driving. "They're saluting the commission," he told me, which they knew given the commissioned officer sticker that now resided on the bumper of our car.

"So that means," I continued, realization dawning, "that when I am old enough to drive, they will salute for me too?"

Daddy smiled and indicated that they would.

I had seldom imagined myself marrying someone in the military, but, all of a sudden, I thought that was something I could get used to. He would definitely have to be an officer, I decided.

April 19, 1967, Fort Lee, Virginia

Hi Honey,

Just a few lines this morning before I go to classes. This school sure does keep us on the go—to school at 0800 till 1200, one hour for dinner and to school from 1300 till 1600, 5 days a week.

Sugar, I love you oh so much. You are my everything. I will be so glad when we are together again.

June 27, 1967, Albany, Georgia

Dear George,

It's not easy to always be leaving you or for you to be leaving me! As much as I love being your wife and living with you, it's terrible to have to be away from you so much. I love you very dearly and never want anyone but you. It was good to talk to you last night. I wanted to call you but decided maybe it would be rather silly. So I'm very glad you were 'silly' and called to see about me.

WHILE WE WERE ALL happy to have the additional prestige, and money, that went with Daddy's commission, in the end, it was that promotion to commissioned officer that ended up taking him away from us again. In April 1967, less than a year after his promotion, the Marine Corps sent him for two and a half months to Fort Lee, Virginia, to attend the U.S. Army Quartermaster School and complete their Food Service Supervision course. Once again, our family was thrown into familiar patterns of missing husband/father and staying connected mainly through letters.

Located in Southeastern Virginia not far from Petersburg, Fort Lee had the advantage of being only 30 miles south of Richmond, where Uncle J.B., his wife, our Aunt Jeannette, and our cousins Bruce and newborn Beth were living. As such, it was fairly easy for Daddy to visit on the weekends or even drive up to their place for supper. Beth was just three and a half months at the time, and Daddy remarked, after one visit, how "perty" she was. And on the weekends, he could sometimes get away to drive the just-under 200-mile trip to visit all the family in Greensboro.

At times, however, his weekend plans were foiled by schoolwork. *I just don't know yet,* he wrote Mother after suggesting that he may go to see her brother on the weekend. *I don't know what kind of homework we will have to do this weekend. It seems they always give us something for the weekend.*

Daddy threw himself into this course as he had with everything in the Marine Corps, striving to do his best. *I want to get an "A" out of this school if I can,* an admission that I'm sure did not surprise our Mother. He kept us apprised of his success— *We had our test today and I only missed one, so I still have my "A"*—as well as when the course work became a little more challenging.

May 17, 1967, Fort Lee
I sure am glad that test is over. It took 4 hours. It had 235 questions. I missed

14. I think that is still an "89"; will know for sure in a few days. We started bak-
ing today, and you know I don't like baking, but will try and do the best I can.

May 23, 1967, Fort Lee

We have been baking bread for the last two days. In the morning we start on
sweet dough and cookies. I must say that this baking leaves me cold. I just don't
like it. Must study hard for this baking test. Then we go on to cooking, which I am
looking forward to.

May 24, 1967, Fort Lee

Well, I made my first "B" in the school; got a "B" on meat cutting. I just
missed an "A." Will tell you all about it when I see you. I made a 91 or 92 on the
test, so I had a high "B." I hope I get an "A" or even a "B+" out of this baking. I
will say again that this baking leaves me cold. I just don't like it.

The "B" on meat cutting must have left Daddy exasperated with himself,
since he had served as a meat cutter in the Corps. But, as usual, he simply looked
ahead, this time to conquering the dreaded baking requirement.

His biggest scholarly challenge while there may have been tackling the oral
part of the course. Not a man of words, he wrote one Monday night of needing
to close his letter in order to prepare for a fifteen-minute talk he had to give, not
the following morning, but on Wednesday.

As always, Mother served as his biggest fan and encourager—*hope your talk
went well; I'm sure it did*—and letting him know that we were thrilled with his
success.

May 5, 1967, Albany

I'm proud of your A. I know you must be working hard. Jeff was as pleased as
punch. He said, "I knew Daddy could do it."

Despite how busy Daddy was with school and the distractions on the weekends with family close by, or that Mother, Jeff, and I were frantically finishing
up the school year, the reality was that all of us, once again, had to endure

separation. Phone calls were easier, cheaper, and more frequent than either Oki-nawa or Newfoundland, which helped some, and Daddy encouraged Mother to take full advantage of any opportunity to call. Mostly, though, there was the constancy of their letters.

May 8, 1967, Fort Lee

Honey, anytime you need or want to call me, please do. I am here most of the time. About the only thing I do is go eat, and some time [go] to the show.

Sugar, I love you with all of my heart. You are the only one for me. I love you more than words can ever tell. I wish I had you in my arms now and could hold and love you, honey.

May 5, 1967, Albany

In case I haven't told you lately, I love you with all my heart. You are the only one for me. I don't believe I have ever missed you this much before. I need you so much. Always love me, dearest. You are my very heart.

It was a mixed bag, this life that Daddy had chosen and Mother had agreed to when she married him. It provided a good living, but, as with everything, came with its challenges. But Daddy loved it, and Mother understood that about him, accepting the difficulty along with the advantages. And she certainly couldn't deny the joy of the previous year that saw Daddy's promotion to officer. *I love you so and am so pleased with the way things have turned out for you,* she wrote one Tuesday night. *But you have deserved it and more. I just wish our kind of life didn't mean so much separation.*

May 28, 1967, Albany

We had brunch today with Sue Hurley and kids. Robert just arrived in Viet-nam Friday. They kept him on West Coast all this time. Stuck him in to train some kind of something. Sue has been very upset over it, because of course his time has just started.

IT WAS A SUNNY afternoon in Albany and my brother and I were home together after school. I guess our maid Frances was there—who was employed mostly for me but also to make sure Jeff didn't blow something up—but to tell the truth, in this strikingly vivid memory of our youth, I don't remember her presence. Maybe she had to leave early that day and Mother wasn't yet home from teaching. Perhaps she was sick. Or perhaps she *was* there but, with this memory being so focused on my brother, Frances's presence, over time, has faded far into the background.

I was probably six at the time, maybe seven, Jeff eleven or twelve. He had a couple of friends over and they were intensely busy outside with something. I slipped out of the sliding glass door on the side of the house that led to the patio to try to investigate, but Jeff shooed me back inside. Clearly, I thought with the exasperation that only a seven-year-old can muster, they're cooking up something and don't want me to be part of it. When Jeff had friends over, I took a decidedly clear back seat as a rival for his attention.

I had been outside long enough to see a bottle of some kind and a mixture they were working on. I also had had enough experience as a younger sister by now to know that if Jeff didn't even want me observing, then whatever he was involved in would probably not end well.

Back inside, I busied myself doing I'm not sure what. In a few minutes, I heard a crash from outside in the direction of my brother and his friends, and I strategically positioned myself along the passageway that led from the sliding glass door, between our dining room table and living room, and into the hallway of bedrooms and bath. It did not take long for the sliding glass door to open and my brother to enter the house clutching his knee, fresh with blood and glass shards protruding. As he rushed past me headed to our bathroom, he said in a distinctly frantic voice, "Don't tell Mama and Daddy; don't tell Mama and Daddy!"

I watched him go by, saying nothing.

Some short minutes later, he passed by again, limping and clutching his knee gingerly, carrying something to try to stem the tide of blood and doctor the wound as best he could.

His refrain was the same…"Don't tell Mama and Daddy; don't tell Mama and Daddy!"

I shook my head back and forth, but again, was silent.

I would like to say that I was not much of a tattle tell, but truth is, at that age, I had a penchant for that kind of thing—after all, a girl has to have something in her arsenal when her brother is five years older!—so Jeff's plea was not unfounded. Despite my relative inexperience with life at that age, I distinctly remember understanding that in *this* situation, I would not have to say a thing. Even if Jeff attempted a cover-up, the evidence was in plain sight and utterly damning.

Only later did I find out that my brother and his friends had been mixing up their own, homemade version of an incendiary device with baking soda and vinegar. I'm not entirely sure what possessed them to do so. Inquisitive souls? A science experiment? Boys will be boys? Influence of the Vietnam War? It was probably a combination of all those things. But when the bottle, shaken and under pressure, slipped out of Jeff's hands and onto our patio, their homemade effort at an incendiary device was a success. It exploded, right into my brother's knee.

I never said a word to Mother and Daddy. They found out anyway.

BY THE SUMMER OF 1967 when Daddy was at Fort Lee, the United States was in its second decade of involvement in Vietnam. True, President Johnson had just ordered ground troops to the area in 1965, and the official beginning as acknowledged by the Vietnam Veterans Memorial dates to November 1955. But, in reality, our involvement dated back to the Truman administration, which began providing military aid and equipment to the French to help fight off the attempt by the Vietnamese to throw off colonial rule.

In many ways, our concern and subsequent mistakes in Vietnam paralleled those of Korea. The country had been divided toward the end of WWII along the 17th parallel, with communist insurgency, led by Ho Chi Minh, in the North, and British and French influence in the South. As with Korea, though, Ho Chi

Minh and his followers were much more interested in getting rid of the French than in some kind of plan to bring communism to the world. The North Vietnamese finally defeated the French for an end to colonial rule in 1954. By this time, the United States was fully committed to its domino theory of foreign policy, believing that each fall to communism would result in another falling domino on the path to an eventual communist takeover. So despite the promise at the 1954 peace conference of nationwide elections to unite the country in two years, no elections took place, and the U.S. began propping up the South Vietnamese by training their army.

The number of military personnel in Vietnam expanded from roughly 900 to 16,000 during Kennedy's two and a half years in office, including military advisors, equipment, and air and naval support of the South Vietnamese Army. But none of this aid enabled the South to defeat the North and reunite the country under non-communist leadership, which is the only way we would, at least at this point, settle for unification. In retrospect, then, it seems all but inevitable that the difficult decision of committing ground troops to the cause would fall to President Johnson, as Marines landed on the beaches near Da Nang, South Vietnam, in March 1965.

The reality, then, for military families, particularly those of Marines, soldiers and airmen, shifted dramatically that spring as the threat of war once again loomed large over households. Two years later, with Daddy at Fort Lee, the situation was only worse, and Mother kept Daddy abreast of the comings and goings of families we knew, and the associated horror of war.

May 7, 1967, Albany

The Blackmons are leaving. (Remember the colored family from chapel?) He has orders to Vietnam. They had been here 9½ years.

May 17, 1967, Albany

Honey, a young Albany man was killed in action. The chaplain went to deliver notice today. He and his young wife had been high school sweethearts (Dougherty

High) and were married just 5 days before he left for Vietnam. The wife went into shock. Chaplain Howard has been really busy with those things lately.

Daddy's reply acknowledged that he was sure the chaplain must be busy with all the fighting, and dying, over in Vietnam. It was not an easy time to be a military chaplain, as word came into base headquarters and he was left to deliver notice to the family and then, at times, officiate over the funeral. *Things sure don't look good in this old world today,* Daddy lamented.

Years later, I would read the journal that my brother-in-law Roger kept while a corpsman in Vietnam, and understand through his first-person narrative how truly horrific the situation was over there.

> It is blood chilling to hear the "pop" of a mortar being dropped into its tube; of the sound of someone yelling, "incoming," and the faint whistling sound of the missile itself. One hugs the ground, trying to become part of it, wondering where this round will land. One lone, last mortar fell harmlessly at about 0230. By that time, most people were dug in and I was busy with the casualties. I had two people die while trying to save them. I felt utterly helpless.

Roger had enlisted because he knew his draft number was coming up, choosing the Navy as a way to stay out of the worst action, which took place on the ground and in the air. However, he was summarily sent to train in the medical corps as a corpsman because, well, in someone's mind, he must already possess some medical knowledge since his father was a doctor. Once trained, he was issued a sidearm and attached to a Marine platoon; the man he replaced had died in action. Far from sitting out the war on a Navy cruiser, he found himself in the middle of it. He spent the rest of his life trying to find a way to chase the demons away. When he lay dying from lung cancer years later, the Marines he had served showed up to say goodbye to the man they knew as "Doc."

Our mother must have lived in a somewhat constant state of worry that Daddy would get orders for Vietnam, but she never voiced it to us or let it bleed over into our lives. When one of the other wives told Mother at tea one April Sunday afternoon shortly after Daddy had left that her husband *got orders right after coming back from that <u>same</u> school* and Daddy probably would too, our Mother, usually the soul of Southern decorum, remarked to Daddy, *she's about as friendly as a cobra!* Despite her ability to protect us from certain realities, her comment toward the end of May—*The world situation really looks terrible, doesn't it? I worry so very much*—surely had an underlying meaning.

There were the "lucky" ones who had returned in one piece physically, although who knew what demons lay buried inside. *Don Ivers came home Wednesday,* she wrote Daddy the day after informing him of the death of the young man from Albany. *He is thinner and very brown. The kids are so cute. They won't let him out of their sight.*

There were also the general comings and goings of military life—*the Goodnoes left today*—and other happenings on base. Some were delightful, such as the General and his wife attending after-church coffee—*they sure are lovely people.* Others, as in the death of a sergeant from a heart attack or the chaplain's assistant attempting suicide, were mournful and shocking. As was their way, Mother shared it all.

May 16, 1967, Albany

Honey, some teenage kids have been giving Frances a bad time. They have been laughing at her, even coming up under the carport to the window and laughing, talking, etc. Today, the kids were getting off the bus and they started this "n--, n--" bit.

WHEN THE MOVIE *THE Help* came out in theaters in 2011, my twenty-year-old daughter and I went to see it. Neither of us had read the book, although we both subsequently would, but we knew enough about the film and its story surrounding Black women who served as domestics in early 1960s Mississippi to recognize that it was fairly familiar territory for me. My own daughter had grown up just outside Washington, D.C., but had had experiences with the South since we still went down there each summer to visit family.

At the end of the film, as the lights came up and the credits rolled, Anna turned to me. I was just on the verge of asking her what she thought of the movie when she said, "Oh my gosh, you're Mae Mobley." She was referring to the three-year-old that the Viola Davis character, Aibileen, took care of while she cooked for, and cleaned the home of, the Leefolt family. The film was set in 1963. I turned three in 1963. Off and on, I grew up with a maid helping to take care of me. I nodded and affirmed, "Yes, I guess I am."

We were not wealthy like the characters in *The Help*. There were no dinner parties or afternoon teas that Frances cooked and served for. She did not work for us on weekends. As far as I remember, she was there to do some housework and take care of Jeff and me until Mother got home from school. I like to think that my parents were good employers, who, thanks in part to being part of a military that had desegregated in 1948, were fair-minded people who tried to treat all people well.

And yet, our father, whom I adored during my growing up above all other men, who worked alongside people of color most of his life and who, in his later years, counted at least one as a good friend, also, at times, privately told racist jokes and held fast to certain racial stereotypes. We were, in truth, still part of a racist system that, though perhaps more obvious in the South, defined the entire country and institutionalized the ways of White privilege that continue to this day.

At the age of six, I didn't know that I was living in a time of great turmoil and change in the country. The boycotts, marches, freedom rides, sit-ins, and other nonviolent protests of the fifties and sixties had brought enough pressure to bear that Congress, with significant support from President Johnson, had finally passed the Civil Rights Act in 1964. The 1965 Voting Rights Act followed on its heels. We didn't know it yet, but a tumultuous 1968 was just on the horizon, a year that would see the tragic assassinations of Martin Luther King Jr. and Bobby Kennedy, race riots throughout many U.S. cities, and Black athletic protests throughout the country that culminated in Tommie Smith and John Carlos's raised, gloved fists at the Mexico City Olympics in September. Toward the end of the decade and early into the next, protests against the Vietnam War would continue to grow as public opinion turned against our involvement there, and Blacks who had witnessed their own make up a disproportionate share of combat deaths during the mid-sixties, joined the anti-war movement.

No, at the age of six, I didn't know any of this. I lived in a somewhat blissful state of ignorance to it all. I was yet to grapple with the effects racism and its twin, White privilege, have had on our society, on me, and with my participation in a system that has privileged White skin over all others and made our lives far easier and safer than persons of color. I never stopped to consider what maids gave up to be with White families, what it meant to them to leave their own children in the afternoon, what it meant to these kids to come home to what was probably an empty house, their mothers off taking care of some White family's children. All I knew was that, in the afternoons, I had Frances.

It was as if my parents had brought her there just for me. Jeff was usually off doing his own thing, playing with friends, at ball practice or scouts, or doing homework, so I often had Frances all to myself. She played games with me, my favorite of which was to chase her around the house in order to catch and tickle her. She was frightfully ticklish, although, in retrospect, I wonder how much of it was an act meant to entertain me, particularly given my tiny little fingers. Whichever, it did the trick. Mother confessed that she came home many an afternoon to the sight of Frances flying around the front of the house with me trailing behind, both of us laughing and me squealing in delight. I can still remember Mother admonishing me to let poor Frances rest.

The reality, though, was that we did live in the Deep South, and no military base would insulate Frances or the other people of color from the racial slurs that were a regular part of our society. In an earlier time, we might never have found out about it, Frances may have just figured it was her "place" to endure such behavior, that no good would come out of saying anything to any White person. But for whatever reason, perhaps because of the advances earlier in the decade or because she knew the kind of person our mother was and felt she could talk to her, Frances came to Mother to tell her what was going on.

Mother confessed to Daddy that she didn't know what to do. Our mother didn't particularly like conflict, but she also couldn't abide meanness, and she certainly didn't shy away from standing up for what she felt was right. But she also understood the South, having lived in it most of her life. She must have also still been adjusting to her relatively new role as an officer's wife and how heavily or lightly she should tread in different situations. In the end, she decided to seek help.

May 16, 1967, Albany

I didn't know what to do about it. So I talked to Father Berulio; Chaplain Howard wasn't available. He said he would handle it and use no names and would first discuss it with Chaplain H. in the morning. I hope I did the right thing. He said I did, that neither Frances should have to put up with it, nor should I have to worry about it.

There was no more discussion of it in Mother's letters, and the letter where Daddy referenced the situation is consigned to the ages, although I imagine his reply going something like, honey, I'm sorry you had to deal with that, you did the right thing, and I hope you and Frances don't have to put up with anymore of that mess.

At the age of six, though, all I knew was that, in the afternoons, I had Frances.

TO SAY THAT MOTHER got used to dealing with situations while separated from Daddy may not exactly reflect her lived reality. But she certainly had a variety of things to deal with while he was gone that spring and summer of 1967, some of them far beyond anything she might have imagined.

I've had a couple of blows lately that have left me rather shaken, Mother confessed to Daddy in early May, just a couple of weeks after he had left for Fort Lee. The first "blow" was that one of her teacher acquaintances *has been almost too friendly since you left and today she almost propositioned me.* Questioning whether it had really happened—*I thought perhaps I had imagined it*—but clearly upset and unsure how to handle the delicate situation, Mother found an opportunity to speak with another friend as they rode together to a teacher's meeting, and she assured Mother that there had been no imagining, for she had had a similar encounter with their mutual acquaintance.

May 2, 1967, Albany

Helen said she had been worried with you gone that I might have her over but didn't know how she could tell me. I have plans to eat at Shoney's with her next week (the children are going too) and our librarian is meeting us also. Helen said she wouldn't worry about that just steer clear after that. This has been so disappointing to me. Please try not to worry. I'm going to keep distance, and plenty of it.

Daddy wrote immediately after receiving her letter that he was sorry to hear about what had happened. *Those things do go on. Just stay away from her,* he assured her.

Still needing additional reassurance, Mother decided a couple of days later to go talk with the chaplain about the incident. Chaplain Howard, the protestant chaplain stationed at the base chapel in Albany, had by this time become a good friend of our family. It seemed wherever we went our parents befriended the local clergy, in part because that's just who they were but also because they became active in whatever church or chapel we attended. *He said I had handled it well and he didn't think I'd have any more trouble, but to make sure someone is always around.*

Things finally settled down, for Mother indicated that everything had been *as normal as can be,* which might have been at least in part due to the woman in question having hooked up with a Marine whose wife had left him with five children. Mother told Daddy that the two had been sitting together at PTA (Parent-Teacher Association) meetings and there seemed to be no mentioning one name without the other. *Maybe this will help her,* our mother observed, *but I don't know what it will do to him!*

The second "blow" that had lately shaken Mother concerned her teaching position. She was in the process of changing her teaching certificate over to general classroom since the few music jobs available were much harder to come by. However, she was not going to be able to do the course work necessary that summer to continue working on the change because we planned to leave as soon as school was out to stay in Greensboro for the first part of the summer so we would be closer to Daddy and see him on the weekends. The school superintendent explained that if she didn't do the summer course work, she would put the school in jeopardy of losing its accreditation. Mother told the superintendent she would just have to be replaced, then; she clearly was not giving up the plan for us to be closer to Daddy as soon as she could make that happen.

Fortunately, however, when Mother returned to school after her conversation with the superintendent, she spoke with her principal who informed her to sign her contract and forget about it, that she could have some teachers teaching out of field without the threat of losing accreditation, and she only had a few at present. She assured Mother she could have a fifth-grade classroom next year.

Daddy had written her not to worry about the job; *you don't have to work if you don't want to anyway.* But as hard as it could be to manage a teaching career, raise two children and be a Marine, now officer's, wife, I think our mother really enjoyed working. She loved learning herself and she adored children, so it was a good combination. She even had a way of engaging us in ways to help. *This is report card weekend,* she wrote Daddy right after he left, *and Jeff and Mike [spending the night] helped me average some grades tonight.* But I think she also liked contributing to the family income. Their financial situation had strengthened considerably since the Okinawa years so that Daddy could reassure her periodically that she didn't *have* to work, but I believe it made her feel better about the money she spent to know that she was bringing some in as well. That said, she and Daddy used to joke about the pittance of a teacher's salary she received. Clearly, she didn't do it for the money, and I'm sure there were times, particularly when she was left to handle things on her own, when she wondered if it was all worth it. But she poured out her worries to Daddy so that she could stay positive for Jeff and me.

It had been ten years earlier that Daddy had been in Okinawa; for our mother, that must have seemed a lifetime before. She had been thirty-one at the time, a young mother of a bright, active twenty-month-old son, living with her parents. Now here she was a decade later with a son on the cusp of his teen years and a daughter in her first year of elementary school. She was a wife, a mother, a teacher, a newly commissioned officer's wife, and a church choir member. Makes me tired just to think about it. In some ways, the three months that Daddy spent at Fort Lee that summer must have seemed longer than those fourteen he had spent on Okinawa. I'm sure she considered herself one of the lucky ones that her husband was in Virginia rather than Vietnam. Still, staying positive for Jeff and me couldn't have been easy. I like to think that, in the absence of family, two things helped tremendously—having a network of good friends on base, and the joy of keeping our father up to date on their children.

12

It Takes a Village

I T WAS A TYPICALLY COLD WINTER EVENING IN Argentia, Newfoundland, and snow lay on the ground. Jeff was involved with some extracurricular activity or perhaps over at a friend's, while Mother and Daddy both had evening commitments and had gotten their calendars crossed up so that they had not made any arrangements for their three-year-old daughter. They checked around with friends, but it seemed as if everyone was tied up. When Mother finally got around to calling our good friends, the Sassamans, it was the same story; Helen had something going on and Glen had his bowling league. But Mr. Sassaman said he wouldn't mind watching me as long as it was okay that I went with him to the bowling alley. Desperate at this point to find a solution, she agreed.

I guess this was my first memory because I can still see the bowling alley in my mind, remember skipping and hopping up and down the few steps that led to the chairs and tables situated around each lane. It was a glorious evening unlike any other I had spent up to that point. And I was completely comfortable with Mr. Sassaman; he was funny and would joke with me to see how high I could raise my arms and then tickle me when I did. It was our version of Charlie Brown and Lucy and the football. I would protest that I knew what he was up to and he would say no, not this time, he just wanted to see how high I could reach, how much I'd grown. So I would fall for it, he would tickle me, and I would erupt into little-girl giggles.

When Mother pulled up into the parking space later in the evening to pick me up, she found me outside, jumping up and down the steps in front of the bowling alley with a huge smile on my face. Clearly it didn't take a lot to entertain me at the age of three. I raced into her arms and told her how much fun Mr. Sassaman and I had had; she took my hand and we entered the bowling alley to say goodbye to my newfound babysitter. He and Mother chatted a bit, I gave him a big hug, and Mother and I left, my big adventure over.

I found out a few years later that, as Mother thanked Mr. Sassaman, he said it was his pleasure, that I was no trouble at all. And, as a bonus, I had been a wealth of information. I knew Mr. Sassaman well enough and felt so comfortable with him that, although reticent with most people, I had been all talk that evening, letting forth on some innocent family secrets. With a wicked grin that characterized this Naval and future NASA engineer, he told Mother he would be happy to watch me anytime they needed him to.

May 27, 1967, Albany

Babe, this hasn't been much of a letter. I hope I haven't depressed you; just a bunch of things happening at once. I'm doing fine, with the help of the Hemlepps. Maybe when Mick leaves we'll be able to repay some of their kindness.

ONE OF THE GREAT privileges of being part of the military is the huge village of friends who steps in to help when the Marine, soldier, sailor, or airman is deployed or away on temporary assignment. You have a sense that if you are on the receiving end now, there will come a day when the situation will turn around and you will have the opportunity, as Mother wrote, to repay some of their kindness.

Throughout the time Daddy was at Fort Lee, there were all manner of difficulties that Mother did not have to face alone thanks to our own village. Car trouble cropped up often—the back wheel bearing, motor mount, problems with the accelerator—these were all left to her to handle and, though Daddy was more accessible than he had been ten years earlier in Okinawa, she usually had to figure a course ahead without passing it by him. But, generally, there was someone right there living in base housing who stepped up to help.

May 27, 1967, Saturday morning, Albany

When I got in the car at school, I noticed that the clutch was dragging or "grabbing" and planned to come home, see Jeff, and go back to the service station. When I got on base, I heard a scrape. It got worse so I turned around in front of the Hemlepps and headed toward the S.S. [service station]. I pulled in GySgt. Shaeffer's drive just at the beginning of housing. He talked to me and listened and called the garage. It is the right back wheel bearing. He said he would call me before noon today, that he couldn't get to it yesterday. I don't know how bad or how much, but I didn't know what else to do.

We also became friends with one of the Naval doctors stationed there, as Marines get their medical care from the Navy. Mother and Mrs. Robeson sang in the choir together and often sang duets, or trios with one of the other doctor's wife. *The Robesons ask about you and send a greeting each time I see them,* she relayed to Daddy in mid-May. A couple of weeks later when Jeff returned from a weekend campout with the Boy Scouts, Mother needed to rely on Dr. Robeson for his medical expertise.

June 1, 1967, Albany

Jeff has an infected bite from the swamps. Right on the front of his leg. I was shocked when I saw it tonight. All red streaked and full of pus. I called Jim Robeson and he said Jeff really needed to be on penicillin. He called down to the dispensary and I drove down to pick it up tonight. He warned me that he might run a fever. He said he was glad I saw it 'cause Jeff really needed penicillin. Of course, he sends greetings. I really think he hates the fact that you won't be back before he leaves.

Unfortunately, the Robesons had orders for transfer to a new duty station, one of the great sadnesses of military life.

We also became close to Chaplain Howard, who was available for counsel and dinners, and his friend, Clarence Fuquay, one of the chapel deacons. Both of them were sources of joy, comfort, and laughter.

May 21, 1967, Albany

Today Clarence F. asked me after church if the children and I would come over for homemade ice cream. I said yes, and that I had some frozen peaches that he could use. The Hemlepps were invited, too. We really had a good time and the ice cream was "delicious." But it was a little hard to swallow sometimes for thinking of you, knowing how you like homemade ice cream and especially peach.

Chaplain Howard told me to say hello to you. He said he really misses having you around to harass him.

Yet no one was more present for us during that time nor came to mean as much to us as our close friends the Hemlepps. They had two daughters around my age and we were fast friends. We were constantly popping over to one another's homes for dinner or a visit, often without Mr. Hemlepp, who *has worked the awfulest hours for the past few weeks.* Mrs. Hemlepp had been sitting with me the evenings Mother had choir practice, so when we got the chance to help them out, she jumped at the chance to return the kindness.

May 5, 1967, Albany

I'm down at Ruth's "sitting" tonight. She has been keeping Jenny for me during choir practice—Jeff has his patrol meeting then. I had asked for them to let me sit sometimes. They needed to do some shopping so I'm down here. Jeff is at home and Mike Forrester is staying with him. He and Mike get along so well.

Of course, Jenny loves to be here. She thinks there's no one like the Hemlepp girls.

It was fitting, then, that they were available to help Mother and me through one of the most difficult situations we were to encounter while Daddy was away.

Mother and I had seen Jeff off on a Friday afternoon as he left to go with an advance group out to Okeenefenoke Swamp to help set up for the Scouts' weekend camping trip, the very same trip that gifted him the infected bite on his leg. After we had dinner that evening, the Hemlepps called and invited us to go see *Born Free*, the movie playing at the base theater. But when we were getting ready to leave, Mother noticed our dog Rusty had come outside to go to the bathroom. Frances had told her that he had been sick, so she had planned for us to take him to the vet on Saturday when she got the car back from the garage, for it was the same day she had stopped to seek help for our ailing car at GySgt. Shaeffer's. But Rusty's condition was clearly not going to wait. *He was having convulsions. It was just terrible, shaking and drawing up all over*, she recounted to Daddy in her letter the following day.

Mr. Hemlepp tried contacting first the Game Warden, then the vet, but it was Friday evening and both places were already closed. They finally hit upon the idea of calling the MPs (military police) to come pick him up and put him to sleep, and Mr. Hemlepp stayed behind while Mrs. Hemlepp skirted Mother and me away in their car.

But as she tried to get an update on our beloved dauchsand the following day, she couldn't get any information, and the weekend had been just about more than she could handle.

May 27, 1967, Saturday afternoon, Albany

I can't seem to find out anything about Rusty. I called this morning (County Health) and they're closed over the weekend. I hope they went ahead and put him to sleep. I'd sure hate to think he was over there suffering.

May 27, 1967, Saturday night, Albany

My darling George,

How wonderful to hear your voice. I feel so terrible that it was so obvious how miserable I was. Talking to you helped more than I can say. I had been so disgusted with myself that I had had so many things happen that I couldn't work out by myself.

Honey, I sure am sorry about Rusty. Jenny was sure upset for a while. She didn't see any of it, but I had to tell her because the Magers' kids had seen him convulsing and kept asking, "Is Rusty dead?" Today I had to tell her. She just cried and cried, but seemed to understand. (I just told her he died.) I sure dread to tell Jeff about him tomorrow.

The most heartbreaking part of the whole episode was yet to come, though.

May 28, 1967, Sunday night, Albany
Dearest George,

Jeff got home about 5:30 and he was one tired, dirty boy. I don't know when I've ever been madder! The Magers' kids all raced up yelling, "Guess what? Rusty's dead!" By the time Jeff got to the house he was all to pieces. He really was hurt and it embarrassed him that he had broken down in front of everyone. Dorothy P. told them how cruel it was, but of course the damage was done.

Rusty died from heartworms, a disease that plagued any number of dogs until veterinarians found a way to monitor and prevent them. I have images from that night, mostly a realization that Rusty was sick. Mother, with considerable help from the Hemlepps, protected me from the worst of it, from seeing the convulsions and understanding how sick a dog he really was. But sadly, and to her considerable anger, she was unable to protect Jeff from hearing about this stinging loss from someone besides her.

May 20, 1967, Albany
Dear Dad,

We just got through playing a game of ball. As usual, we lost. I played first base for about two and a half innings. I pitched the rest of the game.

The scouts are going to the swamps next weekend. I hope I can go, and Mother said I could. Mr. Patton asked me if I was going. When I said, "Yes, I am," he said, "I'll feed you to the crocks." Ha, ha, fat chance. They could not chew me up; I'm so tough.
Love,
Jeff

IT WAS MY GOOD fortune to grow up in a time when little league base ball was the game of choice for most young boys who played team sports, at least in the South. If I was going to have to sit there for my brother's games, at least it could be baseball. Football wouldn't come until high school for Jeff, and I'm not even sure we knew that soccer existed.

Jeff ended up pitching quite a bit during his little league career and, though inconsistent, at times was pretty good. He was to earn the distinction one year of being the only pitcher to pitch a no-hitter, and lose, 1–0, which can happen when you walk a batter who ends up stealing a couple of bases and then comes home on a wild pitch. He was thoroughly disgusted with himself at the time but it became good legend in our family.

That spring season of 1967 was to be a rough one for Jeff and his team, the Dodgers, who ended up winning their first game of the season but then lost their final thirteen, sometimes with wildly unbalanced scores. With Daddy gone for pretty much the entire season and longing to be there—*wish I could be there to see him play some*—descriptions of Jeff's games filled Mother's letters. Despite the losses, Jeff was one of the cornerstones of the team and made some important contributions on offense, as in a game in early May when he hit a triple, reached base twice more, and scored each time. *Jeff's playing good ball*, Mother wrote, *but they only have about 5 that can play, and they can't be everywhere.* Mother tried to encourage them early in the season by reminding Jeff and his friends that the previous year the Mets lost their first four games but then ended up in first place by the end of the season. But eventually, there was no sugar coating the unending string of losses, and the team was pretty discouraged.

Jeff's early forays into pitching proved a difficult learning experience.

April 25, 1967, Albany

Jeff pitched part of a game tonight and I'm glad you weren't here to see it. He was put in to pitch in the 2nd inning when the score was 13–0, favor Yankees. Some other kid had pitched. By then the Dodgers were scared to death. Jeff walked a couple, struck out a couple, and went completely wild. When the inning was over,

18–0. Mike Forrester finished the game and he didn't do too well. The other team was starting to play poorly and didn't get more runs but the final score was 18–6.

A week later, a blow struck when Jeff's friend Mike, one of the other corner-stones of the team, was out for the rest of the season with a hernia. Jeff had not pitched since the April 25 game, but had been practicing because, with Mike out, he knew he'd be in there again before long. He pitched again on May 20 and did a lot better, but the game was pretty much lost before he got up to pitch. Despite the loss, he caught the attention of an assistant to the opposing coach.

May 20, 1967, Albany

Mr. Curtis, who assists Mr. Henne, came up after the game and said, "Son, I'd like to tell you what you're doing wrong," and talked to Jeff awhile. He said he'd sure like to work with Jeff, that he showed great promise. Someone said that Curtis knew more than any coach there and had played semi-pro ball for a few years. He sure has the respect of all the coaches. I told him I'd be glad for him to, but perhaps Jeff ought to tell his coach, so it wouldn't look bad.

May 24, 1967, Fort Lee

By all means, let Mr. Curtis work with Jeff. If he played semi-pro ball he must be good and if he thinks Jeff has good promise.

A few days later, Jeff pitched his first complete game, to an 11–5 loss. *I thought he would be terribly discouraged,* Mother related to Daddy, *but he said, "Mother, 11–5 is better than 33–3, isn't it?"* If there was a bit of sage wisdom our mother left with us besides "life isn't fair," it was to try to always look for the silver lining.

When he wasn't pitching, Jeff usually played first, except for the game when one of the coaches told him to get on the catcher's gear, and he had fun relating the story to our father.

May 10, 1967, Albany

I said, "Me? I've never caught before." "You don't won't [want] to," he asked. "Yes," I said. "What have we got to lose?" At that time, they were ahead by some

20 odd points. I caught pretty good for my first time.

That was the game they ended up losing 33–3.

Mother did not limit the baseball news to simply recounting the games. Like any seasoned parent of a child playing team sports, she provided commentary on what went on in the stands and her thoughts on the coaching staff. A losing season, in particular, often generates strong feelings from the stands, and little league in 1967 Southwest Georgia was no different. Following their fourth straight loss, Mother commented on the ugly behavior of the parents, and many of them mothers from their own team—*the crudest, most big mouth women I have ever seen.* She considered taking Jeff out for a bit but was concerned that everyone would think she had done it because the Dodgers were having such a lousy season. *I just sit there and grade papers between times and try to ignore them.*

By the end of the horrible season, Mother used her letters to Daddy to do her own venting.

May 31, 1967, Albany

Jeff played again tonight...and they lost. It's just tragic! Jeff stole bases and got one fabulous run. Then later in the game he was put out of the game. The coach put him out because he threw the helmet down. Of course, I didn't tell Jeff, but I would have probably thrown it at him! Jackson knows too little about ball and boys to be coaching—12 straight losses!

June 3, 1967, Albany

What a relief—this horrible ball season is over! Jeff's last game was today. That was another loss. He's so glad it's over.

Jeff got selected for All-Stars, but the game was to be June 19, after we were scheduled to leave for Greensboro. The coaches tried to get the game changed to June 10 so that we could delay by a couple of days and Jeff could play in the game, but it turned out the trophies wouldn't be ready in time, so unfortunately, Jeff missed the game. By that time, though, while I'm sure he was excited to be selected, he was also just ready to be done with a thoroughly horrible season.

April 22, 1967, Albany
Dear Daddy:

I miss you. I love you very much. We get our report Wednesday. Who will give me my dollar? Write soon to me.
Love,
Jenny

AFTER DADDY RETIRED FROM the Marine Corps and we moved from one side of Albany to another, our parents purchased a house on Acker Drive, just half a block from both the Baptist church we joined and from Sherwood Elementary School, where I attended third through sixth grades. I think our mother finally gave up the dream of returning to Beaufort once Daddy got the job at Doublegate. The proverbial handwriting was on the wall at that point. They held onto our house there for a while longer but eventually sold it.

Although by the time I graduated from college I could not imagine returning to Albany, Georgia, the area where we lived was a pretty great place to grow up. I walked the short half block to and from school, sometimes by myself, sometimes with friends, and my friends and I had the run of the subdivisions in the area on our bikes. In the summer following third grade, my best friend Gina and I daily checked out the construction sites of the new houses, scavenging for Coke bottles the workmen left behind, collecting them to turn in for the ten-cent deposit at the Quickie, our local convenience store. Our collection of dimes we then used to buy Coca-Cola Icees, our frozen drink of choice and the perfect refreshment on a hot and humid Southwest Georgia day. Once empty, we would tear the coupons off the cups, add them to our stash, and re-count them until the day we had enough to send off for our prizes. For eight-year-olds, we had quite an operation going.

During the school year, however, I was pretty much all business. By fourth grade, two years into Sherwood school, I had developed a reputation among the teachers as a good, dedicated student. These were the days before I professed to our father my hatred of school, and I was happy to be so designated.

Following the close of the third grading period of that fourth-grade year, we arrived to what was known as "report card day," when, at the end of the day, the teachers passed out the stiff, letter stock report cards that had the new grades added in, handwritten by our teachers. I waited with contained excitement, anticipating that I might have done well enough to get all "A"s, although I was never quite sure about math and science; there could be a couple of "B+"s. By that time, Daddy was paying us a dollar for each "A" we earned, and I anticipated collecting a nice little sum. I was, after all, my father's daughter.

I usually waited until I got outside to pull my card out of its little jacket so that I had some privacy and didn't have to go through the awkward moments of sharing my grades with inquiring friends. As I began the short walk home, I pulled the report card out to a collection of "A"s. But all I could focus on was a big fat "C." For what subject, I wondered, as my eyes began to blur a bit. I looked across the row and read "Social Studies." Completely distraught, tears rolled down my cheeks. Social studies was my favorite subject and I just couldn't believe I had earned a "C." Our parents never put pressure on us to make certain grades; they only asked us to do our best, which, in this case, I knew was above a "C." I have since come to re-evaluate my thinking on grading and what it means, but then, well, I was pretty devastated.

I made my way to the house quickly, trying to keep things together as best I could until I walked in and dissolved in a mass of tears into my mother's arms.

"Sweetie, what's wrong," Mother asked me as she gently patted my back.

"I got a "C" on my report card," I wailed. "In social studies!"

"Oh no, that *can't* be right. There must be some mistake. I saw all the papers you brought home; you never had anything less than a 'B+'."

"But it's right there," I pointed. I was still at the age where what a teacher had written down in ink surely was infallible. I continued wailing. I was on the verge of what Papa Jack used to call the "snubs," the point where you've cried so hard that you have to stop for a few, intermittent sniffs.

Mother hugged me some more and insisted that it was going to be all right. She knew Mrs. Horton, my social studies teacher, well, and said she would call her and simply ask if there had been a mistake. Which she did, almost immediately, and there had been.

Mrs. Horton's response was virtually the same as Mother's—oh no, that can't be right—as she went on to tell my mother that I was one of her best students. She went straight to her grade book and discovered that she had picked up the student's grade in the row just below mine. I had made an "A," and she would change it on my card if I would bring it back the following day.

She hung up the phone and told me the good news—"now, see there, it was nothing to get upset over"—and I let relief wash over me.

It was to be my only close call with a "C" until Georgia Tech, when I did get a "C" in Geology my first semester. I thought I had signed up for the science elective that Management majors affectionately called, "Rocks for Jocks," an easy way to get three of our nine-credit science/engineering electives, but I found out too late that I was in the introductory course for Building Construction majors. I have never been so happy to see a "C" in all my life and could have kissed Dr. Pollard for what I'm sure was a serious exercise in curving. (My fellow GT Yellow Jackets, you know what I mean!)

In the spring of 1967, though, finishing up my first year in elementary school, my two, very different, encounters with what I considered the dreaded "C" were all ahead of me. My major concern when it came to report card time was, with Daddy gone for so long and so far away, who would give me my dollar? I suppose I felt sure enough of myself to think that a dollar, which is what we earned at that time for a good report, was safely in my future.

April 26, 1967, Albany
My dearest husband,

We are getting along fine. Everything is going very nicely, if you don't count loneliness or an ache for someone you love! The children really are doing well. I was so pleased with their report cards. Jeff brought Arithmetic and Science up to 1E and both children got 1E on Respect for Authority. Jeff did an amazing thing; he dropped to a 3S in Reading. All the rest were 2s. Jenny is the "gal" of the moment. All 1S, and all habits and attitudes Excellent, but [for] 2 that were S. Isn't that wonderful? She is very proud and Jeff and I are so proud of her.

Jeff and I are so proud of her. That and my own satisfaction with a job well done were, in truth, more important than the dollar, although my brother would probably take issue with that, insisting that I still own the first nickel I ever made. But at the age of six, I was still enough in awe of my bubba that his praise and admiration were nourishment that lit me up from inside. If he was willing to bring me in on a plan, then I was all in. And once in awhile, that plan did *not* involve blowing something up, but rather quite the opposite.

May 24, 1967, Albany
My dearest,

These days are very long and lonely. Things are going all right but we sure do miss you around here. I went to choir practice and Jeff and Jenny stayed here. I got back before dark. Those kids had weeded the flower beds and washed the dishes. I hadn't even asked them to. I was so pleased and very touched. They said they did it because they wanted to!

With five years between us, he was very much my protector, and, while once he was "grown up" enough to be in junior high school he didn't seem to want me tagging along much, no one was allowed to disrespect or mess with his little sister. In truth, Jeff has always been very protective of me. Sometimes that extended to him protecting me from his own superior knowledge, him being vastly older and wiser than me.

Hard though it must have been for him, he kept the mystery of Santa Claus sacrosanct for me long after he had given up believing. Although, come to think of it, he did it partially under the threat of our father and with good reason. Jeff had announced to our parents that the game was up, that he knew that *they* were really Santa. To which our father replied, "Boy, you better not ruin this for your sister." And in case he needed further incentive, Daddy added, "and if there is no Santa, then your Mother and I don't have to bother putting out presents." My brother rapidly became a believer once again, allowing me to live in blissful, youthful innocence for a few more years.

It was one of those years while we were still living on the Marine Base in Albany when that youthful innocence, some Christmas excitement, and, well, okay, a certain amount of disobedience if I'm totally honest, all came together to produce a close encounter with that jolly guy himself. I was five or six at the time; it was Christmas Eve and past my bedtime, but I just could not settle. The tree glistened with lights and a number of presents adorned its base. The promise of Santa was that he would bring more sometime in the night, and our parents were staunch believers that no presents should be opened until Christmas morning. It could almost be too much for a little girl to bear, but there it was; I knew by now there was no changing their minds on this.

Mother and Daddy had told me a number of times that I needed to get to bed, but in an unusual bout of defiance, I danced and hopped around, laughing and playing and wondering with Jeff if tomorrow morning would bring the special stuff we had requested from Santa.

"You know, sweetie"—Mother was being beyond patient with me but was pulling out every idea in her arsenal to get me in bed—"Santa won't stop at our house if you're not in bed."

I wasn't quite sure what Mother was thinking. Of course I knew that. This was *not* my first Christmas. I had been around the block a few times with the holiday and considered myself a seasoned professional, but I wisely kept that strain of reasoning to myself.

"Oh, he doesn't come till later," I responded. Mother let it go. She was always pretty good about choosing her battles.

So I danced and hopped around some more until...I thought I heard the sound of sleigh bells and a faint "ho ho ho," in the distance. No, I thought. It can't be. But it caught my attention so I halted my antics to listen more closely.

"Ho, ho, ho, Mer-ry Christmas." This time there was no mistaking. Santa had arrived and it sounded as if he was right outside our door.

I wasted no time. My bedroom was down the hall on the right. It wasn't a long hall, but Jeff's was even nearer, the first bedroom, just to the left. I quickly calculated that his bedroom was the better option, and took off like a shot. I was still in my "athletic" phase of childhood so figured I could easily make it there and feign sleep before Santa arrived. As for Jeff, well, I loved my bubba but, in this case, it was every woman for herself.

Only, I realized I wasn't getting anywhere. Jeff had grabbed the back of my pajamas and was trying to tell me it was okay. "Let. Me. Go." I screamed the words out with both fierceness and intensity, holding on to each one. He tried reasoning with me, saying something about an initial stop to drop off some candy. Santa's real stop would come later, some such nonsense. I think our parents were saying something along the same lines, but seriously, I could not be bothered. They all were chuckling a little too, which I really could not understand. Had my family completely lost its mind? Did they think this was funny? Christmas was on the line here, for heaven's sake. "No, no," I pleaded with Jeff. "Let me go!"

I'm not really sure how I got away. I'm guessing that Jeff figured there was no reasoning with me, and turned loose of my pjs. But, then, you never know; you hear of amazing feats of strength when people are under a state of duress. Miraculously, I realized I was free, and by this point, I *knew* I had to reach the closest bedroom. In a flash, I was in Jeff's bed with the covers pulled up over my face, eyes closed, thanking God that I was swift of feet and promising that I would never, ever, disobey our parents again, at least on Christmas Eve when they told me it was time for bed.

I heard a knock on our front door. Whew, I thought, I made it. Although then reason started to kick in. Why is Santa knocking? I wondered. Daddy answered the door and I heard a very distinct and disturbingly close "Ho, ho, ho, Mer-ry Christmas" from a deep, happy voice. I stopped worrying about it, squeezed my eyes closed more securely, and made sure every inch of me was covered with Jeff's bedspread.

Next thing I knew, Mother and Jeff came into his bedroom and were trying to get me up. Thoughts raced through my mind. What were they thinking?! And, poor Jeff, why doesn't he go hop in my bed? Well, he'd have to figure that one out for himself. I'm "asleep."

"Jenny," Mother began. "You can get up. Santa is just visiting the neighborhood and handing out some candy before he starts making his run to deliver presents."

Okay, on one hand, this didn't make any sense to me; he'd never done that before. But on the other, I knew I could always trust our mother. Jeff was there in the background, trying to reassure me it was okay, so I slowly lowered the bed covers just enough so that my eyes were showing. I guess I looked skeptical because they both said, "Really, it's okay."

For the opportunity to see Santa on Christmas Eve before he started his run, I decided to chance it. I hopped down from Jeff's bed and slowly walked to the front door where the big guy himself stood, chatting with Daddy.

"Ho, ho, ho, Mer-ry Christmas, Jenny." I think he confirmed what Mother had said, but to be honest, I was so enthralled with the experience that, standing there mute, it was lost on me. He handed Jeff and me some candy, said goodnight, and, because you can't say it enough, another Merry Christmas, and left to pay a visit at the next house.

For some reason, Santa's visit calmed me down. I bid Jeff and Daddy goodnight and Mother tucked me into bed, this time, my own. Sure enough, Santa made another stop later that night, as evidenced by the additional, unwrapped presents under the tree the following morning. (In our house, the presents Santa left under the tree always greeted us unwrapped that morning.) For the rest of my believing days, Mother and Daddy never had trouble getting me to bed on Christmas Eve. And, Jeff? Well, true to his promise to our father, just like that evening, he played along, kept mum, and let me grow up on my own.

It's probably no surprise, then, that I held the same reverence for the tooth fairy, or, in my lexicon, the "Good Fairy," as I did for Santa Claus. Let's face it, at six, and losing teeth at an early and rapid pace, I was happy to believe in the mystery that produced a Kennedy half—a half dollar coin with our recently slain president's bust on the front—under my pillow just for losing a baby tooth. Really, how easy could it be to get a cool, half dollar?

May 4, 1967, Albany

Jeff and Jenny are doing so well. Guess what? Jeff lost a tooth last week, has another right ready, and Jenny lost a bottom one yesterday. She woke up crying this morning, crying the "good fairy" forgot. I recovered quickly tho' and told her she'd have to put it under her pillow. She was sleeping with me. I have it all fixed now. The "good fairy" can't goof many times!

May 8, 1967, Fort Lee

You had better watch about that Good Fairy, ha. That Jenny is not going to have any teeth left!

Tell Jeff and Jenny that Daddy said hello and I sure do love them and want to see them so much.

AS GRAND A BIG brother as he was and is, we were still siblings vying for our parents' attention, he prone to teasing, me to tattling. I came to understand at an early age that Daddy put women on a pedestal, especially the ones in his life, and raised his son to do the same, which gave me a bit of an upper hand. "Daddy, make Jeff stop it," or, when I was very young, "Jeff's being rouge [rude]" were standard arsenal in my toolkit. However, no amount of intervention, correction, or admonition from our parents could prevent him from teasing me with the nickname I acquired during our time on MCSC Albany.

It happened the end of the summer of 1966. I was five, and Mother had enrolled me in swimming lessons there at the base pool. Jeff was already completely at home in the water, and she and Daddy intended for me to acquire a similar set of skills. As enticement to successful completion of the lessons, each child received a small trophy with his or her name engraved on it during an awards presentation in the base theater. This was thrilling stuff for a five-year-old.

I completed the lessons with little trouble, for I already loved the water, and looked forward to the trophy presentation. Jeff already had a nice collection of trophies for baseball. This was to be my first and I envisioned my own burgeoning collection.

We gathered in the base theater, the children and families who had taken beginner, intermediate, and advanced lessons. To a five-year-old, it seemed like the theater was filled, although it was just the front part of the center section. All of a sudden, I realized that I really hadn't thought this through; that was a lot of people to walk up to the stage in front of. The fluttering butterflies started up in my stomach as I waited for my name to be called.

As the person calling the names arrived at the "H"s, I squirmed a little in my seat. Any minute now, I thought. I reassured my internal self that I could do this.

There was a moment of hesitation, and then the announcer called my name. Only, it wasn't my name. I mean, it kind of sounded like my name, and miracle of miracles, they had pronounced Hobaugh correctly, no small feat. But the first name sounded off, not quite like Jennifer—Mother always went with the long version of our names on trophies, certificates, and awards— but there were no other Hobaughs in Albany, let alone the small community of the Marine base. I shifted a little in my seat, but waited to be sure, and when they called the second time, I knew the worst nightmare of my young life had come true. "Jemmifred Hobaugh," I heard again, and, with what I knew was a quiet yet distinct, "Bahahaha," from my brother and a somewhat less quiet and rigid "Shhhing" from our mother, I resigned myself to the embarrassment of the ages, wriggled out of the theater seat, and walked up on stage to receive my trophy, elegantly engraved with "Beginner" on the first line, and "Jemmifred Hobaugh" on the second. Even at the age of five, I knew that this was something my brother would *never* let go of. At some point, well into adulthood, I realized that I was glad he hadn't.

———

June 28, 1967, Greensboro

Darling,

One day nearer to being with you. We are really very anxious. Jeff is rather excited about going home, especially the game and Stone Mountain idea. Jenny just wants to go to the beach or a pool all summer. And I just want to be with you anywhere.

Mrs. Emma, Mother and the kids and I went to the [Guilford] dairy tonight. I believe that Jeff could eat 2 banana splits. He finished his and asked for a cone! O yes, your phone call to me cost a cool $6.16, and I loved every minute of it. I paid Mrs. Emma tonight.

Babe, will see you soon. I'll be so glad when we will settle down again. I have already put your hat, briefcase, etc. in the trunk. Don't want to forget!

Goodnight, dearest. I love you dearly.

Forever yours,

Becky

WE SPENT THE LAST month of Daddy's course up in Greensboro where we were able to see him on the weekends. The course officially concluded on July 7, but there was some kind of ending celebration the evening of July 6, which Daddy had written Mother about back in late May and invited her to attend. *By the way, I didn't tell you,* she wrote back in early June, *but I accept your invitation to party with you on July 6th. We'll work it out some way!*

He graduated from the Food Service Supervision course, six out of forty-two. I would expect that was good enough to secure his "A," or at least an "A-" but no records exist to confirm that. His academic report indicated that he was an eager participant in the course, and the lieutenant colonel evaluating him recommended Daddy as a potential instructor at the school in the Subsistence and Food Service Department.

We spent a wonderful few weeks of summer at the beach, and at Stone Mountain and a Braves game in Atlanta, together again as a family. And then we returned to MCSC Albany for Daddy to resume work and Mother, Jeff, and me to prepare for the coming school year.

In October of that year, Daddy was promoted to 1st lieutenant. He was, gratefully, no longer on the bottom rung of the officer corps.

In January 1968, now settled into his position as Mess Administrator, he received a glowing fitness report:

> Lt. Hobaugh, as this center's mess administrator, is responsible for the operation of one of the few in the Marine Corps that is staffed almost exclusively by civilian personnel. Lt. Hobaugh consistently runs an excellent/outstanding mess hall in every sense of the word. Innovations set up in this general mess have subsequently been recommended for use in other messes throughout the Marine Corps. Primarily this is due to his constant drive to improve the entire mess administration. His pride, sense of responsibility, attention to duty and initiative are of such caliber that they are seldom, if ever, matched by his contemporaries or seniors and stand out as an excellent example to his subordinates. His growth potential is virtually unlimited.

That was to be his final report.

His initial obligation of three years as a commissioned officer was up in a few months, and, except for the Vietnam War, remaining on active duty would have been something of a no-brainer. He had 20 years in but would only be 38 the following month and could make captain if he remained. But the MCSC in Albany was humming with activity as a central supply center for the war. Not only was Daddy fully aware of the brutality of war given his experience in Korea but he also had served as Casualty Assistance Officer, working with Chaplain Howard to inform families of the death of their Marine and serving as their liaison to the Corps in the days leading up to and after the funeral. And we had seen a number of friends say goodbye to their dads and husbands as they were deployed to Vietnam; the situation over there grew worse rather than better.

So as Daddy mulled over another three years' commission versus retirement with 20 years, he decided to go to his commanding officer and ask his thoughts on the chance of him being shipped over to Vietnam if he stayed in. His C.O. looked him in the eyes and said, "George, there are two kinds of Marines; the kind that have been to Vietnam, and the kind that are going."

When he got home to talk things over with Mother, he told her what his C.O. had said. She looked at Daddy, and said in no uncertain terms, "George Hobaugh, I have never said anything to you about your career. I have followed you wherever the Marine Corps has sent us and tried to be a support to you. But you are not getting yourself shipped off to Vietnam to get killed over there and leave me with these two children to raise by myself."

As Daddy had learned over the years, his wife was not shy of speaking her mind when the situation called for it. He put in his retirement papers the next day. In four short months, the civilian part of our lives began and our father escaped the violence and vagary of another war.

There were other separations, of course, but they were short, mostly as we went off to spend some time in Greensboro during the summer and Daddy couldn't get away from the club. But, thankfully, the extended separations were over. And as Daddy's income increased, our parents relied more and more on phone calls, which had become more reliable and less expensive, to stay connected while apart.

Their love continued for another 43 years, and our family made many more memories as it did. But just like that, the beautiful, sometimes mundane, correspondence that Becky and George Hobaugh had intermittently carried on for sixteen years, came to an end. Sometimes I wish there was more, but there isn't. I'm grateful for the words they left.

May 18, 1967, Albany

Babe, I'll write very often, every night if possible, but it may be rather short sometimes. The stuff is really loading up at school—end of the year.

I know what you mean by "life complete." I'm just part of a person without you. I love you very dearly. Keep the letters coming. We really enjoy them.

I love you,
Becky

May 24, 1967, Fort Lee

Baby, I get so lonesome for you all, and I know you all get lonesome for me. When you love like we do you just miss one another. I will be so glad when we are together again.

Well, honey, I guess I will come to a close for tonight. Will write you again Thursday night.
All my love,
George

Epilogue

FOR YEARS, I TRIED TO CONVINCE MY SECOND husband John to spend our annual beach vacation down in Panama City Beach, Florida, with my parents.

Panama City, or PC as it was known in our church youth group, was where our family had spent at least a week every summer after moving to, and then staying put in, Albany, Georgia. Situated on the Florida panhandle's Gulf Coast, it boasts gorgeous white sands, and calm, crystal blue waters that warm over the summer to bathtub-like temps. And, it was only a three-hour car ride from Albany, which I know our parents saw as a distinct advantage when traveling with my brother and me during those years when the backseat was never big enough for the both of us.

There was just one problem in the plan to get John down there. From Northern Virginia where we lived, it was a plane ride away, and my husband hated to fly. He had done enough of it with work to last a lifetime, and the idea of boarding a plane for a vacation seemed like an oxymoron to him. So we continued to go places like Rehoboth Beach, Delaware, a three-hour car ride for us, with its darker sands, boardwalk, and rougher, much colder waters. They were nice enough. I tolerated the boardwalks of the northern beaches, a strange thing to me, but longed for a place where I could leave the grounds of the hotel or condo, walk down the wooden steps, and step right onto the beach. Nothing to attract yet more crowds or mar the view where the sun seemed to drop right into the Gulf at sunset. I figured if I could get him down there just one time, he would be hooked like me.

As any good wife would do, then, I gently persisted, and when our son David went off to college and our daughter Anna entered her tweens, he finally relented.

And, of course, I was right. From the time Anna was about nine until she graduated from high school, we spent the end of the summer down there and I luxuriated in the sands of my youth, giving my daughter wonderful beach memories with her grandparents.

In truth, John wasn't much of a beach person. He was allergic to the sun and would break out in this little red rash unless he covered up, doused the rest of himself in sunscreen—a practice he was loathe to do—and do his best to stay out of the sun. But he soon learned that there were several advantages to the beach situation in PC. First, Daddy would rent the beach chairs and large umbrellas from the guy who ran the business outside the condo we frequented, thus providing ample shade for my sun-tortured husband. Second, John loved good food, especially seafood and steak, and he came to look forward to eating at the wonderful restaurants that my parents had discovered over the years. Third, there were an ample number of pawnshops in the area where he could browse and supplement his airgun collection. But most importantly, we would generally fly into Albany and spend a few days with my parents there before packing up to drive with them to the beach. For him, this became the best part of the vacation, as he relaxed on the screened-in porch and studied the birdlife that skimmed the pond or perched on the branches in the woods just beyond. Plus, he told me one year, it didn't seem quite right if we missed the ritual of my parents packing up for the beach.

Years before, when Mother retired from teaching, Daddy surprised her that fall with an anniversary present of a month at Panama City. He rented a condo on the beach, right next to the St. Andrews State Park, on the lovely, natural section of the shore away from the worst crowds. She went down for most of the month, Daddy came and went as he could get away from the club, and they invited family and close friends to join them on and off throughout the month. I told Daddy at the time that he had made the biggest mistake of his life, since I figured Mother would love the time down there so much he would have to turn it into an annual event. Sure enough, that is exactly what happened. By the time John, Anna, and I started joining them annually for our week down there, Mother was a seasoned pro, having devised a list of what they needed to take, especially in the way of food, to keep from having to buy everything when they got down there.

As Daddy packed the car, I could have written the script for the conversation between our parents. If it had ever been different, I would have worried that something was wrong between them. Mother and I would place things by the door, and Daddy and John would begin the tricky dance of fitting everything into the trunk of the two cars we were taking. As Daddy saw the pile of things by the door grow and the car trunks would begin to fill, he good naturedly began the familiar refrain. "How long are we staying for? We're never going to get all this into these two cars. I don't know why we can't just buy this stuff when we get down there." Mother would roll her eyes and then issue the rejoinder. "The one year we waited and bought all the food when we got down there, he complained about how much it cost," she said, always within earshot of him. He would just smile. We used to call our father, "the great agitator" because he knew how to stir things up. He had struck again, and Mother knew to expect it. It really was an essential beginning to the annual beach vacation.

Once we arrived, the routine was familiar, the same each year. Breakfast in the condo, beach time in the morning, back to the condo for lunch and to get out of the sun during the hottest part of the day, more beach time in the afternoon, and then showers and an early dinner out for anyone who wanted to go. Mother always said that the beach was for doing what each of us wanted. If someone didn't want to go to dinner, just wanted to stay in and relax and eat leftovers, then that was fine. No one was to put pressure on anyone else to always be part of the group. It was a real vacation. Most of the time we all did dine out together, and, for sure, no one *ever* turned down going to Ruthie T's, one of our favorite local restaurants.

It was an easy, relaxed setting, with wonderful food, excellent service, and on certain nights of the week, live music. Our favorite entertainer was Pat, who played the guitar and sang old favorites with her rich, easy alto voice. They were there so often, she came to know Mother and Daddy and would speak with them every year when they were in town.

One year we drove the short distance down Hwy 90 to Ruthie T's, and discovered that the owners had retired and sold the restaurant. We tried the new place, but it was not the same, and our singer no longer performed there. We set out to find a better alternative.

April 30, 1958, Okinawa
My Dearest darling,

I am so much in love with you. You are the only one for me. Oh, honey, I will be so glad when these next 4 months are over and I can be back home with you, for that is where my heart is.

Baby, I am so lonesome when I am not with you. No matter how many people I am around, I am still lonesome because I am not with you. Baby, I love you more than I can ever put into words. You are my everything, and I love you, love you, love you.

WE SAT TOGETHER IN somewhat unfamiliar surroundings. Anna was in high school and she, John, and I had come down for the annual beach vacation with Mother and Daddy. Ruthie T's was no longer Ruthie T's, but we had learned from the owners of the new place that Pat was now playing at the Boar's Head, a restaurant further down the beach that we had not been to in years. So for the sake of hearing her and in hopes of what Daddy and John were trusting would be a good steak, we had driven the extra fifteen minutes to give it a try.

Pat had arrived and set up, happy to see that we had tracked her down. The five of us sat there in easy conversation, listening to her play the guitar and sing covers from several decades.

I excused myself and went over to request a song. "Would you play something of Norah Jones's, please?" To which I received a smile and an, "of course"— and I rejoined my family to wait. I knew which one she would sing. I had made the request a year or two before at Ruthie T's, expecting something like "Come Away with Me," or "Don't Know Why," but instead getting "The Nearness of You," the last song on Jones's *Come Away with Me* album. I remembered the effect the old Hoagy Carmichael song had had on Mother and wanted to gift it to her again.

We sat, talked, and laughed, waiting on our main course. In a few minutes, the first guitar chords of my request sounded, and Pat began in with her smoky voice...

> It's not the pale moon that excites me,
> That thrills and delights me,
> Oh no, it's just the nearness of you.

I looked over at Mother as she immediately recognized the song, and saw her drift away into another time and place as she sat, soaking in the Ned Washington lyrics.

> It isn't your sweet conversation
> That brings this sensation,
> Oh no, it's just the nearness of you.

And there she sat, luxuriating in memories, until Pat finished the final chord. I knew it was one of her absolute favorites from that era. It's a hard one not to like, a seemingly perfect combination of seductive melody and lyrical magic.

I had never asked why she liked it so, but in reading their letters, I think I came to understand the song's allure for our mother. Woven through their correspondence, I discovered the frustrating—broken-down cars, mounting bills, worrying illnesses; the exciting—challenging work, exotic places, growing children; and the seemingly unending day-to-day of carrying on through those days, weeks, months, even years apart. But mostly, I discovered the core of our family story, our parents' love for one another, expressed through repeated vows of tenderness, assurance, trust, and firm commitment to each other. So I imagine that that song captured for Mother the truth that she and Daddy both felt during each of their separations—their own longing to be together that they shared through the letters that sustained them until they could, once again, experience what the songwriter so beautifully penned...

> When you're in my arms
> And I feel you so close to me,
> All my wildest dreams come true.
>
> I need no soft lights to enchant me,
> If you'll only grant me
> The right
> To hold you ever so tight
> And to feel in the night
> The nearness of you.

Notes

One

"**At present,** I have $.22 in my pocket..." Lawrence W. Levine and Cornelia R. Levine, *The People and the President: America's Conversation with FDR* (Boston: Beacon Press, 2002), p. 86.

"**He is** representative of thousands of farmers in North Carolina..." Ibid., p. 83.

Information on the textile mills, construction projects, and Greensboro during the Depression comes from the following websites: Greensboro, North Carolina Convention and Visitors Bureau, "Life during the Great Depression," https://www.visitgreensboronc.com/about-us/greensboro-history/great-depression/; University of North Carolina at Greensboro Digitals Collections, Marvin Brown, "Greensboro, 1808–1941: A Brief History," http://libcdm1.uncg.edu/cdm/ref/collection/ttt/id/37137; University of North Carolina, Chapel Hill, "Documenting the American South," http://docsouth.unc.edu/sohp/H-0161/H-0161.html.

Background on the Ohio Yearly Meeting of Friends and conservative Quakers comes from Snow Camp, North Carolina, "A Short History of Conservative Friends," http://www.snowcamp.org/shocf/shocframes.html.

Two

"**At that** time, Guilford provided a five-part educational program..." 1947 Guilford College Academic Catalog.

David Troll Rees was an organist, choir director, and private teacher, predominately in New York City and Italy. When he passed away in 1945, he left the bulk of his estate for scholarships at Guilford and the College of the Ozarks, two colleges whose philosophies had attracted him.

INFORMATION on the twelve-week basic training program at Parris Island for Marine recruits comes from my brother, and the official Marine Corps website, training summary by week for recruit training, http://www.mcrdpi.marines.mil/Recruit-Training/Training-Summary-By-Week/.

Three

BACKGROUND on the lead up to the Korean War and U.S. involvement up to the landing of Inchon is drawn from Thomas McKelvey Cleaver, *The Frozen Chosen: The 1st Marine Division and the Battle of the Chosin Reservoir* (Oxford, UK: Osprey Publishing, 2016), pp. 31–120. For a good and thorough monograph on the war, see Clay Blair, *The Forgotten War: America in Korea, 1950–1953* (New York: Doubleday, 1987).

I WAS able to track our father's whereabouts during the landing at Inchon and the Chosin Reservoir campaign, and obtain background on his colorful regimental commander from Burke Davis's excellent biography on Puller, *Marine!: The Life of Chesty Puller* (New York: Bantam Books, 1964), particularly chapters 14–18.

Five

HISTORY on Camp Fuji can be found at https://www.fuji.marines.mil/About/History/.

INFORMATION on the economic boom in postwar Japan comes from Andrew Gordon, *A Modern History of Japan: From Tokugawa to the Present* (New York: Oxford University Press, 2009), pp. 243–248.

Six

INFORMATION on Okinawan history and strategic importance of the island comes from Congressional Research Service, *The U.S. Military Presence in Okinawa and the Futenma Base Controversy*, by Emma Chanlett-Avery and Ian E. Rinehart, 7-5700, www.crs.gov, R42645. https://fas.org/sgp/crs/natsec/R42645.pdf.

Ten

FOR MORE information on the Naval Air Station at Argentia, see "Argentia Naval Air Station and Fort McAndrew," HiddenNewfoundland.ca. https://www.hidden-newfoundland.ca/argentia-naval-station.

Eleven

BACKGROUND on the Limited Duty Officer Program comes from Bernard C. Nalty and Lieutenant Colonel Ralph F. Moody, USMC, "A Brief History of U.S. Marine Corps Officer Procurement, 1775–1969," Marine Corps Historical Reference Pamphlet (Washington, D.C., 1970), pp. 19-22, https://www.marines.mil/Portals/59/Publications/A%20Brief%20History%20of%20USMC%20Officer%20Procurement%20PCN%2019000414000.pdf?ver=2012-10-11-163207-097.

FOR A brief overview of the Vietnam War, see Scott Michael Rank, "The Vietnam War: Background and Overview," History on the Net, https://www.historyonthenet.com/the-vietnam-war-background-overview. An excellent memoir on the Vietnam War is Philip Caputo, *A Rumor of War*, 40th Anniversary ed. (Picador, 2017).

MY BROTHER-IN-LAW served in Vietnam from April 1967 to April 1968. His journal was subsequently published as "Notes between Two Worlds: The Diary of Roger Lansbury, 2nd Battalion, Fifth Marines, *The Pennsylvania Magazine of History and Biography*, July 1985, 257–97. The quoted excerpt is from June 5, 1967, p. 271.

Epilogue

"THE NEARNESS of You," Hoagy Carmichael, melody, and Ken Washington Lyrics, 1938.

Acknowledgements

———

THE BIRTH OF THIS BOOK TOOK PLACE AT A ROOM in the North Lodge of Lost River Retreat Center in West Virginia a number of years ago when I first drafted the prologue. Since then, many iterations of chapters and sections found their way to the page there, at the biannual Poets, Writers, and Artists retreats, the brainchild of my friends Myra Bridgforth and Anne Mugler. I am grateful to them and the other retreat participants who listened to my stumblings during "open mic night" every six months and encouraged me in the process.

My dear friend Eric Larson traveled from New York to Albany, Georgia, to help me begin the process of cleaning out Mother and Daddy's home in the wake of Daddy's death. I am beyond grateful that he was with me when I began discovering the letters and thank him for being there throughout, as he has been so many times over the years.

Our late uncle on our father's side, Elmer Hobaugh, was invaluable with information about our grandparents' work at the mill, Grandad's death, and the time surrounding our brother Samuel's stillbirth. I am grateful to our cousins Ruth Amelia Mayo and Ruth Ann Phillips—Mother's first cousins—who helped with family stories and the identity of previous generations in pictures. A big thank you to Ruth Ann for putting me up when I traveled to Greensboro for research.

Many thanks to Liz Cook at the Guilford College archives and Amy Yuncker-

McCoy at the Malone College (formerly Cleveland Bible College) archives for help in filling in the gaps about our mother's time at those two institutions.

Elaine Porter, Allison Stiller, and Suzanne Smith, friends, reading enthusiasts, and, in the case of Suzy, fellow scholar, read an earlier draft. I am incredibly grateful for their honest assessments, insights, and comments that went into making this a better narrative than the one they slogged through.

My dear friend Arlene Decina carefully read the final draft and applied her fine eye to grammar and clarity. I am beyond grateful and assure her that any mistakes that remain are mine alone.

For the beautiful cover and interior design of the book, I bow in thanks and awe to the giftedness of my graphic designer son-in-law, Joseph Dente.

A special thank you to many other friends who supported and encouraged me along the way. From my Georgia "gals,"—Lisa Crockett, Tammy Putnal, Lynne Travis, Kathy Young, and our two Leahs, Leah Masters and Leah Sowell—who have known me longer than most; to my dear friends who helped me survive my first husband's death— Courtney and Mike Flores, and Jennifer and Andy Brent; all the way to my friend Shawn Sledge who came into my life much more recently but has felt like she's been there forever and kept pushing me to find the right title, and everyone else in between.

These acknowledgements would not be complete without thanking my family—John, Steve, and David (the "boys" as their dad always lovingly referred to them) who many years ago accepted me as part of the Lansbury family when I married their father, a bizarre thing for them, I'm sure, since I was much closer in age to the older two than their dad; and Anna, who took on three older brothers with the love and exuberance that only a two-year-old can. Since that time, the Lansbury clan has grown to include wives and children (numbering 16 at present!) and I am blessed to have each and every one of them in my life. Their love, encouragement, and support—especially after John died and more recently throughout this project—have been the rock upon which I wrote.

And finally, to my brother Jeff, my deepest thanks for filling in the gaps, helping with the military aspects, reading through and correcting the first draft, listening to my joys and frustrations, but, mostly, for living part of the story. Without you, Jeff boy, this would have been a lesser story, by far. Bubba, I love you more than words can ever tell.

Made in the USA
Middletown, DE
10 January 2021

31232568R00175